The Rhode Island
—1777—
Military Census

THE RHODE ISLAND
— 1777 —
MILITARY CENSUS

Transcribed by Mildred M. Chamberlain

Published Under the Direction of
THE RHODE ISLAND GENEALOGICAL SOCIETY

GENEALOGICAL PUBLISHING CO., INC.
Baltimore 1985

ACKNOWLEDGEMENTS

The following are gratefully acknowledged for their contributions to this work: Bruce Campbell MacGunnigle, C.G.; Jane Fletcher Fiske, F.A.S.G.; John D. Bacon; Elsie B. Williams; Robert S. Trim, C.G.; Robert M. Sherman, F.A.S.G.; and Ruth Wilder Sherman, F.A.S.G.

THE RHODE ISLAND 1777 MILITARY CENSUS

transcribed by Mildred Mosher Chamberlain

In March 1777, the Rhode Island General Assembly passed an act ordering an enumeration of all males in the state who were 16 years of age or older. John D. Bacon suggested that we publish this enumeration and, through the kindness of Secretary of State Robert F. Burns, we have permission to do so.

Six towns are presently missing from the census records in the State Archives: Exeter, Little Compton, Middletown, Newport, New Shoreham (Block Island), and Portsmouth. Since Exeter and Little Compton were among the towns for which census committee men were appointed, we assume that censuses were taken for them, but they had not been discovered by the fall of 1984.

The following is a transcription of the act of the General Assembly of 1777, from the original volumes of Rhode Island Colonial Records at the State Archives [9:645-647].

AN ACT FOR NUMBERING ALL PERSONS ABLE TO BEAR ARMS WITHIN THIS STATE.

Be it Enacted by this General Assembly and by the Authority thereof, it is Enacted, That the Following Persons be appointed Committee-Men for the Towns to which their names are respectively ascribed, for the Purposes herein after mentioned, to wit:

For Providence, Mr. Martin Seamans; Warwick, Mr. James Jerauld; Westerly, Joseph Crandall Esq.; North-Kingstown, Joseph Coggeshall Esq.; South-Kingstown, Thomas Potter Esq.; East-Greenwich, Benjn. Tillinghast Esq.; James-town, Benjn. Underwood Esq.; Smithfield, Daniel Mowry Esq.; Scituate, Mr. Joseph Davis; Gloucester [sic], Capt. Asa Kimbal; Charlestown, Joseph Hoxsie Esq.; West-Greenwich, Samuel Hopkins Jun. Esq.; Coventry, Samuel Wall Esq.; Exeter, George Peirce Esq.; Bristol, Daniel Bradford Esq.; Tiverton, Walter Cooke Esq.; Little-Compton, Phillip Taylor Esq.; Warren, William T. Miller Esq.; Cumberland, John Dexter Esq.; Richmond, Captn. Sim. Clarke Jun.; Cranston, Nehemiah Knight Esq.; Hopkinton, Thomas Wells Esq.; Johnston, Richard Eddy Esq.; North-Providence, Captn. Joseph Olney; Barrington, Mr. Henry Bowen.

And be it further Enacted by the Authority aforesaid, That the said Committees make regular Lists or Registers of the Names of all the male Persons inhabiting or residing within their respective Towns.

From sixteen to Fifty years of Age, whom they shall judge able to bear Arms.

From ditto to ditto, whom they shall judge unable to bear Arms.

From fifty to sixty able to bear Arms.

From ditto to ditto, not able; and

From sixty upwards.

That lists be made of those who are transient or resident Persons in the same manner; as also of those belonging to the Towns within this State in the Possession of the Enemy; of Negroes and Indians in the same Manner; and also of those who have taken the Affirmation or produced Certificates from the Friends-Meeting to excuse them from Military Duty; as also of those who have inlisted into the Continental Battalions or into the service of this State for fifteen Months; setting Down the Names of all the Persons numbered in seperate Columns: And after the Lists aforesaid are made, the said Committees shall make Oath before some Magistrate or Justice of the Peace, that the same hath been justly and truly made, according to the best of the Knowledge of such Committee-Man; which lists so made and sworn to, shall be returned by the said Committees to the General-Assembly at their next Session, to be holden at South-Kingstown on the seventeenth Day of April next.

And be it further Enacted That in Case either of the said Committees shall refuse to serve, that either of the Deputies of the Town where such Committee resides be empowered to appoint other suitable Persons in their Places.

And it is also Enacted, That the Commanding Officers of the Two Continental Battalions raised by this State, and of the two Regiments and train of Artillery inlisted by this State for fifteen Months, be requested to make return to the General Assembly on the said seventeenth Day of April next, of the Soldiers they shall then have inlisted, with the Towns to which said Soldiers belong, in order that the General Assembly may then know the Strength of the State.

And it is further Enacted, That the Secretary, as soon as may be, furnish the said Committees with Copies of this Act, and with blank Columns for the Purposes aforesaid.

*

Key to Abbreviations

16-50 A	From 16 to 50 years and able to bear arms
16-50 U	From 16 to 50 years and unable to bear arms
50-60 A	From 50 to 60 years and able to bear arms
50-60 U	From 50 to 60 years and unable to bear arms
60+	60 and upwards
Aff	Those who have taken the Affirmation
Cert	Those who have certificates from the Friends Meeting
T	Transient persons and to what places they belong
R	Residents and to what places they belong
N	Negro
I	Indian
SM	State Militia
CS	Continental Service
[]	Names in brackets were supplied from the handwritten 1898 copy of the census, at the Archives.
?	Question marks appear with names whose spelling is uncertain.

1777 MILITARY CENSUS

BARRINGTON, RHODE ISLAND

Page 1

Nathanel Martin	50-60 A
Luther Martin	16-50 A
Anthony Martin	"
Joseph Gladding	"
Samuel Bosworth	"
Nathanel Smith	"
Pawl Mumford	"
Newdigate Adams	"
Samuel Adams	16-50 U
Joshua Kent	16-50 A
Edward Bosworth	50-60 U
Hezekiah Kinnicutt	16-50 A
Daniel Kinnicutt	"
George Salsbury	"
Hezekiah Tiffeny	60+
Joshua Bicknel	50-60 A
Joshua Bicknel Jr.	16-50 A
[torn]ah Viall	"
[torn] Allen	"
[torn]n Andrews	50-60 A
[torn]h Traffarn (SM)	16-50 A
[torn] Bowen	"
[torn]liam Brown	"
[torn]s Brown Jr.	"
[torn]l Allen	"
[torn]anel Heath	"
[torn]g Heath	"
[torn]mon Peck	"
[torn]der Tripp	"
[torn]h Remington	"
[torn] Peck	"
[torn]uel Peck	16-50 U
[torn]nd Peck	16-50 A
[torn]ard Adams	50-60 A
[torn]h Adams	16-50 A
[torn]w Watson Jr.	"
[torn]w Watson	60+ 2 N
[torn] Watson	16-50 A
[torn]anel Clerk	"
[torn]eazar Tiffeny	"
[torn]y Humphry	"
[torn]h Humphry	50-60 A
[torn] Humphry Jr.	16-50 A
[torn] Sabin (CS)	"

Page 1

| [torn]eas Barns | 60+ |

Totals:

34	16-50 A	2	16-50 U
5	50-60 A	1	50-60 U
3	60+	2	N

Page 2

Benjamin Mumford	60+
Benjamin Mumford Jr.	16-50 A
Peter Mumford	"
Benjamin Garner	"
David Reed	"
Eleazer Reed	"
Gideon Reed	"
Levi Barns	"
Peleg Barns	"
Samuel Barns	"
John Barns	"
Samuel Humphry	50-60 A
James Humphry (CS)	16-50 A
Joseph Viall Jr.	"
Joseph Viall	60+
Samuel Viall	16-50 A
Silvester Viall	"
Thomas Allen (CS)	" 2 N
Mathew Allen	" 1 N
Comfort Stanly	"
Richard Harding	"
William Harding	"
Joseph Allen	50-60 A
Benjamin Allen	16-50 A
Joseph Grant	50-60 A
Joseph Grant Jr.	16-50 A
Shubal Grant	"
Thomas Grant	"
Ebeneazer Grant	"
Abiel Grant	"
Moses Horton	60+
Moses Horton Jr.	16-50 A
Benjamin Horton	"
James Martin	"
Edward Martin	"
Rufus Martin	"

1777 MILITARY CENSUS

BARRINGTON, RHODE ISLAND

Page 2 (cont.)

Benjamin Hathaway	16-50 A
James Bowen	50-60 A
Josiah Bowen	16-50 A
John Kelly	60+
Dunkan Kelly	16-50 A
Moses Tyler	"
Samuel Kent	"
John Kent	"
Spicr Hews	"
Benjamin Drown	50-60 U
Benjamin Drown Jr.	16-50 A
Daniel Drown	"
Jonathan Jenks Drown	"
Mihal Cary	"
John Short	"
John Short Jr.	"
Samuel Short	"
John Martin	50-60 A
Benjamin Martin	16-50 A
William Buffington	16-50 U

Totals:

79	16-50 A	3	16-50 U	
10	50-60 A	2	50-60 U	
6	60+	3	N	

Page 3

Simon Smith	16-50 A
Caleb Drown	"
Simeon Drown	"
Benjamin Grant	"
James Bushe	"
Daniel Bears (CS)	"
David Luther	"
Scipio a Negro Man	N

Totals:

86	16-50 A	3	16-50 U	
10	50-60 A	2	50-60 U	
6	60+	6	N	

BRISTOL, RHODE ISLAND

A list of all the Persons from Sixteen years and upwards who have removed out of the town of Bristol since the fleet first came to Newport viz:

Page A

Joseph Russell	Daniel Lefavour
Jonathan Russell	William Lindsey
Benjamin Smith	James Smith
Samuel Smith	James Nooning [?]
Isaac Wardwell	Joshua Sanford
Jonathan Wardwell	Joshua Sanford Jr.
John May	Royal Sanford
John May Jr.	James Willson
William Lindsey Jr.	Sebry Manchester
William Coxx	Simeon Ingreham
Josiah Finney	Josiah Smith

1777 MILITARY CENSUS

BRISTOL, RHODE ISLAND

Page A (cont.)

Edward Pain
Stephen Pain
Royal Pain
Thomas Pain
Joseph Wardwell
John Higgins
Charls DeWolf
Nathaniel Munro 2^d
Samuel Munro
Nathan Munro 2^d
William Hoar
Benjamin Hoar
Joseph Diman
Richard Smith
Richard Smith Jr.
John Gladding Jr.
Archibald Munro
Benjamin Wardwell
Joseph Oldridge
Nathaniel Smith 2^d
Nathaniel Manchester
Anthony DeWolf
Edward Talby
Edward Talby Jr.
John Oldridge
Cornelius Waldron
Nathaniel Waldron
Nathaniel Waldron Jr.
Solomon Drown
Richard Drown
William White
Samuel Wardwell
Daniel Wardwell
William Wardwell
John Pratt
Joseph Pratt
John Gladding
Daniel Gladding
Peter Gladding
Solomon Gladding
Joshua Gladding
Nathaniel Smith
Nathaniel Bosworth
William Gladding

William Gladding Jr.
Joseph Gladding
Ebenezer Gladding
John Norrice
John Norrice Jr.
Jeremiah Diman
Samuel Lindsey
Nathaniel Pearse
Richard Pearse
Samuel Pearse
Thomas Pearse
William Munro
George Munro
John Usher
Samuel Usher
Henry Munro
Barnard Sailsbury
Job Coggeshall
Samuel Oxx
John Smith
Joseph Reynolds Jr.
James West
Benj^a Sialsbury
Benj^a Sailsbury Jr.
Isaac Waldron
Samuel Liscomb
Samuel Liscomb Jr.

(93)

Page 1

William Bradford	50-60 A
Lebaron Bradford	16-50 A
John Eastabrooks	50-60 A
Charles Eastabrooks	16-50 A
John Eastabrooks Jr.	T-Newport
George Oxx	16-50 A
Aaron Bourn	"
Allen Usher	16-50 U
James Usher	T-Providence
Thomas Usher	"
William Christophers	16-50 A
Isaac Eslick	"
Benjamin Bosworth	"

1777 MILITARY CENSUS

BRISTOL, RHODE ISLAND

Page 1 (cont.)

Jonathan Drown	16-50 A
Phillip Drown	"
Nathanil Church	"

Totals:

10	16-50 A	1	16-50 U
2	50-60 A	3	T

[illegible] and fifteen month service in the Town of Bristol
Sion Martindule Capt of the fort
Benjamin Sailsbury 3^{d} in the Continantal Service.

In the Fifteen month Service in Coll. Smiths Regiment:

Lieut. William Lawless	)	
Lieut. Thomas Swan	)	in Capt.
Ensign Thomas Pearse	)	
John Pearse	)	Allens
Daniel Maxfield	)	
Thomas Jethro	)	Company
Privits David Maxfield	)	in the
Leanox Bullock Jr.	)	
Thomas Holmes	)	Same
James Allen	)	
Samuel Wardwell	)	Regiment
Nathaniel Willson	)	
Samuel Martin	)	under
Joseph Shearman	)	Capt. Carr

Danl Bradford) Committee for the Town of Bristol

Bristol April 16, 1777
Appeard the above named Danl Bradford and made Solemn Oath that the above and foregoing list is justly and truly made according to the best of his knowledge. Before me
Shearj^{a} Bourn Just. [illeg]

Page 2

Joseph Reed	60+ A
Leanox Bullock	16-50 A
Leanox Bullock Jr.	"
Simeon Bullock	"
William Harding	"
Shearjashub Bourn	50-60 A
Frank	N
Nathan Munro	16-50 A
Nathan Munro [sic]	"
Nathaniel Fales	50-60 A
Thomas Fales	15-60 A
Stephen Fales	"
William Fales	"
John Fales	"
Ruben	N
Jonathan Diman	15-60 A
William Pearse	60+ U
Dick	N
London	N
William Lake	50-60 A R-Newport
Oliver Earl	15-60 A R-Portsmouth
Oliver West	15-60 A
Nathaniel Fales Jun.	"
Timothy Fales	"
John Waldron	50-60 A
Shearjashub Bourn Jun.	16-50 A
William Bosworth	50-60 A
Benjamin Bosworth 2^{d}	16-50 U
William Bosworth Jun.	16-50 A
Timothy Bosworth	"
Prince	N
Jeremiah Willson	60+ U
Thomas Willson	16-50 A
William Willson	"
Thomas Gray	"
Thomas Gray Jun.	"
John Gray	"
William Munro	60+ U
Hezekiah Munro	16-50 A
James Munro	"
Peleg	N

1777 MILITARY CENSUS

BRISTOL, RHODE ISLAND

Page 2 (cont.)

Charls	N
John	N
George Coggeshall	16-50 A
Stephen Munro	"
Moses Davis	Cert
John Howland	60+ A

Totals:

27	16-50 A	1	16-50 U
5	50-60 A	5	60+
1	Cert	2	R
8	N		

Page 3

John Howland Jun.	16-50 A
Samuel Church	"
Samuel Howland	"
Jonathan Glover	"
Benjamin Harding	"
Simon	N
Newport	N
Joseph Reed Jun.	16-50 A
Samuel Reed	"
William Holems	50-60 A
James Diman	16-50 A
Timothy Diman	"
Jeremiah Bosworth	60+ U
Zeikel	N
Stephen Wardwell	50-60 A
Stephen Wardwell Jun.	R-Providence
Josiah Wardwell	15-60 A
Stephen Smith	"
Samuel Bosworth	[torn]
William West	[torn]
Nathaniel West	16-50 A
William Ingreham	"
John West	60+ A
Hix West	16-50 A
Aseph West	"
Anthony VanDorn	"
Newton Waldron	"
Lenord Waldron	"
Jeremiah Ingreham	"
Prince	N

Page 3 (cont.)

Stephen Whitting	R-Boston
Moses VanDorn	16-50 A
Plato	N
Joseph Lindsey	16-50 A
Nathaniel Diman	"
William Diman	"
Lemuel Clark	16-50 U
Joseph Eddy	16-50 A
Simeon Munro	60+ A
Jonathan Munday	60+ U
Edward Munro	16-50 A
Simeon Potter	16-50 U
Hertford	N
Quam	N
Hezekiah Usher	50-60 A

Totals:

25	16-50 A	2	16-50 U
3	50-60 A	5	60+
2	R	7	N

Page 4

John Jolls	16-50 A
Ebenezer Jolls	"
John Throop	60+ A
Simon Burn	16-50 A
Thomas Champlin	"
Thomas Champlin Jun.	"
Samuel West	50-60 A
Robert Jolls	16-50 A
John Coomer	50-60 A
John Coomer Jun.	16-50 A
Thomas Coomer	"
Charls	N
Jeremiah Finney	16-50 A
Thomas Finney	"
Loring Finney	"
Caleb Seulsbury	60+ A
Theophilous Seulsbury	16-50 A
Newby Coggeshall	50-60 A
William Coggeshall Jun.	16-50 A
James Coggeshall	"
George	N

1777 MILITARY CENSUS

BRISTOL, RHODE ISLAND

Page 4 (cont.)

William Throop	16-50 A		Daniel Bradford	50-60 A
David Maxfield	"		John Dyer	50-60 U
Ebenezer Blake	"		Benjamin Bosworth	16-50 A
Jonathan Peck	"		Joseph Reynolds	50-60 A
Jonathan Peck Jun.	"		George Reynolds	16-50 A
Nino	N		Samuel Reynolds	"
Nathaniel Pearse	16-50 A		Samuel Reynolds	"
Sion Martindale	"		Cato	N
Charls Thurill	16-50 U			
Nathaniel Cary	60+ A		Totals:	
Cudgo	N		27 16-50 A 1 16-50 U	
Ichabod	Mulato		5 50-60 A 1 50-60 U	
Loring Peck	16-50 A		3 60+ 6 N	
Peter Church	"		1 Mulato	
Abraham	N			

CHARLESTOWN, RHODE ISLAND

Page 1   Page 1 (cont.)

‡Ebenezer Addams	16-50 A	William Bassett	60+
John Addams	16-50 A	Caleb Bassett	16-50 A
Thomas Addams	16-50 A	John Bartlett	"
	R-Richmond	John Bartlett Jr.	"
Stephen Allen	50-60 A	Peter Boss	"
Christopher Allen	16-50 U		R-So Kingstown
	R-So Kingstown	Caleb Boss	16-50 A
Elemuel Allen	16-50 A		R-So Kingstown
Stephen Allen Jr.	"	Jeremiah Browning (Cert)	50-60 A
William Allen	"	Jeremiah Browning Jr. "	16-50 A
Silas Austin	"	Ephraim Browning (Aff)	16-50 A
Robert Austin	50-60 U	William Browning	"
Jonathan Austin	16-50 A	John Browning	"
Joshua Austin	"	Sam[ll] Burdick	"
Stephen Austin	"	Ichabod Burdick	"
Eldredge Austin	"	Walter Burdick	"
	R-So Kingstown	Jonathan Burdick	"
George Austin	16-50 A	Ephraim Burdick	"
Christopher Babcock	"	Nathaniel Burdick	"
Christopher Babcock Jr.	"	‡Silvester Burdick	"
‡Caleb Babcock	"	‡Gideon Burdick	"
	R-Hopkinton	John Card	50-60 A
Simeon Babcock	16-50 A	Weeden Card	16-50 A

1777 MILITARY CENSUS

CHARLESTOWN, RHODE ISLAND

Page 1 (cont.)   Page 2 (cont.)

Aechus Card	16-50 A	John Champlin	16-50 A
Jonathan Card	"	Asa Champlin	"
Joshua Card	50-60 A	Michal Champlin	"
Joshua Card Jr.	16-50 A	‡Jonathan Champlin	"
William Card	"	‡William Champlin	"
John Card Jr.	"	Charles Church	"
Job Card	"	Isaac Church	"
Augustus Card	"	James Congdon	60+
Elias Cary	"	John Congdon	60+
	R-So Kingstown	William Congdon	50-60 U
Jonathan Clark	60+	Robert Congdon	16-50 A
Elisha Clark	60+	James Congdon 3ᵈ	"
Caleb Clark	60+	Joseph Congdon	"
Abraham Clark	16-50 A	Joseph Congdon/of Jos(Cert)	"
Joseph Clark	"	John Congdon Jr.	"
Job Clark/son of Elish	"	John Collier	"
		Joseph Coon	"
Totals:		Daniel Crandal	"
45 16-50 A 1 16-50 U		Abijah Crandal	"
4 50-60 A 1 50-60 U			R-Richmond
4 60+ 1 Aff		Oliver Crandal	16-50 A
2 Cert 7 R			R-Richmond
		Caleb Crandal	16-50 A
Page 2		Augustus Crandal	"

John Champlin 16-50 A — (repeats noted in right column)

Jonathan Clark/son of Josᵃ	16-50 A		R-Stonington
Job Clark	16-50 A	Ezekil Crandal	16-50 A
Rowland Clark	"		R-Stonington
Jonathan Clark Jr.	"	Simeon Crandal	60+
William Clark	50-60 A	Simeon Crandal Jr.	16-50 A
Joseph Clark/of Job	16-50 A	Gideon Crandal	"
Joshua Clark	"	Samuel Crandal	50-60 A
David Clark	"	Samuel Crandal Jr.	16-50 A
Oliver Clark	"	Ethan Crandal	"
George Clark	"	Jesse Crandal	"
William Clark/of Elish	"	Edward Crandal	50-60 A
William Clark Jr.	"	James Crandal	50-60 A
Nathan Clark	"		R-Stonington
Edward Clark	"	Eber Crandal	16-50 A
James Clark	"	Peleg Cross	50-60 U
Ichabod Clark	"	Peleg Cross Jr.	16-50 A
Ephraim Clark	"	Samuel Cross	16-50 U
Jesse Champlin	"	Jos. Cross	I
Jabez Champlin	"		
	T-Newport		

1777 MILITARY CENSUS

CHARLESTOWN, RHODE ISLAND

Page 2 (cont.)   Page 3 (cont.)

Totals:

45	16-50 A	1	16-50 U
4	50-60 A	2	50-60 U
3	60+	1	Cert
1	T	5	R
1	I		

Page 3

Joseph Cross	16-50 A	
Joseph Davis	"	
Edward Deake	"	
Immanuel Deake	"	
Daniel Edwards	50-60 A	
Daniel Edwards Jr.	16-50 A	
Clark Edwards	"	
Jesse Enos	16-50 U	
Stephen Enos	16-50 A	
	R-New Shoreham	
Joseph Eyeres	16-50 A	
William Gardiner	"	
	R-Newport	
Daniel Gardiner	16-50 A	
Thomas Green	60+	
Amos Green	60+	
Amos Green Jr.	16-50 A	
Benjamin Green	"	
John Green	"	
Reuben Green	16-50 U	
William Green	16-50 A	
Allen Green	"	
David Green	"	
Thomas Green Jr.	"	
John Green/of Thos.	"	
Edward Green	"	
Samuel Green	"	
Joshua Green	50-60 U	
Silas Greenman	60+	
George Griffen	16-50 A	
Thomas Grinnel	"	
	R-So Kingstown	
George Grinnal	16-50 A	
	R-So Kingstown	
Jonathan Hall	50-60 A	
Peter Hall	60+	

Page 3 (cont.)

George Hall	60+
Nathan Hall	60+
Ephraim Hall	16-50 A
Theodaty Hall	"
Thomas Hall	50-60 U
John Hall/of Peter	16-50 A
Jonathan Hall Jr.	"
Silas Hall	"
‡John Hall	"
William Harvey	50-60 A
William Harvey Jr.	16-50 A
Joseph Harvey	50-60 U
John Harvey	16-50 A
Peter Harvey	"
Uriah Harvey	"
James Harvey	"
James Harvey Jr.	"
‡Jonathan Hazard	"
Jonathan Hazard Jr.	"
Robert Hazard	"
John Hennon	50-60 A
	R-Ireland
Joseph Holloway	50-60 U
Joseph Holloway Jr.	16-50 A

Totals:

39	16-50 A	2	16-50 U
4	50-60 A	4	50-60 U
6	60+	5	R

Page 4

Joseph Holloway 3^d	16-50 A
	R-Coventry
Joseph Hoxsie	16-50 A
Benjamin Hoxsie (Cert)	60+
Benjamin Hoxsie Jr.	16-50 A
Benjamin Hoxsie/of Lod	"
	R-Newport
Thomas Hoxsie (Cert)	16-50 A
Gideon Hoxsie	16-50 U
Gideon Hoxsie Jr.	16-50 A
Peleg Hoxsie	"
Stephen Hoxsie (Cert)	"
Stephen Johnson	60+

1777 MILITARY CENSUS

CHARLESTOWN, RHODE ISLAND

Page 4 (cont.)

Stephen Johnson Jr.	16-50 A	
Gideon Johnson	60+	
Nathaniel Johnson	50-60 A	
Job Johnson	16-50 A	
Theodaty Johnson	"	
Jared Johnson	"	
Paul Johnson	16-50 U	
[Lot] Johnson	"	
[Robert] Jones	16-50 A	
[Joseph] Kinyon	60+	
[Enock] Kinyon	60+	
[Samuel Kinyon]	16-50 A	
[James Kinyon]	"	
Jonathan [Kinyon]	50-60 U	
Caleb [Kinyon]	16-50 A	
Alexander [Kinyon]	"	
Elijah [Kinyon]	"	
Joshua Kinyon	"	
Daniel Kinyon	50-60 U	
‡Jos. Kinyon/of Dan [?]	16-50 A	
Joseph Kinyon Jr.	"	
Elisha Kinyon	"	
Jonathan Kinyon/of Jas[?]	"	
Sam¹¹ Kinyon Jr.	"	
Amos Kinyon	"	
Jas. Kinyon/of Sam¹	"	
Joshua Kinyon/of E	"	
Roger Kinyon	"	
John Kinyon	"	
Lodowick Kinyon	"	
Reynolds Knowles	"	
	R-So Kingstown	
Daniel Knowles	16-50 A	
Daniel Knowles Jr.	"	
Thomas Knowles	50-60 U	
Kinyon Larkin	16-50 A	
Moses Larkin	"	
Peter Lee	"	
Joseph Levit	"	
Beriah Lewis	"	
Augustus Lewis	"	
Richard Lewis	"	
	R-Newport	

Page 4 (cont.)

John Lloyd	16-50 A	
	R-Newport	
Joseph Lock	16-50 A	
	R-New Shoreham	
Joseph Lock Jr.	16-50 A	
	R-New Shoreham	

Totals:

43	16-50 A	3	16-50 U
1	50-60 A	3	50-60 U
5	60+	3	Cert
7	R		

Page 5

Jonathan Macomber	16-50 A	
Hobart Mason	50-60 A	
	R-Stonington	
John Millard	16-50 A	
Benjamin Millard	"	
Jonathan Nash	"	
	R-So Kingstown	
Isaac Ney	60+	
Stephen Ney	16-50 A	
James Ney	"	
Joseph Nichols	"	
	R-Richmond	
John Park	16-50 A	
George H. Peckham	16-50 U	
Benjamin Peckham	16-50 A	
Nathan Peirce	50-60 A	
Edward Peirce	50-60 U	
Edward Peirce Jr.	16-50 A	
Simeon Perry (Cert)	50-60 A	
Samuel Perry	16-50 A	
Simeon Perry Jr. (Cert)	16-50 A	
Edward Perry (Cert)	"	
Edward Perry Jr. (Cert)	"	
John Perry	"	
Joseph Petty	"	
Arnold Procer	"	
Robert Reynolds	60+	
Daniel Saunders	60+	
Isaac Saunders	50-60 U	

1777 MILITARY CENSUS

CHARLESTOWN, RHODE ISLAND

Page 5 (cont.)

Caleb Saunders	16-50 A
Augustus Sanders	16-50 U
Luke Saunders	16-50 A
	R-Westerly
Isaac Saunders Jr.	16-50 A
John Saunders	"
Luke Saunders/of Tobias	"
Tobias Saunders	"
Mial Saulsbury	"
Amon Sunderland	"
	R-Exeter
Samuel Shearman	"
	R-Newport
Nathaniel Sheffield	60+
Thomas Sheffield	16-50 A
Benja Sheffield	16-50 U
	R-New Shoreham
Daniel Stafford	16-50 A
Joseph Stanton	60+
‡Joseph Stanton	16-50 A
Daniel Stanton	60+
Daniel Stanton Jr.	16-50 A
Samuel Stanton	50-60 U
Stephen Stanton	16-50 A
Gardiner Stanton	"
Marlborough Stanton	"
Augustus Stanton	"
John Tallman	"
	R-Hopkinton
Job Taylor (Aff)	50-60 A
John Taylor	16-50 A

Totals:

36	16-50 A	3	16-50 U
4	50-60 A	3	50-60 U
6	60+	1	Aff
4	Cert	9	R

Page 6

Jeremiah Taylor	16-50 A
Joseph Taylor	"
Thomas Tew	"
	R-Newport
Simeon Tucker (Cert)	60+

Page 6 (cont.)

Jabez Tucker	50-60 U
Nathan Tucker (Cert)	16-50 A
Joshua Tucker (Cert)	"
Josias[?] Utter	"
Jesse Wilbour	"
	R-Hopkinton
	60+
William Welch	
Henry Welch	16-50 U
William Welch Jr.	16-50 A
‡John Welch	"
Edward Willcox	60+
Joseph Willcox	16-50 A
Edward Willcox Jr.	"
Jeremiah Worden	60+
Gideon Worden	16-50 A
John Worden	"
Benjamin Worden	"
Chris^r Worden	"
William Yorke	"
Stanton Yorke	60+
Nicholas Young	16-50 A
	R-Westerly
Saml Young	60+ ditto
Thomas Young	16-50 A
	R-Westerly

Totals:

18	16-50 A	1	16-50 U
1	50-60 U	6	60+
3	Cert	5	R

INDIANS

Samuel Niles	60+ I
James Niles	60+ I
Ephraim Coyhis	60+ I
William Sachem	60+ I
John Stattock	60+ I
John Anthony	60+ I
James Caff	60+ I
Anthony Willson	60+ I
William Skisuck	60+ I
Daniel Harry	50-60 A I
Cozen Joes	" I
‡Harry Hazzard	" I

1777 MILITARY CENSUS
CHARLESTOWN, RHODE ISLAND

Page 6 INDIANS (cont.)

James Wappy	50-60	A	I
Daniel Skisuck	16-50	A	I
James Niles Jr.	"		I
James Niles 3	"		I
Benjamin Garrit	50-60	A	I
Thomas Sachem	16-50	A	I
John Toohigh	"		I
David Secaton	"		I
John Skisuck	"		I
Chris^r Harry	"		I
‡Silas Harry	"		I
‡Gideon Harry	"		I
Samuel Niles Jr.	"		I
‡Joseph King alia Anthony	"		I

Totals:
   12 16-50 A   5 50-60 A
    9 60+

Page 7 INDIANS (cont.)

John Wappy	16-50	A	I
Daniel Wappy	"		I
James Wappy Jr.	"		I
Harry Hazard Jr.	"		I
Roger Wappy	"		I
Joe Cummuck	"		I
Joe Jeffery	50-60	U	I
Toby Coyhis	16-50	A	I
‡Harry Perry	"		I
‡Daniel Perry	"		I
‡John Perry	"		I
‡Benedict Aaron	"		I
Toby Skisuck	"		I
‡Will Copper	"		I
John Daniel	"		I
‡James Daniel	"		I
Thomas Dick Jr.	"		I
	R-Jamestown		
Isaac Dick	50-60	A	I
	R-Jamestown		
John Johnson	16-50	A	I
	R-Jamestown		
John Brown	16-50	A	I
	R-Jamestown		

Page 7 INDIANS (cont.)

James Stattock	16-50	A	I
	R-Jamestown		
Thomas Packey	16-50	U	I
Tyas Tyken	50-60	A	I
Primas Hoxsie	60+		I
Gideon Nocake	16-50	A	I
Simeon Niles	16-50	U	I
John Oney	16-50	A	I
Amos Hoxsie	"		I
‡Pharash Hazard	"		I
James Peckham	"		I
‡John Cheats	"		I
‡Joshua Cheats	"		I
Charles Dick	"		I
Ephraim Charles	"		I
Henry Matthews	60+		I
Simeon Matthews	16-50	A	I
‡James Treddles	"		I
‡Charles Treddles	"		I
‡John Cheats	"		I
‡John Lewis	"		I

Totals:
   33 16-50 A   2 16-50 U
    2 50-60 A   1 50-60 U
    2 60+
brt forward 12 16-50 A   5 50-60 A
                 9 60+
Total of Indians:
   45 16-50 A   2 16-50 U
    7 50-60 A   1 50-60 U
   11 60+   66 I

NEGROES

Dick Browning	16-50	A	N
Caesar Congdon	50-60	U	N
Hod Cross	16-50	A	N
Bristol Congdon	"		N
Bristol Champlin	"		N
James Champlin	60+		N
London Champlin	16-50	A	N
Conga Champlin	"		N

Totals:
   6 16-50 A   1 50-60 U
   1 60+   8 N

1777 MILITARY CENSUS

CHARLESTOWN, RHODE ISLAND

Page 8

NEGROES (cont.)
Caff Congdon	50-60 U	N
Caff Hoxsie	16-50 A	N
Jack Stanton	50-60 A	N
Tom Perry	16-50 U	N
Cesar Babcock	16-50 A	N

Totals:
2	16-50 A	1	16-50 U		
1	50-60 A	1	50-60 U	5	N
6	16-50 A	1	50-60 U		
1	60+			8	N

Total of Negroes:
8	16-50 A	1	16-50 U		
1	50-60 A	2	50-60 U		
1	60+			13	N

Total of White Persons brt forward:

Page 1	45	16-50 A	1	16-50 U	4	50-60 A	1	50-60 U	4	60+	1	Aff
	2	Cert	7	R								
Page 2	45	16-50 A	1	16-50 U	4	50-60 A	2	50-60 U	3	60+		
	1	Cert	1	T	5	R						
Page 3	39	16-50 A	2	16-50 U	4	50-60 A	4	50-60 U	6	60+	5	R
Page 4	43	16-50 A	3	16-50 U	1	50-60 A	3	50-60 U	5	60+		
	3	Cert	7	R								
Page 5	36	16-50 A	3	16-50 U	4	50-60 A	3	50-60 U	6	60+	1	Aff
	4	Cert	9	R								
Page 6	18	16-50 A	1	16-50 U			1	50-60 U	6	60+		
	3	Cert	5	R								

Total of

Whites	226	16-50 A	11	16-50 U	17	50-60 A	14	50-60 U	40	60+ [sic]		
	2	Aff	13	Cert	1	T	38	R				
Negroes	8	16-50 A	1	16-50 U	1	50-60 A	2	50-60 U	1	60+		
Indians	45	16-50 A	2	16-50 U	7	50-60 A	1	50-60 U	11	60+		
	279	16-50 A	14	16-50 U	25	50-60 A	17	50-60 U	52	60+		
	2	Aff	13	Cert								

The whole number from 16 and upwards Indians and Negroes included: 402

Charlestown, April 17, 1777
Agreeable to a Resolve of the Honble General Assembly I the Subscriber have
taken an Acct of the Number and Names of the Male Persons in the Town of
Charlestown of 16 Years of Age and upward, and do Report as followeth, from
16 to 50 Years of Age 226 White able to bear Arms, Eleven unable; from 50 to

1777 MILITARY CENSUS

CHARLESTOWN, RHODE ISLAND

Page 8 (cont.)
60 able to bear Arms, Seventeen; unable Fourteen; from 60 and upwards Forty;
including Transient and Resident Persons, who are noted in their several Col-
unns, Two of whom have taken the Affirmation, Thirteen are excused by Certificate from Friends Meeting, that there are Thirteen Negroes of Sixteen Years
old and upward, Sixty-six Indians from 16 Years and upward, 4 of which belong
to Jamestown. There are included in the foregoing Numbers those in the Continental Service and in the Publick Service of this State for 15 Months,
whose Names are marked thus ‡ included in this Report Seven Persons from Newport, and Three from New Shoreham. Those in the Publick Service 29. The
whole of which is Submitted by the publicks Humble Servt.

James Congdon 3[d]

Kings County South Kingston April 18th 1777, Personally appeared James Congdon 3[d] & on his Solemn Oath declared that he hath Justlly & Truly made the
aforegoing List of all the Male Persons of Sixteen Years of age & Upwards in
the Town of Charlestown According to the best of his Knowledge.

Before Inian Case, Justice Common Pleas

COVENTRY, RHODE ISLAND

Page 1				Page 1 (cont)		
James Arnold	16-50	U		Job Wood	16-50	A
Job Arnold	16-50	A		Samuel Strate	"	
Ephariam Tingley	"			John Strat Jr.	"	
Nathanael Lindul	"			Stephen Capwell	50-60	A
Joseph Strate	"			Stephen Capwell Jr.	16-50	A
William Collins	"			James Capwell	"	
Tho[s] Mantchister	"			Jeremiah Capwell	"	
Tho[s] Mantchister Jr.	"			Richard Matteson	16-50	U
Gideon Arnold	"			Nehemiah Potter Esq[r]	16-50	A
Daniel Gardner	50-60	A		Job Goff	16-50	U
Joseph Gardner	16-50	A		Spink Tarbox	16-50	A
John Wood Jr	16-50	U		Ezekiel Potter	"	
Job Mantchester	16-50	A	R-E. Greenwich	Fons Potter	"	
				George Potter	"	
Noel Andrew	16-50	A		Henry King	"	
Nathan Goff Esq[r]	60+			John Johnston Jr.	50-60	A
John Wood	60+			Rubin Johnson	16-50	A
John Potter	60+			John Johnston Esq[r]	60+	
Ichabod Printis	16-50	A	R-E. Greenwich	John Cassell	16-50	A
				Benj[a] Johnston	"	
David Potter	16-50	A		Joseph Johnston	"	
William Potter	"					
Hecter Beatman	"					

1777 MILITARY CENSUS

COVENTRY, RHODE ISLAND

Page 1 (cont.)

Totals: [Full]

352	16-50 A	11	16-50 U
31	50·60 A	5	50-60 U
43	60+	1	I
5	N		

Page 2

Robert Greene	16-50 A
Timethey Greene	"
Jonathan Greene	"
Elisha Johnson	50-60 A
Ezekiel Johnston	16-50 A
Ebenezer Johnson	"
Elkanah Johnston	50-60 A
Silvester Johnston	16-50 A
Rufous Johnston	"
Elisha Johnston Jr.	"
Uzal Johnson	"
Ezekiel Johnston Jr.	"
Henry Johnston	"
Joseph Mallen [?]	"
Elnathan Andrew	"
John Andrew	60+
William Andrew	16-50 A
James Andrew	"
Joseph Nichols	"
John Letson	60+
Ephariam Letson	16-50 A
Ebenezer Greene	60+
Stephen Greene	16-50 A
Tho[s] Whaley	60+
Tho[s] Whaley Jr.	16-50 A
Job Whaley	"
Samuel Whaley	"
George Potter	"
Warddell Greene	50-60 A
Phillip Greene	16-50 A
Nathaneal Greene	50-60 A
Isaac Greene	"
John Greene Son James	16-50 A
William Greene	"
Othanial Greene	"
John Rice Son of Richard	"

Page 2 (cont.)

James Phillips	16-50 A
James Phillips Jr.	"
Benj[a] Hackstone	"

Totals:

30	16-50 A	5	50-60 A
4	60+		

Page 3

John Rice	16-50 A	
Joseph Rice	"	
Allin Matteson	"	
Randall Rice Junr	"	
Richard Rice Junr	"	
Nathean Scott	"	R-Scituate
Henry Rice	"	
John Burlison	"	
John Burlison Junr	"	
Samuel Johnson	"	
Abner Goff	50-60 A	
Daniel Goff	16-50 A	
Caleb Goff	"	
William Kirk	"	R-Georgea in South Coralina
Andrew Young	"	
Josiah Gibbs	60+	
Stephen Colegrove	60+	
John Colegrove	16-50 A	
Samuel Gibbs	"	
Thomas Knox	"	
Robert Wood	"	
Caleb Rice	"	R-Warwick
James Gibson	"	
James Gibson Jr.	"	
William Love Junr	"	
Ebenezer Perkins	50-60 A	
Ebenezer Perkins Junr	16-50 A	
Joshua Spencer	"	
Richard Herrington	50-60 A	
Francis Herrington	16-50 A	
Thomas Eddy	50-60 A	
John Leyon	16-50 A	
Benjamin Tripp	"	
Thomas Parker	50-60 A	

1777 MILITARY CENSUS
COVENTRY, RHODE ISLAND

Page 3 (cont.)

Ezekiel Parker	16-50 A	
Samuel Parker	"	
Jonathan Wilbur	"	
Abel Bennet	"	

Totals:
31 16-50 A 5 50-60 A
2 60+

Page 4

Richard Nichols	16-50 A	
Abel Bennett Jr.	"	
Joseph Bennett Jr.	"	
Jonas Bennett	"	
Andrew Bennett	"	
Joseph Bennett	60+	
Hazekiah Bennett	16-50 A	
John Blanchard	"	
Caleb Blanchard	"	
Abel Potter	"	R-West Greenwich
Isaac Rice	60+	
James Rice	16-50 U	
Richard Rice	60+	
George Rice	16-50 A	
Nathan Rice	"	
Daniel Rice	"	
Ebenezer Rice	"	
Edward Jurdin	50-60 A	
Johnston Jurdin	16-50 A	
Edward Jurdin Jr.	"	
Isaac Greene Jr.	"	
Nathean Cory	"	
Benj[a] Sweet	"	
Joseph Kinyon	"	
Joseph Kenyon Jr.	"	
Tho[s] Matteson	60+	
Solomon Matteson	16-50 A	
Neubary Bolten	"	
James Andrew son Charls	"	
Randall Rice	60+	
Phillip Aylsworth Jr	16-50 A	
John Cory	"	
Adam Kasson	60+	
Archabiald Kasson	16-50 A	

Page 4 (cont.)

John Lad	60+	
James Lad	16-50 A	
John Lad Jr.	"	
Timmethy Bennett	"	
Benj[a] Mott	50-60 A	
Caleb Nichols	16-50 A	
Phillip Jurdin	"	
Isaac Rice Jr.	"	
Olney Whitman	"	R-Scituate
Pirziller Scott	"	
Ebenezer Collins	"	R-Providence

Totals:
35 16-50 A 1 16-50 U
1 50-60 A 7 60+

Page 5

Samuel Johnston	16-50 A	
William Johnston	"	
John Robert	60+	
James Robert	16-50 A	
Jeremiah Letson	"	R-West Greenwich
Isaac Johnston	"	
Job Johnston	"	
George Johnston	"	
Jonathan Johnston	"	
Bennadick Colvin	"	
John Wall	50-60 A	
Elisha Potter	16-50 U	
Tho[s] Matteson Esq[r]	60+	
Henry Matteson	16-50 A	
Jonathan Nichols	60+	
Jonathan Nichols Jr.	16-50 A	
Jonathan Nichols third	"	
David Nichols	"	
Jonathan Matteson	50-60 A	
Nathan Matteson	16-50 A	
Amas Matteson	"	
Stephen Matteson	"	
Jonathan Oldin	"	
Tho[s] Staffard	50-60 A	
John Staffard	16-50 A	
Tho[s] Staffard Jr.	"	
Richard Staffard	"	

1777 MILITARY CENSUS

COVENTRY, RHODE ISLAND

Page 5 (cont.)

Joseph Staffard	16-50	A
Benj^a Sweet	50-60	A
Job Sweet	16-50	A
Micheil Sweet	"	
Benj^a Sweet Jr.	"	
Micheil Letson	"	
John Scranton	16-50	U
James Greene	50-60	A
Henry Greene Jr.	16-50	A
Charls Andrew	60+	
Benj^a Andrew	16-50	U
Uzal Greene	60+	
Henry Greene	16-50	A

Totals:
    27 16-50 A   3 16-50 U
     5 50-60 A   5 60+

Page 6

Richard Chadsey	16-50 A	R-North Kingstown
Francis Brayton	50-60 U	
Francis Brayton Jr.	16-50 A	
George Brayton	"	
Thomas Brayton	60+	
Jonathen Brayton	16-50 A	
Joseph Brayton	"	
Charls Spencer	"	
William Phillips	50-60 A	R-North Kingstown
Thomas Colvin	60+	
Joshua Colvin	16-50 A	
Yelverton Wiate [?]	"	
William Brayton	"	
David Brayton	"	
Benj^a Cahoon	"	
Joseph Cahoon	"	
Josiah Colvin	60+	
Benj^a Briggs	16-50 A	
Amas Turner	"	R-Cranston
Daniel Matteson	"	
Samuel Baley	"	
John Briggs	"	R-Warwick
Benj^a Reed	"	
Benj^a Reed Jr.	"	
Stephen Potter	"	

Page 6 (cont.)

William Potter	16-50	A
Noel Potter	"	
Ichabud Potter	60+	
Ichabud Potter Jr.	16-50	A
William Briggs	60+	
Peleg Potter	16-50	A
Stukly Westcot	50-60	A
Arnold Wescot	16-50	A
Stephen Wescot	"	
James Tripp	"	R-Warwick
Benj^a Arnold Jr.	"	
Jonathen Robert	"	

Totals:
    29 16-50 A   2 50-60 A
     1 50-60 U   5 60+

Page 7

James Greene	60+	
Thos Greene	16-50 A	
Increese Greene Jr.	"	
Henry Briggs	"	
Jeremiah Whitman	"	R-Sciteueate
Ammezir King	"	
John King	16-50 U	
Samuel Basett	16-50 A	
Daniel Wever	"	
Elisha Greene	"	
Samuel Greene	"	
Charls Greene	"	
Benj^a Greene son Isaac	"	
Benj^a Brayton	"	
Thos Gibbs	"	
Joseph Commins	50-60 U	
William Commins	16-50 A	
Peleg Gorton	"	
Samuel Dorrance	"	
Thos Wood	50-60 U	
John Wood	16-50 A	
Thos Andrew	"	
Charls Andrew	50-60 A	
Silvister Andrew	16-50 A	
Jonathan Wever	"	
George Wever	"	
Nathean Wever	"	
Samuel Greene	50-60 A	
Nathean Greene	16-50 A	

1777 MILITARY CENSUS

COVENTRY, RHODE ISLAND

Page 7 (cont.)

Jesea Greene	16-50	A
George Gorton	"	
Robert Letson	50-60	A
William Letson	16-50	A
Robert Letson Jr.	"	
Daniel Budlong	50-60	A
Daniel Budlong Jr.	16-50	A
Aaron Budlong	"	
Edward Greene	"	
Joseph Budlong	"	
Samuel Budlong	"	
Benj^a Budlong	"	

Totals:

33	16-50 A	1	16-50 U
3	50-60 A	2	50-60 U
1	60+		

Page 8

Nathean Fisk	16-50	A
Johnston Fisk	"	
Joseph Colvin	50-60	A
Thomas Colvin Jr.	16-50	A
Phillip Colvin	"	
Ebenezer King	50-60	A
Jesea King	16-50	A
Benj^a King	"	
Lankfard Wever	"	
James Stone	"	R-Cranston
John Johnston	"	
Benj^a Burlinggam	"	
Daniel Burlinggam	60+	
Eseik Burlinggam	16-50	A
Edmond Johnston	"	.
Daniel Cumins	50-60	U
William Goff	16-50	A
William Stafford	50-60	U
David Bucklin	16-50	A
John Bucklin	16-50	A
Benj^a Bucklin	"	
John Arnold	"	
Phillip Arnold	"	
Ezra Knight	"	
Isaac Sweet	"	N
Petter Capwell	50-60	A N
William Capwell	16-50	A N

Page 8 (cont.)

Thomas Watson	16-50	A N T-Uropin
Peter Colvin	16-50	A N I
Pardon Abbitt	16-50	A
Edward Casey	"	
Thomas Brayton Jr.	"	
Benj^a Blanchard	60+	
William Fowlar	16-50	A R-North Kingstown
William Stone	"	
William Stone Jr.	"	
Jessea Potter	"	
Phillip Potter	"	
Judiah Greene	"	
Finneas Currin	"	R-Long Island

Totals:

33	16-50 A	3	50-60 A
2	50-60 U	2	60+
5	N	1	I

Page 9

William Edmonds	50-60	A
William Edmonds Jr.	16-50	A
Job Greene	50-60	A
William Greene	16-50	A
Fons Greene	"	
Stephen Greene	"	
Pardon Parce	16-50	U
John Nichols	16-50	A
Thomas Remington	"	
William Remington	"	R-Porthmath
Hezekiah Remington	"	R- "
Jeremiah Fenner	"	
Joseph Fenner	"	
Jeremiah Fenner Jr.	"	
Jeremiah Hopkins	"	
Stephen Colvin Jr.	"	
John Colvin	"	
Stephen Burlinggam	"	
David Spencer	16-50	U R-East Greenwich
Joseph Burlinggam	16-50	A
Daniel Colvin	60+	
Griffin Andrew	16-50	U

1777 MILITARY CENSUS

COVENTRY, RHODE ISLAND

Page 9 (cont.)

Samuel Colvin	16-50 A	
James Colvin	"	
Samuel Cook	60+	
John Cook	16-50 A	
Robert Cook	"	
Stephen Colvin	60+	
John Colvin Jr.	16-50 A	
Thomas Remington Jr.	"	
Josiah Potter		
Thomas Utter	16-50 U	
Thomas Hathuway	16-50 A	
John Greene	60+	
Lawduick Greene	16-50 A	
Benj^a Greene	"	
Gideon Greene	"	
Zaphanier Lanard	"	
Eliheu Greene	"	

Totals:
29 16-50 A   4 16-50 U
 2 50-60 A   4 60+

Page 10

Robert Green Son of		
Ebnezer	16-50 A	
Obediah Johnson Esqr	50-60 A	
Isaiah Johnston	16-50 A	
Hozah Johnston	"	
John Wever	"	
William Burlinggam	"	
Elijah Wever	"	
Bennadick Weeks	"	
Abel Weeks	"	
Olliver Weeks	"	
Increese Greene	60+	
John Greene Son of		
Increese	16-50 A	
Joseph Walker	"	
Nathean Greene	"	
Joseph Cummins Jr.	"	
Bowen Greene	"	
Cheafea Greene	"	
John Wever Son of John	"	
Reicum Percee	"	
Elkanah Sharemon	60+	
William Sharemon	16-50 A	

Page 10 (cont.)

Stephen Cummins	16-50 A	
Thomas Cummins	"	
Samuel Tarbox	60+	R-East Greenwich
Nicholas Whitfard	16-50 A	
Joseph Weeks	60+	
William Roy	16-50 A	
Elkanah Johnston	"	
Ebenezer Weeks	"	
Ebenzer Perce	"	
Phillip Aylsworth	60+	
James Hearington	16-50 A	
Stephen Pettis	"	
Nichals Coggashall	"	R-East Greenwich
Jeremiah Strat	"	"
Nathean Munrow	"	R-Bristol
Samuel Munrow	"	"
Daniel Fox	"	
John Fox	"	
Petter Parker	"	
William Parker	"	
Clark Parker	"	
Jonathen Parker	"	
Nathean Nichals	"	
Joseph Place	"	R-East Greenwich
Dennis Dunn	60+	
Robert Wever	16-50 A	

Totals:
40 16-50 A   6 60+

Page 11

Asaph Bennet	16-50 A	
Moses Blanchard	"	
Thomas Greene	"	R-West Greenwich
Samuel Blanchard	"	
Anthony Corey	60+	
William Corey	16-50 A	
Anthony Corey Junr	"	
Lazarous Corey	"	
John Love	"	
William Love	"	
Ezekiel Bennet	"	

1777 MILITARY CENSUS

COVENTRY, RHODE ISLAND

Page 11 (cont.)		Page 12			
Rubin Tarbox	16-50 A	This is the Mens Names that has inlisted			
James Bates	50-60 A	into the Continental and fifteen months			
William Bates	16-50 A	Service:			
Asaph Bates	"				
Jonathan Knight	"	Samuel Mearihew	(CS)	16-50 A	R-Cranston
Jeremiah Greene	60+	Samuel Davis	(CS)	"	R-Warwick
Joseph Matteson of		Daniel King	(CS)	"	R-Coventry
Jos	16-50 A	Benj^a Brown	(CS)	"	R-Wast
John Greene Esqr	"				Greenwich
Charles Cooke	"	Nicholas Teylor (CS)		"	R-Coventry
Richard Waterman	"	Warddel Greene Jr. (SM)		"	R-Coventry
Caleb Vaughan	50-60 A	Leut. Job Greene	(SM)	"	R-Coventry
Caleb Vaughan Junr	16-50 A	Capt. John Gasze	(SM)	"	R-Newport
John Kelley	"	[Capt] Josiah Gibbs Jr			
Philip Bowen	"		(SM)	"	R-Coventry
Ichabod Bowen	"	Leut Elisha Parker (SM)		"	R-Coventry
Benj^a Westcot	60+	Abel Gibbs	(SM)	"	R-Coventry
Israel Bowen	16-50 A	Insine Lias Blanchard			
Aaron Bowen	"		(SM)	"	R-Coventrry
Amos Perry	"	John Gibson	(SM)	"	R-Coventry
Benjamin Matteson	"	John Staffard (SM)		"	R-Coventry
Ephraim Westcot	"	John Nichols Jr. (SM)		"	R-Coventry
Silas Westcot	"	Robert Love	(SM)	"	R-Coventry
Ephraim Westcot Junr	"	James Herrington (SM)		"	R-Coventry
James Waterman	"	Theophalis Herrington			
Thomas Waterman	"		(SM)	"	R-Coventry
Stuckely Hudson	"	Thomas Kittle (SM)		"	R-Coventry
Wescot Stone	"	Ellicksander Love (CS)		"	R-Coventry
Joseph Scott	"	James Fenner	Indian		
			(SM)	"	R-Coventry

Totals:
  34 16-50 A   2 50-60 A
   3 60+

Total:
  21

The Sheets that is hereunto annexed is a list of all the male persons that I
have any knowlidge of in the town of Coventry from Sixteen Yers of age and
upwards that is able to bare arms and those that is not able and those that
have inlisted into the Continental Battalions and those that have inlisted
into the Service of this State for Fifteen months and the Negroes and Indians
in said town.

Taken this 19th day of April AD 1777

                   Sam. Wall Committee

South Kingstown April 19, 1777
  Sworn to before me

        Wm. Greene C. Jus^t Sup^r C^t

1777 MILITARY CENSUS

CRANSTON, RHODE ISLAND

Page 1

Benjamin Congdon	60+
John Congdon	Affirm
John R. Arnold	16-50 A
Nath[l] Stone	"
Rufus Stone	"
John Hudson	50-60 U
Israel Barney	16-50 A
Ebenezer Hill	50-60 U
Eben[r] Hill Ju[r]	16-50 A
Elisha Carpenter	"
Stephen Dexter	"
William Fenner	60+
Stephen Fenner son Wm.	16-50 A
Nath[l] Williams	60+
Fradick Williams	16-50 A
Abner Williams	"
Nath[l] Williams 3rd	"
Benajah Williams	"
James Williams	"
Eleazar Shearman	"
Jeremiah Williams	60+
Caleb Williams	16-50 A
James Harris	"
John Harris	"
George Waterman	"
Mesheck Potter	"
Abednego Potter	"
Holiman Potter	"
Walter Clark	" R-Newport
Zuriel Waterman	"
Christopher Waterman	"
Stephen Waterman	50-60 A
Stephen Waterman Jun[r]	16-50 A
Daniel Fenner	"
Zuriel Waterman 3rd	"
William Waterman (son Wm)	"
John Payn	50-60 U
Oliver Payn	16-50 A
William Payn	"
John Field	"
James Field	"
Jeremiah Field	"
James Burgis	"
Joseph Burgis	60+

Page 1 (cont.)

W[m] Hammon Ju[r]	16-50 A
Edward Edwards	"
Nathaniel Fuller	"
Reuben Baker	"
Caleb Henry	"

Totals:
    39   16-50 A   1   50-60 A
     3   50-60 U   5   60+
     1   Affirm

Page 2

Stephen Remington	60+
Peleg Arnold	16-50 A
Israel Arnold	"
Anthony Aborn	"
Rhodes Arnold	"
Benj[a] Sheldon	50-60 U R-Tiverton
Stephen Brown	50-60 A
James Sheldon	16-50 A
Thomas Corpe	60+
Joseph Rhodes Ju[r]	16-50 A
Joseph Wanton	50-60 A R-Newport
Benoni Lockwood	16-50 A
Nehemiah Rhodes	"
Zachariah Tucker	"
William Hager	" R-Newport
Josiah Haines	16-50 A
John Smith	"
Daniel Aborn	"
Benj[a] Smith	"
Zebedee Hunt	"
William Waterman	"
Caleb Corpe	"
Silas Carpenter	60+
Peter Rhodes	16-50 A
Jonathan Pitcher	"
Samuel Dunton	"
Benjamin Rhodes	"
Joseph Rhodes 3rd	"
Joseph Edmunds :	" R-Warwick
John Smith Ju[r]	"
William Wood	" R-Warwick
Stephen Potter	60+
Daniel Burrough	16-50 A R-Connecticut
Thomas Potter son [?Ec[d]]	"

1777 MILITARY CENSUS
CRANSTON, RHODE ISLAND

Page 2 (cont.)

Amos Potter	16-50 A	
Jonas L. Wanton	"	
John Corpe	60+	
Philip Sheldon	60+	
William Field	16-50 A	
Abnir Field	"	
Nehemiah Field	"	

Totals:
   32 16-50 A   2 50-60 A
    1 50-60 U   6 60+

Page 3

Peter Sprague	60+	
Nathaniel Sprague	50-60 A	
William Field (son James)	16-50 A	R-Providence
Benj^a Sprague	60+	
Christopher Williams	16-50 A	
Benjamin Williams	"	
Jonathan Sprague	50-60 A	
Jon^a Sprague Ju^r	16-50 A	
Stephen Sprague	"	
Thos Williams	60+	
John Williams	16-50 A	
Jabez Williams	"	
John Williams Junr	"	
Nathaniel Williams Junr	"	
Thomas Williams Ju^r	"	
Gideon Comstock	60+	
William Comstock	16-50 A	
Andrew Pitcher	60+	
John Pitcher	16-50 A	
John Pitcher Junr	"	
Nathan Williams	"	
Stephen Sheldon	"	
Benoni Bates	"	R-Scituate
Stephen Knight	"	
Jeremiah Utter	"	
Thomas Knight	"	
Richard Knight	"	
Reuben Knight	16-50 U	
Barzilla Knight	16-50 A	
William Knight	60+	

Page 3 (cont.)

Job Knight	16-50 A	
Henry Knight	"	
Noah Fisk	"	R-Scituate
Benjamin Knight	"	
John Fisk Ju^r	"	R-Scituate
William Collins	50-60 A	
[blank] Collins	16-50 A	
William Field Ju^r	"	
Thos Field	"	
Job Manchester	"	
Edward Knight	"	

Totals:
   31 16-50 A   1 16-50 U
    3 50-60 A   6 60+

Page 4

Joseph Harris Esqr	60+	
Andrew Harris Esqr	16-50 A	
John Clark	60+	
John Greene	16-50 A	
Abraham Clark	"	
Eleazar Clark	"	
Zuriel Potter	"	
Peleg Briggs	"	
Joseph Stone	50-60 A	
Nathan Salsbury	16-50 A	
Joshua Allen	"	R-Island of Prudence
Jonathan Carpenter	"	
Charles Goof [?]	"	
Edward Card	60+	
Thomas Waterman	16-50 A	R-Coventry
William Stone	60+	
Jabez Stone	16-50 A	
Roger Burllinggame	"	
Samuel Burllinggame Ju^r	"	
John Stafford	"	
Jeremiah Potter	"	
Peter Taylor	"	R-Warwick
David Relph	"	
Peter Stone	60+	
Peter Stone Ju^r	16-50 A	
Peter Stone 3rd	"	
Josiah Westcot	60+	

1777 MILITARY CENSUS

CRANSTON, RHODE ISLAND

Page 4 (cont.)

Josiah Battey	16-50 A	
Joseph Lockwood	"	
John Lockwood	"	
James Lockwood	"	
David Burton	"	
Josiah Westcot Junr	50-60 U	
Samuel Westcot	"	
Daniel Westcot	16-50 A	
Urian Westcot	"	
Jonathan Westcot	"	
Jacob Westcot	"	
Benjamin Westcot	60+	
Robert Henry	60+	
John King	60+	
Jonathan King	60+	

Totals:
```
   29  16-50 A    1  50-60 A
    2  50-60 U   10  60+
```

Page 5

Henry Randall	60+
Henry Randall Ju^r	16-50 A
Samuel Tompkins	50-60 U
Charles Dyer	16-50 A
Eseck Dyer	"
Jeremiah Williams Junr	"
Thomas Dyer	"
William Sprague	"
Samuel Fenner	"
Stephen Fenner	"
[blank] Fuller	"
Joseph Fenner	60+
Stukley Westcot	60+
Reuben Westcot	16-50 A
William Randall	"
William Randall Junr	"
Joseph Randall	60+
Joseph Randall Junr	16-50 U
Eleazer Randall	16-50 A
Benajah Randall	"
Anthony Randall	"
Zuriel Randall	"
Waterman Randall	"
Stephen Beverly	"
Robert Briggs	"

Page 5 (cont.)

Randall Briggs	16-50 A	
Andrew Knight	"	
Charles Atwood	"	R-Johnston
Samuel Pratt	"	
Peter Howard	"	
Rufus Barton	60+	R-Warwick
Job Joy	16-50 U	
Peter Joy	16-50 A	
Arthur Fenner	"	
Thomas Relph	60+	
Samuel Morris	Old country man	
Christopher Roberts	16-50 A	
John Rutenbur		R-Johnston
Nickolas Sheldon	60+	
Nickolas Sheldon Junr	16-50 A	
John Sheldon	16-50 A	
Pardon Sheldon	"	
John Burton Junr	"	
John Waterman	60+	
John Waterman Ju^r	16-50 U	
Zuriel Waterman Junr	16-50 A	
Martin Salsbury	60+	
William Potter	50-60 A	

Totals:
```
   33  16-50 A    3  16-50 U
    1  50-60 A    1  50-60 U
    9  60+
```

Page 6

Samuel Stone	Affirm	
Nicholas Battey	"	
James Congdon	"	
Amos Turner	"	
John Dyer	"	
~~Thomas Baker~~ John Dyer Ju^r	~~Cert~~	
Richard Sarle	16-50 A	
Peter Burllinggame 3rd	"	
Nehemiah Burllinggame	"	
Anthony Potter	"	
Elisha Burllinggame	"	
William Aldrich	"	
John Aldrich	"	R-Gloucester
William Baker	Cert	
Thomas Mason	16-50 A	
Seth Keech	"	

1777 MILITARY CENSUS

CRANSTON, RHODE ISLAND

Page 6 (cont.)

Jeremiah Potter	16-50 A	
Joseph Coggeshell	"	R-Warwick
Benj^a Greene	50-60 A	R-Warwick
Thomas Gould	16-50 A	R-Warwick
Thomas Potter	50-60 A	
Nathan Potter	16-50 A	
Christopher Lippitt	"	
Moses Lippitt	"	
Charles Lippitt	"	
Waterman Lippitt	"	
William Wight	50-60 A	R-Situate
James Burllinggame	16-50 A	
Robert Knight	50-60 U	
Lippitt Remington	50-60 A	
Christopher Smith	16-50 U	
John Remington	16-50 A	
Stephen Remington Ju^r	"	
Philip Burllinggame	50-60 A	
Samuel Burllinggame Ju^r	16-50 A	
Pardon Burllinggame	"	
Jonathan Burllinggame	50-60 A	
Jeremiah Burllinggame	16-50 A	
Benj^a Burllinggame	"	
Hopkins Burllinggame	"	

Totals:
```
25  16-50 A    1  16-50 U
 6  50-60 A    1  50-60 U
 6  Affirm     1  Cert
```

Page 7

Jonathan King Junr	16-50 A
Asa King	"
Jeremiah King	"
John King Ju^r	"
John Andrews	60+
Caleb Potter	50-60 U
William Potter son Caleb	16-50 A
Thomas Baker	Cert
John F. Fedderman	16-50 A
John Thurman	"
Thomas Potter Esqr	"
Joseph Potter	"
Peter Burllinggame	60+

Page 7 (cont.)

Pardon Briggs	16-50 A	
Stephen Burllinggame	60+	
Caleb Burllinggame	16-50 A	
Edward Sarle	50-60 A	
Thomas Sarl Ju^r	16-50 A	
Joseph Sarle	"	
Silas Sarle	"	
Joshua Burllinggame	60+	
Nathan Burllinggame	16-50 A	
Christopher Townsend	"	R-Newport
Ephraim Congdon	16-50 U	
Ephraim Congdon Ju^r	16-50 A	
James Congdon Ju^r	"	
Joseph Knight	"	
Jacob Lockwood	50-60 U	
Abraham Lockwood	16-50 A	
Philip Knight	"	
James Knight	"	
Obediah Higinbotham	"	
Samuel Burllinggame	"	
Samuel Smith	"	
Thomas Hunter	"	
Adam Philmore	"	
Jon^a Knight	50-60 A	
Benajah Knight	16-50 A	
Jon^a Knight Ju^r	"	
John Nicholas	"	
James Briggs	"	
Oliver Briggs	"	
Elisha Briggs	"	

Totals:
```
33  16-50 A    1  16-50 U
 2  50-60 A    2  50-60 U
 4  60+        1  Cert
```

Page 8

Ezekiel Warner	16-50 A
William Warner	16-50 U
Moses Warner	16-50 A
John Warner	"
William Westcot	60+
William Westcot Ju^r	16-50 A
Thomas Congdon	"
William Carpenter	"
Josiah Potter	"

1777 MILITARY CENSUS

CRANSTON, RHODE ISLAND

Page 8 (cont.)

Edward Potter Ju[r]	16-50 A	
George Colvin	"	
Samuel Philips	60+	
Elisha Philips	16-50 A	
Caleb Philips	"	
William Philips	"	
Zorobable Westcot	"	
Sylvenus Relph	50-60 A	
John Randall	60+	
John Randall Jun[r]	16-50 A	
Israel Randall	"	
Rufus Randall	"	
Noel Randall	"	
John Randall 3rd	"	
Edward Potter	60+	R-Coventry
William Burton	16-50 A	
Benjamin Burton	"	
Thomas Sarle	"	
Ezekiel Sarle	"	

Page 8 (cont.)

Israel Gorton	60+
John Gorton	60+
Israel Gorton Ju[r]	16-50 A
Pardon Gorton	"
Benjamin Gorton	"
Peter Burllingame	60+
David Robarts	60+
William Robarts	60+
Ephraim Robarts	16-50 A
Caleb Robarts	"
Oliver Robarts	"
Sam[l] Robarts	"
Samuel Congdon	60+
Benj[a] Blanchard	16-50 A
John Burton	60+
George Burton	16-50 A
Rufus Burton	"
William Bennet	60+
Jos. Burgis Ju[r]	16-50 A
Jeremiah Knight	50-60 A
Nehemiah Knight	16-50 A

Totals:

34	16-50 A	1	16-50 U
2	50-60 A	12	60+

Whereas I the Subscriber being appointed by the Honorable General Assembly of the State of Rhode Island etc., at their Sessions held at South Kingston March 1777 to Take an account or list of all the male Persons in the Town of Cranston of 16, to 50, Years of age, who I should Judge able to bear Arms, from Ditto to Ditto whom I shall Judge unable to bear arms, from 50, to 60, able to bear Arms, from Ditto to Ditto, unable, and from 60, upwards. -----and Likewise Indians & Negroes.
Agreeable to Said appointment, I have ascertained the Number of each Class, which, with each persons name is Humbly Submitted by your Honor's Humble Ser[t].

Nehemiah Knight

The whole amount as Follows viz,

256	16-50 A	7	16-50 U	17	50-60 A	10	50-60 U	53	60+	7	Affirm
2	Cert	22	N	4	I			Total	378		

Providence Ss, in Providence April 17th 1777

Personally appeared the above Named Nehemiah Knight and made Solemn Oath that the above List or Estamate is Justly and Truly made, according to the best of his Knowledge.

Before me. --- Theodore Foster, Jus. Peace

1777 MILITARY CENSUS

CRANSTON, RHODE ISLAND

(cont.)

The State of Rhode Island etc   D^r _____
To my Service in performing the above Business
    Six Days at 6/   £1...16...0
    To Horse Hire   0...18...0
                             £2...14...0

True Acct E Excepted
Ex: Nathl Mumford & Nehemiah Knight

[on the side of above statement is following]
N.B. I have not Included those Persons that are already Engaged in the 15
    months Service, and Continental Army.

                              Nehemiah Knight

CUMBERLAND, RHODE ISLAND

Page 1

Aldrich Jonathan Capt	50-60	A
Aldrich Squire	16-50	A
Aldrich Robert Esqr	Affirm	
Arnold Levi	"	
Aldrich Baruch	16-50	A
Aldrich Laban	"	
Arnold Moses	60+	
Arnold Joseph	16-50	A
Arnold John	"	
Arnold Amos	50-60	U
Arnold Nathan	16-50	A
Angell Abraham	"	
Allen Timothy	50-60	A
Anderson Thomas	16-50	A R-Smith-field
Allen Nehemiah Capt	60+	
Alexander Roger	16-50	A
Angell Thomas	50-60	A
Angell George	16-50	A
Amsbary Jeremiah	"	
Aldrich Abell	"	
Aldrich Philip (SM)	"	
Aldrich Joseph	"	
Ballou Ariel	60+	
Brown Stephen	60+	
Ballou Abner	16-50	A
Ballou William	"	
Ballou Nathan	"	
Ballou Levi	"	

Page 1 (cont.)

Ballou Ezekiel	50-60	A
Ballou Edward	16-50	A
Bartlet Jacob	"	
Bartlet Abel	"	
Bartlet Eber	16-50	U
Bartlet Abner	16-50	A
Bartlet Joseph Junr	"	
Bartlet Joseph	60+	
Braley Roger	50-60	A
Braley Roger Junr	16-50	A
Braley Lemuel	"	
Ballou Noah	"	
Ballou David	"	
Braley John	16-50	U
Brownell George	16-50	A
Bishop Simeon	"	
Bartlet John	"	
Bartlet Daniel	"	
Bartlet Asa	"	
Bartlet Jeremiah	"	
Brown Jesse	"	
Bragg Daniel (CS)	"	

Page 2

Ballou Noah Junr	16-50	A
Edward Butterrix (CS)		T-Grafton
Brown Joseph Capt	50-60	A
Captain in the alarm List Company		

1777 MILITARY CENSUS

CUMBERLAND, RHODE ISLAND

Page 2 (cont.)

Brown Joseph Jun[r]	16-50 A	
Ballou Elisha (SM)	"	
Ballou James	"	
Bragg Nehemiah	"	
in the Continental Fleet		
Blie John	16-50 A	
Blie Oliver	"	
Bicknell Thomas	"	
Bowen William	"	
Brown John	"	
Butterworth Noah	50-60 A	
Butterworth Noah Jun[r]		
(SM)	16-50 A	
Butterworth John	"	
Bishop John	60+	
Bishop John Jun[r]	16-50 A	
Bishop William	"	
Brown Nicholas	16-50 U	
Boyce Joseph	16-50 A	
Bradford George	"	
Bradford George Jun[r]	"	
Blanding Ephraim	"	
Blanding Samuel	"	
Brown Ephraim	"	
Brown Stephen Jun[r]	"	
Brown Elijah	"	
Brown Elihu	"	
Bartlet Jehu	"	
Bartlet Israel	"	
Bartlet Rufus	"	
Brown Abiel	"	
Bowen Thomas	"	
Bowen Amos	"	
Brown Christopher	"	
second Leu[t] in the alarm List Company		
Brown Cyril	16-50 A	
Bartlet Job	"	
Brown Ichabod	"	
Brown Ichabod Jun[r]	"	R-Smith-field
Brown Amos	16-50 U	
Butler Benjamin	16-50 A	
Burllinggame John	60+	
Burllinggame John Jun[r]	16-50 A	
Burllinggame Daniel	"	
Ballou Joseph	"	
Ballou Benjamin	"	

Page 2 (cont.)

Ballou Reuben Cap[t] (SM)	16-50 A	
Brown Sylvanus	16-50 A	
Ballou Asa	"	
Ensign in ye alarm List Company		
Ballou Absalom	16-50 A	
Ensign in the second Company of Militia		
Bishop Gideon	16-50 A	
Bennet Timothy	"	

Page 3

Blie Jeremiah	16-50 A	
Brown Levi	"	R-Rehoboth
Brown Caleb	"	"
Bates John	50-60 A	R-Attle-borough
Cook Abraham	50-60 A	
Cook David (SM)	16-50 A	
Cook Stephen	"	
Cook Eleazer	"	
Cook Asahel	16-50 U	
Cook Hazekiah	50-60 A	
Capron Charles	"	
Cook Abraham Jun[r]	16-50 A	
Capron Joseph	"	
Capron Philip	"	
Chace Isaac	60+	
Nathan Clarke	16-50 A	
Cole John	60+	
Cole John Jun[r]	16-50 A	
Cole Joseph	"	
Cook Ariel	"	
Cook Annanias	"	
Carpenter Asa	"	
Chase Joseph	60+	
Chase Joseph Jun[r]	16-50 A	
Chase John	"	
Chase Stephen	"	
Cargill James	"	
Carpenter William	50-60 U	
Clarke Samuel	50-60 A	
Clarke Edward	16-50 A	
Clarke John	50-60 A	
Clarke Aaron	16-50 A	
Clarke Samuel Jun[r]	"	
Carpenter Ezekiel	"	

1777 MILITARY CENSUS

CUMBERLAND, RHODE ISLAND

Page 3 (cont.)

Crowingshield Richard	16-50	A
Chamberlin Samuel	"	
Carpenter Jotham	60+	
Carpenter Jotham Junr	16-50	A
Carpenter Oliver	"	
Commins Joseph	"	
Cook Nathaniel	"	
Cook Silas	"	
Dexter John	60+	
Dexter James	50-60	A
Dexter David	"	
Dexter David Junr	16-50	A

Captain in the Continental Battalion

Dexter Oliver	16-50	A

Ensign in the Continental Battalion

Page 4

Dexter Esek (CS)	16-50	A
Dexter Daniel (SM)	"	
Dexter Simeon	"	
Dexter Stephen	"	
Darling John	60+	
Davis Benjamin	50-60	U
Davis Joseph Esqr	50-60	A

first Lieu^t in the alarm Company

Darling Joseph	16-50	A
Darling Peter Esqr	"	
Darling Peter Junr	"	
Darling John	60+	
Darling John Junr	16-50	A
Elias Darling	"	
Darling Ebenezer	"	
Estes Richard	60+	
Estes Richard Junr	16-50	A
Estes Stephen	"	
Estes John	"	
Estes John Junr (SM)	"	
Emerson William	"	
Emerson William Junr (CS)	"	
Estes Samuel	"	
Esterbrooks Abiel	"	R-Warren
Fisher Jeremiah	16-50	U
Field Solomon	16-50	A R-Attle-borough
Field John	16-50	U "
Follet Joseph	16-50	A

Page 4 (cont.)

Follet Abraham	16-50	A
Follet William	"	
Follet Benjamin	"	
Fisher Jonathan	"	
Fisher Jonathan Junr	"	
Fisk John	"	

major of one of Regiments of Militia

Fisk Squire	16-50	A

first Lieu^t of a Company in ye 15 months Service

Fisk John Junr	16-50	A
Fuller Peleg	60+	
Fuller Ezekiel	50-60	A
Foster Samuel	16-50	A
Fuller Thomas	"	R-Attle-borough

Page 5

Goold John Esqr	50-60	A
Goold Benjamin	16-50	A
Gaskill William Esqr	"	
Grant John	60+	
Gaskill Samuel	Affirm	
Goold Nathaniel	16-50	A

Lieu^t of the Second Company of Militia

Grant Joseph	60+	
Goold John Junr	16-50	A
Goold Jabez	"	
Grant Gilbert	"	

1st Lieu^t in the Continental Service

Grant Allen	16-50	A
Grant John Junr	"	
Grant Samuel	"	
Grant David	"	
Green Andrew	"	T-Great Britain
Hopkins Asa	"	
Howard Samuel	"	
Howard John	"	
Hogg Abraham	"	
Hawkins Andrew	16-50	U
Harris Christopher	16-50	A
Harris Christopher Junr (SM)	"	
Harris Ezekiel	"	
Harris Oliver	"	

1777 MILITARY CENSUS

CUMBERLAND, RHODE ISLAND

Page 5 (cont.)

Hathway Silvanus	16-50 A
Hathway Melatiah	60+
Haskill Abner	60+
Haskill Comfort	16-50 A
Haskill Samuel	"
Haskill John	"
Haskill Amos	"
Hill Roger	"
Jenks Daniel	60+
Jenks Daniel Jun	16-50 A
Jenks Jeremiah	"
Jenks John	"
Jenks Anthony	"
Jenks David	"
Jenks Joseph	"
Jillson Uriah Esq[r]	60+
Jillson Nathaniel	60+

Page 6

Joslen Thomas	16-50 A	
Jillson Nathan	"	
Inman Stephen	"	
Jillson Nathaniel Jun[r]	"	
Jillson Uriah Jun[r]	"	
Jillson Paul	"	
Jillson Luke	"	
Jillson Enos	"	
Jenks Amos	"	
Inman Jeremiah	"	
Inman Francis	"	
Feffers [sic] Caleb	"	R-Newport
Jones Uriah (CS)	"	
Lapham Abner Esq[r]	"	
Lapham Joseph	60+	
Lovet John	60+	
Lovet John Jun[r]	16-50 A	
Lovett Eliphalet	16-50 U	
Lovett James Cap[t]	16-50 A	
Lovett William	"	
Lee Joseph	"	
Lee Levi	"	
Lapham John	"	
Lovett Peter	Spanish I	
Lapham Saul	N	
Lind William	16-50 A	T-Sweeden

Page 6 (cont.)

Mason Pelatiah	60+
Mason Jonathan	16-50 A
Mosher Jonathan	"
Mosher Gardner	"
Mosher Luthan	"
Miller Daniel	60+
Miller Daniel Jun[r]	16-50 A
Miller Josiah	"
Miller Peter	"
May Benjamin	"
Meads James	"
Metcalf Ebenezer	"
Mason Jonathan Jun[r]	"

Page 7

Newell Jason	16-50 A	
Newell Aaron	"	
Newell Elisha	"	
Newell David	"	
Peck Solomon	"	
Peck Benjamin	"	
Philbrook Elias	"	
Peck George	"	

    Captain of the Independant Company
    of the Smithfield & Cumberland
    Rangers

Philips Michael	16-50 A	R-Boston
Richmond Ichabod	"	R-Providence
Ray Henry	"	
Ray Daniel [?]	"	
Raze Joseph	50-60 A	
Raze Joseph Juner	16-50 A	

    Ensign in the first Company of
    Militia

Raze Isaac	16-50 A
Richmond Jeremiah	"
Joseph Raze ye 3.	"
Jonas Raze	"
David Raze	60+
David Raze Jun[r]	16-50 A
Ray Joseph	"
Ray Asa	"
Ray Joseph Jun[r]	"
Ray Oliver	"

1777 MILITARY CENSUS

CUMBERLAND, RHODE ISLAND

Page 7 (cont.)

Richmond S[?]igby	N		
Smith John	60+		
Smith Jesse	16-50 A		
Staples Nathan	"		
Staples David	"		
Strange John (CS)	"		
Staples Jonathan (CS)	"		
Smith Benjamin	"		R-Smith-field

Page 8

Smith Chad	16-50 A	
Steeter Joseph	50-60 A	
Streeter Bezeleal (SM)	16-50 A	
Streeter Eleazer	"	
Sly John	"	
Staples Stephen	"	
Sheldon William	"	
Sheldon Roger	"	
Sprague Jonathan	60+	
Sprague Abraham	16-50 A	
Sprague Gideon	"	
Shapardson Nathaniel Esqr	16-50 A	
Shapardson Nathan^l Junr	"	
Smith John Junr	"	
Smith Daniel	"	
Smith Daniel Junr	"	
Smith David	"	
Smith Levi	"	
Smith Jonathan	"	
Streeter Nathan	"	
Streeter Ebenezer	"	
Sprague Amos	50-60 A	
Sprague Seth Ensign (SM)	16-50 A	
Scott Jeremiah	50-60 A	
Scott Jeremiah Junr	16-50 A	
Scott Charles	"	
Staples George (SM)	"	
Trask Daniel	"	R-Mendon
Tower Benjamin Capt	60+	
Thurber Amos (CS)	16-50 A	
Taft Stephen	"	

Page 8 (cont.)

Thurber Barnabas	16-50 A		
Tower Levi Capt	"		
Tower Enoch Capt	"		
Tillson Joseph	60+		
Tower Ichabod	16-50 A		
Trask Edward	"		R-Mendon
Thurston James	50-60 U		R-Rehoboth
Vicory John	16-50 A		R-Chester-field

Page 9

Whipple Jeremiah Esqr	60+	
Wallcott William	60+	
Wallcott Benjamin Junr Leiu^t (SM)	16-50 A	
Wallcott John	16-50 A	
Wallcott George	"	
Whipple Jeremiah Junr	"	
Whipple Simon	"	
Whipple David	"	
Whipple Moses	"	
Whipple Israel	"	
Whipple Israel Junr	"	
Whipple Calvin	"	
Weatherhead John	"	
Weatherhead Daniel	60+	
Willcox Daniel	16-50 A	
Willcox Stephen	"	
Wood Thomas	"	
Weatherhead Levi	"	
Weatherhead Jeram^h Junr (SM)	"	
Weatherhead Enoch Capt in the first Company of Militia	"	
Weatherhead Nathan	16-50 A	
Weatherhead Amaziah	"	
Whipple Christopher	"	
Whipple Peck	"	
Whipple John	60+	
Whipple John Junr	16-50 A	
Whipple Samuel	50-60 A	
Whipple Peter (SM)	16-50 A	
Whipple Joseph	50-60 A	
Whipple Asa	16-50 A	
Whipple Daniel	60+	

1777 MILITARY CENSUS

CUMBERLAND, RHODE ISLAND

Page 9 (cont.)

Whipple Daniel Jun[r]   16-50 A
Whipple Simon Jun[r]   "
Whipple Amos   "
   Cap[t] of the Second Company of
   Militia
Whipple Preserved   16-50 A
Whipple Joel   "
Whipple Comfort (SM)   "
Whipple Job   "
Whipple Eleazer   "
Whipple Eleazer Jun[r]   "
Waterman Amaziah   60+   R-Provi-
                                  dence
Waterman Elisha Cap[t] 16-50 A
Williams Robert   "   R-Great
                                  Britain
Whipple Ibrook   50-60 A
Whipple Ibrook Jun[r]   16-50 A
Whipple Stephen   "
Whipple Ephraim   "

Page 10

Whipple Benjamin   16-50 A
Wilkinson Daniel   60+
Wilkinson Jeremiah   60+
Wilkinson William   16-50 A

Page 10 (cont.)

Wilkinson Benjamin   16-50 A
   Leiu[t] of the first Company of Mi-
   litia
Wilkinson Daniel Jun[r]   16-50 A
Wilkinson Simon   "
Wilkinson Joab   "
Wilkinson Nedabiah   "
   Second Leiu[t] of the Smithfield
   & Cumberland Rangers
Wilkinson Jeremiah Jun[r] Cert
Wilkinson Stephen   16-50 A
Wilkinson Jepthtah   "
Whitaker William   "   R-Bill-
                                   ingham
Wilkinson John   "
Waterman Pero   N

Young Hugh   60+

Totals:
   315 16-50 A   9 16-50 U
    25 50-60 A   4 50-60 U
    41 60+   3 Affirm
     1 Cert   3 T
    20 R   3 N
     1 I
12 Twelve in the Continental Service
16 Sixteen in the 15 month Service
Two have Taken the affirmation
one Certificate from the friends
Twenty Residents
Three Transient Persons

State of Rhode Island Ss Cumberland April 14, 1777. The foregoing is a True
List of all the male persons, inhabiting and Residing within the Town of Cumberland in Said State Taken agreeable to and in obedience To an act of the
Honorable General Assembly of Said State made and passed at South Kingstown
march second session 1777. Taken by John Dexter one of the Committee appointed for that purpose.

Providence Ss Cumberland April 15th 1777
   John Dexter Esq[r] made Solemn oath that the foregoing List of the male persons Inhabiting and Residing within the Town of Cumberland in Said County hath
been Justly and truly made by him, according to the Best of his Knowledge.
            Before me Jeremiah Whipple Justis of Pleas

The State of Rhode Island to John Dexter D[r] To my Time and Expence in Performing the above Service   £2:8:0   Errors Excepted
Examined Nath[l] Mumford   John Dexter

1777 MILITARY CENSUS

EAST GREENWICH, R. I.

[The enumerator for East Greenwich used a different format in tallying his males, apparently using the head of the household in the name bracket.]

Page 1

Frederick Hamilton	one 16-50 A
Richard Briggs	one "
	one 60+
Thos Coggeshall Ju^r	one 16-50 A
Benj^a Godfrey	one "
William Spencer	one "
Richard Spencer	one "
Isack Upton	one " Cert
Samuel Upton	one " "
Nathan Greene	one " "
Samuel Trip	one " "
Daniel Howland	one " "
	one 50-60 A "
Joseph Congdon	two 16-50 A "
Thos Aldrich	two " "
	one 50-60 A "
	one N
William Spencer	
s^n Walter	one 16-50 A Aff.
Walter Spencer	one 60+
John Aylsworth	one 16-50 A Aff
Alexander Nichols	one 60+
Daniel Peirce	one 60+
Stephen Sheppe	one 60+
John Mancester	one 60+
Havens Tabour	one 16-50 A
	T-Warwick
Nicholas Underwood	one 16-50 A
	R-Newport
James Chambers	one 60+ R-Newport
Robert Stephens	two 16-50 A
	one 60+
	R-Newport
John Albro	two 16-50 A
	one 60+
	R-W. Greenwich
Josiah Arnold	one 60+ R-Newport
	one N
William Howard	one 16-50 A
	R-Newport
Stephen Adams	one 16-50 A
Thos Sweet	one "
	R-W. Greenwich

Page 1 (cont.)

Joseph Gardner	one 16-50 A
	R-Newport
Wing Spooner	one 16-50 A
	R-Newport
John Johnson	one 16-50 A
	R-Newport
Edward Stringfeild	one 16-50 A
	R-Newport
William Weaver	one 16-50 A
	R-Newport
Nicholas Matteson	one 16-50 A
	R-Warwick

Totals:

32	16-50 A	2	50-60 A
10	60+	2	Aff
11	Cert	15	R
1	N [sic]		

Page 2

James Searle	one 16-50 A
Richard Aylsworth	one "
Sylvester Greene	one "
Thos Arnold	one "
Isaac Carr	one "
Robart Hall	one "
	one 60+
Joseph Arnold	one 16-50 A
Ephraim Weadon	one "
Elisha Reynolds	one "
Michael Johnson	one "
William Sweet	three 16-50A
	one 60+
Samuel Sweet	one 16-50 A
Thos Wells	two "
Jonathan Weaver	one "
	one N
James Stafford	one 16-50 A
John Mackneear	one "
	R-Warwick
Morgan Calvin	two 16-50 A
William Mosier	one "
Benjamin Vaughn	one "

1777 MILITARY CENSUS

EAST GREENWICH, R. I.

Page 2 (cont.)

Stephen Remington	one	16-50 A
Richard Cornwell	two	"
	one	60+
Jonathan Andrews	two	16-50 A
Benoni Andrews	one	"
Joshua Godfrey	one	"
Gideon Mumford	one	"
William Bentley	two	"
Abraham Greene	one	16-50 U
Ichabod Smith	one	16-50 A
John Shaw	two	"
Benjamin Spencer	one	"
Jerimiah Peirce	one	"
Griffen Greene	one	"
Caleb Sisson	one	"
Samuel Sowl	one	60+

Totals:

42	16-50 A	1	16-50 U	
4	60+	1	R	
1	N			

Page 3

Isack Johnson	one	50-60 A
Colonel Carpenter	one	16-50 A
	one	16-50 U
	one	50-60 U
John Gardner	one	16-50 A
Thomas Spencer	one	"
	one	60+
Griffin Spencer	two	16-50 A
	one	T-Bermudas
Andrew Boyd	one	16-50 A
Pasco Austin (SM)	one	"
Stephen Spencer	one	"
Gideon Casey	one	"
William Bentley	one	"
Smitten Wilcox	one	"
Stephen Mott Ju^r	one	"
Saml Smith	two	"
Richard Matthewson	five	"
William Arnold	three	"
John Gardner	one	"
	one	50-60 U
Anthony Holden	one	"
Edward Weadon	one	16-50 A

Page 3 (cont.)

Jabez Finney	one	16-50 A
Samuel Sweet		
ali[a]s Bul	one	"
Stephen Mott	one	"
	one	60+
Samuel Hatch	one	16-50 A
Oliver Peirce	one	"
John Glazier	one	"
Jonathan Capron	two	"
Caleb Weadon Ju^r	one	"
Edmund Andrews	four	"
Abial Hall	four	"
	one	60+
George Weaver	two	16-50 A
Nicholas Goddard	one	"
	one	50-60 U
Oliver Arnold	one	50-60 A
	one	N
Stephen Mumford	one	16-50 U
	one	50-60 A
William Merice	one	50-60 A
Cornelius Clarke	three	16-50 A
	one	50-60 A
Josias Jones	three	16-50 A
	two	50-60 A
Benjamin Sweet	one	16-50 A
	one	50-60 A
Rowland Sprague	three	16-50 A
	one	60+

Totals:

54	16-50 A	2	16-50 U	
8	50-60 A	4	50-60 U	
4	60+	1	R	
1	N			

Page 4

John Arnold	one	60+
John Nichols	one	16-50 A
	one	60+
John Langford	one	16-50 A
	one	60+
Samuel Davis	one	16-50 A
	one	60+
	one	N
Philip Tillinghast	one	60+
	one	N

1777 MILITARY CENSUS

EAST GREENWICH, R. I.

Page 4 (cont.)

John Briggs	one 16-50 A
	one 60+
William Hamilton	two 16-50 A
	one 60+
James Wightman	one 16-50 A
	one 60+
Thos Rumrill	one 16-50 U
William Spencer	two 16-50 A
	one 16-50 U
Chandley Burlingham	one 16-50 A
Ezra Simmons	one "
Remington Kinyon	one "
Stephen Cooper	one "
David Alvason	one "
Thos Spencer	
sⁿ Wal^r	one "
James Budlong	one "
Pardon Mawney	one "
	one N
John Oldfeild	one 50-60 U
	one N
Thos Place Juⁿ	four 16-50 A
Thos Tillinghast	two "
Thos Cory	two "
Jonathan Tibbits	one "
Henry Gardner	one 50-60 A
James Sweet Sⁿ Sylv.	one 16-50 A
William Peirce	one "
	one N
Henry Tibbitts	one 16-50 A
	one 60+
Richard Fry	two 16-50 A
John Millemon (SM)	one "
John Wightman	two "
Richard Nichols	one "
Oliver Sweet	one "
	one 60+
William Bailey	two 16-50 A
	one 60+
John Bailey	one 16-50 A
Yelverton Briggs	one "
Benjamin Dexter	four "
Richard Briggs	one "

Totals:
   45 16-50 A   2 16-50 U

Page 4 (cont.)

Totals: (cont.)
   1 50-60 A   1 50-60 U
   11 60+   4 N [sic]

Page 5

MISSING

Page 6

Job Card	one 16-50 A
Jeremiah Sweet	three "
John Briggs Junr	one "
Nathan Briggs	three "
	one 16-50 U
Cary Briggs	one 16-50 A
Francis Briggs	one "
Peter Wells	one "
John Brightman	two "
	one 60+
Joseph Card	one 16-50 A
Benjamin Caperon	two "
Robart Whitford	one "
	one 60+
Jonathan Hopkins	one 16-50 A
Jonathan Fairbank	one "
Thomas Reynolds	four "
Josph Baley	one "
	one 60+
Benjamin Wood	one 16-50 A
Silas Spencer	two "
Thomas Foster	one "
Anthony Alsworth	one "
William Marks	one 16-50 U
John Cory	one 16-50 A
Thomas Shippy	one "
	one 16-50 U
	one 60+
Job Vaughn	one 16-50 A
Wilson Spencer	two "
Jonathan Grinel	one "
	R-Jamestown
Job Peirce	one 16-50 A
	one 60+
Jeremiah Spencer	two 16-50 A
(three Cert)	one 50-60 U

1777 MILITARY CENSUS

EAST GREENWICH, R. I.

Page 6 (cont.)

Thomas Cogsheal	one 16-50 A
	one 16-50 U
	one 60+
Caleb Spencer	one 60+
Thomas Casey	one 60+
Peleg Cranston	one 16-50 A
	R-Newport
Samuel Arrew	one 60+
	R-Newport
	one N
John Proud	one 16-50 A
	one 60+
	R-Newport
William Tweedy	one 16-50 A
	one 60+
	three N
	R-Newport

Totals:

42	16-50 A	4	16-50 U
1	50-60 U	12	60+
3	Cert	5	R
4	N		

Page 7

Cristopher Vaughn	two 16-50 A
John Langford	one "
Rufus Spencer	one 50-60 A
Silas Jones	six 16-50 A
	one 50-60 A
Job Comstock	one 16-50 A
Able Shearman	one "
Benjamin Spencer S[on] of T	one "
Hopkins Cook	one "
Comfort Searl	one "
Robert Vaughn	two "
Lory Jenks	one "
Jonthan Pitcher	two "
	one 60+
John Grinnel	one 16-50 A
	one 60+
Samuel Tarbox	two 16-50 A
Peleg Weaver	two "
	one N
Joseph Green	one 16-50 A

Page 7 (cont.)

Thomas Spencer S[on] of A	two 16-50 A
Jonathan Weaver	one 60+
Joshua Cogsheal	one 16-50 A
	one 60+
Joseph Hunt	two 16-50 A
	one 60+
Henry Sweet	one 16-50 A
	one 60+
Caleb Briggs	one 16-50 A
	one 60+
Thomas Place	one 60+
Thomas Fish	one 16-50 A
Thomas Briggs	three "
Jobn Cobb	one "
George Baley	one "
Job Briggs	one "
Thomas Vaughn	one "
David Vaughn	one "
John Johnson	one "
James Whitman Jun[r]	one "

Totals:

43	16-50 A	2	50-60 A
8	60+	1	N

Page 8

Nicholas P. Tilling[st]	one 16-50 A
	R-Newport
Benj[a] Gould	one 16-50 A
	R-Newport
Benj[a] Nichols	one 16-50 A
	R-Newport
Benj[a] Brown	one 16-50 A
	R-Newport
Sam[ul] Cranston	one 16-50 A
	R-Newport
Gershom Remington	one 16-50 A
	R-Jamestown
Israel Ambros	one 16-50 A
	R-Newport
John Dyer Alin	one 16-50 A
	R-Portsmouth
Jonathan Nichols	one 16-50 A
Stephen Green	one "

1777 MILITARY CENSUS

EAST GREENWICH, R. I.

Page 8 (cont.)

Totals:
10 16-50 A 8 R

	16-50 A	16-50 U	50-60 A	50-60 U	60+	Cert	Aff	T	R	N
No. 1	32	0	2	0	10	11	2	1	15	1
No. 2	42	1	0	0	4	0	0	0	1	1
No. 3	54	2	8	4	4	0	0	1	0	0
No. 4	45	2	1	1	11	0	0	0	0	4
No. 5	46	1	9	1	2	0	0	0	0	4
No. 6	42	4	0	1	11	3	0	0	5	4
No. 7	43	0	2	0	8	0	0	0	0	1
[No. 8	10	0	0	0	0	0	0	0	8	0]
	314	10	23	7	50	14	2	2	29	15 Blaks
	10									
	23									
	7									
	50									

Total   404
Whites from 16 & upward

The Above is a true Accompt
of all the White males from
16 years and upwards in the
town of East Greenwich As
Taken by me to the Best of
my Knoledge
        Benj^a Tillinghast
Kings County Ss
Ap^r 18, 1777

Soldiers in the 15^mon Servis
    John Spencer
    Pasgo Austin
    Caleb Mathews
    Shippy Reynolds
    Michal Spencer
    Ezechal Warner
    Thos Brocks
    George Sweet
    George Milliman

Soldiers in the Con-
    tinental Servis
    John Dexter Junr
    John Cook
    Charls Peirce
    Michal Whitman
    Daniel Peirce
    Benj^a Jonson
    Gedion Casey
    Nicholas Tiler
    Zebelon Millet
    John Wise

        Personally appeared Before me the above Subscriber and made oath
        to the Truth of the above estimate according to the Best of his
        knowledg the Day and Date aforsaid Witness John Northup Jus^t Pleas

GLOCESTER, R. I.

Totals: Page 1

	16-50 A	16-50 U	50-60 A	50-60 U	60+	Cert	Aff	T	R	N	CS	SM
Page 1	33	8	3	4	0	0	2	0	0	0	0	0
Page 2	41	1	0	0	0	0	2	0	0	0	0	0
Page 3	42	2	0	0	0	0	9	0	1	0	0	0
Page 4	35	2	0	0	0	2	1	0	0	4	5	1
Page 5	43	0	0	1	0	0	0	0	0	1	0	0
Page 6	52	1	0	0	0	0	0	0	0	0	0	0
Page 7	45	3	0	1	0	0	0	0	0	0	0	0
Page 8	36	2	0	0	2	1	12	0	0	0	0	0
Page 9	45	0	0	0	0	0	0	0	0	0	1	0
Page 10	43	0	0	0	0	0	1	0	0	0	0	0
Page 11	32	9	2	1	0	4	2	0	0	0	0	0

1777 MILITARY CENSUS

GLOCESTER, R. I.

Page 1 (cont.)

	16-50 A	16-50 U	50-60 A	50-60 U	60+	Cert	Aff	T	R	N	CS	SM
Page 12	0	1	4	1	39	3	1	0	0	0	0	0
Page 13	52	0	0	0	0	0	0	0	0	0	0	0
Totals:												
	499	29	9	8	41	10	30	0	1	5	6	1

Peter Shippee   16-50 A
Joseph Smith Jr   "
Seth Richmond   "
Job Smith   "
Othinel Herendeen   "
Benj. Thornton   "
Seth Hopkins   "
John Davis   "
Jonathan Wade   "
Joseph Cowen   "
Jedediah Sprague   "
John Cowen   "
Elisha Brown   "
Manariah Killy   16-50 U
Aran Winsor   16-50 A
James Cowen   "
Daniel Owen   16-50 U
Timothy Willmarth   50-60 A
Solomon Owen   16-50 A
Elisha Hopkins   "
Obed Sm[torn]   "
Ezekiel Sayles   [torn]
Stephen Smith   [torn]
Ebenezer Darling   16-50 U
Samuel Cuttler   16-50 A
Samuel Potter   "
Isaiah Inman   16-50 U
Noah Whitman   50-60 U
William Hill   "
Hesediah Mitchel   "
David Burllingame   16-50 A
Obadiah Brown   "
Joram Kinyon   50-60 U
Daniel Evens   16-50 A
Abraham Baker   Aff
David Arnold   50-60 A
John Olney   16-50 A
Benjn Barnes   50-60 A
Jonathan Whipple   16-50 A
John Durfey   "
Noah Aldrich   Aff

Page 1 (cont.)

Peter Crossman   16-50 A
William Bowen   16-50 U
Uriah Hawkins   16-50 A
Luther Hise [?]   "
Peter Place   16-50 U
Benjn Tourtelot   16-50 A
Samuel Wright   "
Jeremh Steere   16-50 U
John Andrews   "

Totals:
   33 16-50 A   8 16-50 U
    3 50-60 A   4 50-60 U
    2 Aff

Page 2

Charles Field   16-50 A
John Howland   "
James Lewis   "
Asa Steere   "
Elisha Steere   "
Stephen Killy   "
David Arnold Jr   "
Jonathan Bowen   "
Asa Potter   Aff
Stephen Whipple   16-50 A
David Bourllingame Jr   "
William Brown   "
Richard Evens   "
William Hawkins Jr   "
Saml Irons ye 3d   "
Joseph Page Jr   "
Stephen Page   "
Elizer Bowen Jr   "
John Bussey   "
Hazakiah Bowen Jr   "
Stephen Keech Jr   "
Abner Cole   "
Lippit Eddy   "

1777 MILITARY CENSUS

GLOCESTER, R. I.

Page 2 (cont.)

James Durfey	16-50 A
John Andrews J^r	"
William Steere	"
Stulley (?) Hopkins	"
Peter Sprague	"
Simeon Steere	"
Othenial Young	"
Enoch Steere Ju^r	Aff
Dean Kimball	16-50 A
Eseck Smith	"
William Coman	"
Charles Wright	"
Thomas Burgess	"
Thomas Hopkins	
Son of Zebee	"
David Hix	"
Benedick Bullingame J^r	16-50 U
Elisha Winsor	16-50 A
Joseph Field J^r	"
Thomas Wever	"
Benj Hawkins J^r	"
Simeon Sweet	"

Totals:
     41 16-50 A   1 16-50 U
      2 Aff

Page 3

David Darling	16-50 A
Epherim Ballard	"
Mierjah Moffit	"
Epherim Phillips	16-50 U
Benjⁿ Salsbuary	16-50 A
Levi Thornton	Aff
Elisha Wood	16-50 A
David Hill	"
Nathan Whipple	"
Elisha Herendeen	Aff
Abraham Fairfield	16-50 A
Jonathan Wood	"
Israel Man	"
Benoni Short	"
Abner Yates	Aff
Luke Ballard	Aff
Icabod Ballard	Aff
Daniel Curtice	16-50 A

Page 3 (cont.)

Thomas Herendeen	Aff
Jeremiah Ballard	
ye 3^d	Aff
James Brown	16-50 A
Constant Vial	"
Silvanus Cook	"
Caleb Loge	"
William Moffitt	"
Joshua Cock	"
Nathan Pain J^r	Aff
James Stone	16-50 A
John Howland J^r	Aff
Enos Eddy	16-50 A
David Comstock	"
Shedarak Wells	"
James Page	"
Simeon Herendeen	"
John Short J^r	"
William Smith	R-Ireland
Peter Thompson	16-50 A
Jonathan Short	"
Israel Brown	"
Ezekiel Brown	"
Israel Herendeen	"
Thomas Curtice	"
James Blackmar	16-50 U
Stephen Shippee	16-50 A
Jeremiah Ballard J^r	"
Eseck Harris	"
Gideon Cook	"
Hazakiah Herendeen	"
George Hunt	"
Aseal Shearman	"
Benoni Page	"
John Kimball	"
Joseph Brown	"
Daniel Whipple J^r	"

Totals:
     42 16-50 A   2 16-50 U
      9 Aff   1 R

Page 4

Job Keech	16-50 U
Benoni Sanders	16-50 A
Samuel Steere	"

1777 MILITARY CENSUS

GLOCESTER, RHODE ISLAND

Page 4 (cont.)

Joseph Sanders	16-50 A
Epheriam Andrews J^r	"
Ishmal Enehes	"
Isaac King	"
Ebenezer Sprague	"
Boomer Sprague	"
Samuel Sprague	"
Simeon Place	"
Thomas Burllingame J^r	"
John Warner	"
Daniel Warner	"
Willard Eddy	"
John Blackmar	16-50 U
Daniel Place	16-50 A
Othaniel Brown	"
Stephen Smith	"
James Bowen	"
John Mathewson J^r	"
Charles Salsbuary	"
Isiael Bowen	"
Joseph Place	"
Caleb Howland	"
Eseck Smith J^r	"
Enoch Place	"
Eseck Whipple	"
Peter Lewis	"
Daniel Barns	"
Uriah Hawkins J^r	"
Rufus Sanders	"
John Tinkcom	"
James Irons	"
Nathaniel Blackmar	"
Joseph Bowen	"
Reuben Sprague	"
Reuben Williams	CS
Amos Woodard	CS
Asa Johnson	CS
Elijah Hawkins J^r	SM
Luke Harris	CS
Epherim Andrews	CS
Benedick Arnold	Cert
Samuel Inman	"
Richard Smith	R-Smithfield
Isaac Walling	Aff
Jam? Gardner	N
Ishmal Brown	N

Page 4 (cont.)

| Yankway Fenner | N |
| Job Millard | N |

Totals:

35	16-50 A	2	16-50 U
1	Aff	2	Cert
5	CS	1	SM
1	R	4	N

Page 5

Joseph Richardson	16-50 A
Charles Colwell	"
Abraham Tourtelot J^r	"
Saml Ross J^r	"
Benejah Whipple	"
Simon Smith	"
John Eddy	"
Stephen Olney	"
Elisha Bowen	"
Benjamin Bourllingame	"
William Page J^r	"
Reuben Steere	"
Negro Mingo	N
Simeon Bowen	16-50 A
Henry Wheler	"
Joseph Arnold	"
Benedick Bullingame	"
William Eddy	"
Hosanah Brown	"
Enoch Steere	"
Thomas Bullingame	"
Abraham Sanders	"
Benjn Hawkins	"
John Steere	"
Samuel Steere	"
William Bussey	"
Vinten Lewis	"
John Place	"
Stephen Aldrich	"
Stephen Salsbaury	"
Richard Tucker	"
David Vallet	"
Ezra Bowen	"
William Bisshop	"
Jesse Aldrich	"
Noah Steere	"
Job Steere	"

1777 MILITARY CENSUS

GLOCESTER, RHODE ISLAND

Page 5 (cont.)

Samuel Steere J^r	16-50 A
Samuel Eddy	"
Stephen Evens	"
Daniel Crossman	"
Resolved Irons	"
Stephen Irons	"
Zep^h Keech	"
Lyonard Smith	50-60 U

Totals:
    43   16-50 A   1   50-60 U
     1   N

Page 6

[Apparently numbered wrong; see 13]

Page 7

Samuel May	16-50 A
Ezekiel Phetteplace	"
Daniel Mathewson	"
James Colwell	"
Stephen Colwell	"
Hosea Steere	"
Ai[sic] Mathewson	"
Abnor Chetson	"
Wilcom Pigsle	"
Reuben Phillips	"
David Phillips	"
Caleb Bartlet	"
Henry Buxston	"
Simeon Herendeen	"
John Inman J^r	"
Ezikiel Inman	"
Joshua Walling	"
Moses Cooper J^r	"
David Inmand	"
Solomon Phillips	"
Daniel Page	"
John Simons	"
Joseph Kelly	"
John Mitchel	"
Mark Bundy	"
Obad^h Bellou	"
Caleb Phillips	"
Edward Salsbuary	"

Page 7 (cont.)

John Inman	16-50 A
Samuel Phetteplace	"
Eseck Comstock	"
Seth Ballou	"
John Salsbury	"
Tom Lapham	"
John Mathewson	"
Jacob Walling	"
Bariah Benson	"
John Walling	"
Jese Armstrong	"
Elisha Bartlet	"
Levi Herendeen	"
Elijah Sprague	"
Israel Cook	"
Gideon Daley	"
Andrew Man J^r	"
Arnold Smith	"
Simeon Smith	"
William Page	"
Job Phetteplace	"
Stephen Cooper	16-50 U
David Ballow	16-50 A
Joseph Easton	"
Elihu Benson	"

Totals:
    52   16-50 A   1   16-50 U

Page 8

Daniel Walter	16-50 A
Noah Millard J^r	"
Christoph^r Winsor	"
Squair Whitman	16-50 U
Hazakiah Herendeen	16-50 A
Abraham Williams	"
Stephen Cook	"
William Arnold	"
Zebelon Wade	"
Jesse Keech	"
Joseph Dexter	"
Richard Lewis	"
William Irons	"
Eseck Phetteplace	"
Charles Smith	"
Nathan Shippee	"

1777 MILITARY CENSUS

GLOCESTER, RHODE ISLAND

Page 8 (cont.)			Page 9 (cont.)	
Thomas Smith	16-50 A		Darius Winsor	16-50 A
Andrew Darling	"		Seth Hunt	Aff
John Fenner	"		John Phetteplace	16-50 A
Stephen Sanders	"		Jethro Lapham	Cert
John Tucker	"		Nathan Pain	Aff
Othinal Sanders	"		Henry Polock	16-50 A
Oliver Stone	"		John Ross	"
Robt Sanders J^r	"		Silas Cook	"
Joshua Phillips	"		Noah Woods	"
Stephen Thornton	"		Gulliver Lennard	"
John Straight	"		Joseph Harris	"
Benjn Colwell	"		Elijah Whipple	"
Epherim Smith	"		Oliver Herendeen	"
Benjn Smith J^r	"		Joshua Mathewson	"
Nathan Andrews	"		John Short	"
Reuben Shippee	"		James Smith	Aff
Luke Phillips	"		Elkanah Shearman	16-50 A
Ebenezer Darling J^r	"		Jonathan Harris	"
Samuel Winsor	"		James King	Aff
Nathl Wade	"		Esick Sheldon	Aff
Abraham Winsor	"		Peter Lewis	Aff
William Phillips	"		Jire Wilcocks	Aff
John Wills	"		Ezra Stone	Aff
Jonathan Smith	16-50 U		Israel Brown	Aff
Thomas Collens	16-50 A		William Ross	16-50 A
Thomas Wood	"		Amaziah Harris	60+
Noah Millard	50-60 U		Joseph Bassett	16-50 U
John Dexter	16-50 A		Noah White	"
James Dexter	16-50 U		Stephen Winsor	16-50 A
William Turner	16-50 A		Aaron Arnold	"
Thomas Williams	"		Isaac Ross	"
Samuel Phetteplace	"		Israel Smith	"
Caleb Arnold	"		Jeremiah Irons J^r	"
			Stephen Harris	"
Totals:			Andrew Ballard	"
45 16-50 A 3 16-50 U			Ozial Hopkins	"
1 50-60 U			Asa Ross	"
			Seth Ross	"
Page 9			John Tucker	"
Benjn Batty	16-50 A		Noah Arnold J^r	Aff
Samuel Ross	"		Elisha Raymond J^r	16-50 A
Daniel Bellou	"		David Cook	Aff
John Allen	"		William Ross	16-50 A
Henry Shippee	"		Zoheth Allen	"
William Herendeen	60+		Thomas Herendeen J^r	Aff
Israel Comstock	16-50 A		Resolved Phetteplace	16-50 A

1777 MILITARY CENSUS

GLOCESTER, RHODE ISLAND

Page 9 (cont.)

Totals:
    36 16-50 A   2 16-50 U
     2 60+   12 Aff
     1 Cert

Page 10

Elezer Harris	16-50 A
Joseph Hawkins	"
Stephen Killy	"
William Howland	"
Francis Hambetton	"
Christoph^r Shippee	"
David Cook	"
Stephen Fairfield	"
Derius Mitchel	"
Joseph Leshure	"
Elisha Mitchel	"
Elezer Killy	"
Stephen Arnold	"
Thomas Shippee	"
Daniel Barns	"
Benjn Pain	"
Stephen Ross	"
Ezekiel Ross	"
Daniel Smith	"
Richard Clemons	"
John Herendeen J^r	"
Jonathan Vallet	"
John Hunt J^r	"
Stephen Evens	"
Solomon Owen J^r	"
Zepeniah Cooke	"
David Dalley	"
Elijah Sprague	"
Silas Shippee	"
Thomas Howland	"
Jonas Sprague	"
Samuel Richardson	"
Israel Hill	"
Benjn Smith	"
Joseph Bellou	"
Stephen Barns	"
Israel Raymond	"
Joseph Ide	"
Isaac Smith	"
Prince Allen	"

Page 10 (cont.)

John Durfey J^r	16-50 A
Elisha Inman J^r	CS
William Barns	16-50 A
William Chace	"
Jesse Bellou	"
Jerrey Bellou	"

Totals:
    45 16-50 A   1 CS

Page 11

Capt. Timothy Wallmarth	16-50 A
David Richmond	"
Martin Smith	"
Caleb Sheldon	"
Edward Greene	"
Joseph Keech	"
Saml Clarke	"
Elijah Armstrong	"
David Colwel	"
Caleb Arnold J^r	"
Mathew Barns	"
Asa Ross	"
Stephen Sheldon	"
Thomas Barns	"
John Ide	"
William Colwell	"
Adam Phillips	"
David Bellou	"
David Richardson	"
Jesse Eddy	"
Richd Sprague	"
Thomas Raymond	"
Eseck Sayles	"
Elisha Burllingame	"
Nathan^l Bowdish	"
Stephen Eddy	"
John Phetteplace	"
Elisha Herendeen	Aff
Jesse Potter	16-50 A
Samuel Cook	"
Mark Petters	"
Thomas Owen J^r	"
John Sprague	"
Elisha Brown J^r	"
George Williams	"
	R-England

1777 MILITARY CENSUS

GLOCESTER, RHODE ISLAND

Page 11 (cont.)

Elijah Cooke J^r	16-50 A
William Tourtelott	"
Benjn Smith	"
Andrew Mowry	"
James Martin	"
Ezekiel Brown	"
John Coller	"
Bennoi Tucker J^r	"
Rufus Steere	"

Totals:
    43   16-50 A   1   Aff
     1   R

Page 12

Joseph Barnes	50-60 U
Nathan Pain J^r	16-50 A
Ebenezer Aldrich	"
Stephen Keech	50-60 A
Jeremiah Keech	16-50 A
Elezer Bowen	"
Elijah Hawkins	"
Abraham Smith	"
William Hawkins	"
Zebedee Hopkins	16-50 U
Enoch Eddy	"
John Mathewson	16-50 A
James Cole	16-50 U
Jonah Steere	"
Benjn Warner	50-60 A
Benjn Warner J^r	16-50 U
Jacob Bowen	16-50 A
Hazakiah Tinkcom	"
Reuben Lewis	16-50 U
Stephen Baker	16-50 A
David Steere	Cert
William Basett	Cert
Joseph Basett J^r	Cert
Preserv^d Herndeen	16-50 A
Solomon Herendeen	"
William Raymond	"
Jeremiah Smith	16-50 U
John Wood	16-50 A
Andrew Herendeen	"
George Brown	"
Christopher Sayles	"

Page 12 (cont.)

Nicholas Battey	16-50 A
Andrew Phillips	"
Joseph Ross	"
Ezikiel Burllingame	"
David Salsbuary	"
Asa Inman	"
Jonathan Phetteplace	"
William Lowen	"
Jonathan Tucker	16-50 U
Elisha Cook	16-50 A
Jieal [sic] Smith	"
Israel Inman	"
Noah Arnold	"
Israel Inman	"
Reuben Mathewson	"
Samuel Comstock	Cert
John Smith son of	
Benj	16-50 U
Jerem^h Thornton	Aff
Stephen Steere	Aff

Totals:
    32   16-50 A   2   16-50 U
     2   50-60 A   1   50-60 U
     2   Aff   4   Cert

Page 13 [sic]

Richd Steere	60+
Thos Owen	Cert
Joseph Winsor	60+
Robt Colwell	60+
Silas Williams	[no listing]
Elisha Inman	Aff
Wait Smith	60+
Nathan Wade	60+
Moses Cooper	60+
Peregreen Mathewson	60+
Elijah Cook	60+
Joseph Olney	50-60 A
Israel Arnold	60+
Abner Bartlet	60+
Ezra Bartlet	60+
Solomon Lapham	Cert
Rufus Smith	Cert
Jonath^n Eddy	60+
Daniel Eddy	60+

1777 MILITARY CENSUS

GLOCESTER, RHODE ISLAND

Page 13 (cont.)

Benj. Brown	60+
John Smith	60+
John Easton	50-60 U
Daniel Whealock	60+
John Hunt	60+
Edward Evens	60+
Elisha Cook	60+
Samuel Irons	60+
Daniel Whipple	60+
Experience Mitchel	60+
Jeremiah Phillips	60+
Zebedee Hopkins	60+
Obadiah Lewis	60+
Enock Whipple	16-50 U
Andrew Brown	60+
Jerem^h Bollard	60+
Joseph Shippee	60+
John Whipple	50-60 A
Nehemiah Bellou	60+
Jerem^h Comstock	50-60 A
David Phillips	60+
Jeremiah Phillips Jr	60+
Jeremiah Brown	60+
John Howland	60+
Jeremiah Irons	60+
James Lennard	60+
Samuel Short	50-60 A
Isaac Richardson	60+
James Bliss	60+
William Harvey	60+
Elisha Greene	60+
Stephen Smith	60+

Totals:

1	16-50 U	4	50-60 A
1	50-60 U	39	60+
1	Aff	3	Cert

Page 13 [sic]

Jeremiah Sanders	16-50 A
Squair Luther	"
Silvanus Keech	"
Ahab Sayls	"
Joseph Phillips	"
Joshua Turner	"
George Rounds	"

Page 13 (cont.)

Rial Inman	16-50 A
John Smith son of Jo^s	"
Reuben Cole	"
Solomon Cuttler	"
Benjn Cowen	"
Ozial Inman	"
Jo^s Smith the 3^d	"
Nedebiah Brown	"
John Smith	"
John Johnson	"
Obadiah Inman	"
Henry Sanders	"
Stutley Turner	"
John Thornton J^r	"
Ezekiel Mitchel	"
Jonathan Cowen	"
Jesse Brown	"
Eseck Brown	"
Jeremiah Merethew	"
Stephen Pain	"
Edward Arnold	"
Jesse Dickerman	"
Elisha Cook	"
Abijah Luther	"
Elisha Cowen	"
Zurial Mitchel	"
Amos Winsor	"
Joseph Davis	"
Peter Greene	"
Jonathan Smith J^r	"
Brezila Dexter	"
Joseph Cowen J^r	"
David Bowdish	"
Humphery Wood	"
Jeremiah Sweet J^r	"
James Potter	"
William Merethew	"
Asa White	"
Gidion Eddy	"
William Wilkinson	"
Reuben Mitchel	"
Stephen Colwell	"
Willard Wade	"
George Bowen	"
John Smith Ju^r	"

1777 MILITARY CENSUS

GLOCESTER, RHODE ISLAND

Page 13 (cont.)

Totals:
  52 16-50 A

In Gloucester in the State of Rhode Island. April 16th 1777. Persuant to an act of the General Assembly made and passd at their Second Session in march Last. I have Cearfully Taken an account of all the mail Persons in Sd Town agrable To said act: and hereby Return all the Lists inclosd

Hn Asa Kimball Committee Man

Fees Left to The Honble house

Providence ss in Gloucester

April 17, 1777 Personaly appeared the above Subscriber Asa Kimball and made oath that he had Taken an account of all the mail Persons in the Town of Gloucester according to the best of his Knowledge agrable To the act of Assembly. before Me Timothy Willmarth Justice of ye Peace

HOPKINTON, RHODE ISLAND

Page 1

Benjamin Barber	60+
John Pirce	T
William Pettis	
Peleg Kinyon	two Aff
John Kinyon, Amos	
Burdick	two Aff
Hezechiah Carpenter	one Aff
Ezekiel Hall	60+
Daniel Nickols,	
Samll Wilkison	two Aff
Joshua Dake,	
Abraham Utter	two Aff
John Robinson,	
Thomas Wilber	two Cert
Stephen Perrey,	
Jedidiah Robinson	two Cert
Gideon Wilber,	
George Kinyon	two Cert

Page 1 (cont.)

Daniel Lewis	16-50 U
Thomas Barber &	
two sons	three 16-50 A
William Herin	50-60 U
Matthew Herin,	
Potter Gardner	two 16-50 A
Samll Gardner,	
Jesse Lewis	" "
John Reynolds	R-Exetor
John Davis &	
John Crandall	two 60+
Samll Brown, Henry Hall	" 60+
Benjamin Coon	16-50 A
John Bent	60+
Exchange Wills	N
Two Negro men	two N

Totals:

16-50 A	16-50 U	50-60 A	50-60 U	60+	Aff	Cert	T	R	N	I
8	1		1	7	9	6	1	1	3	

Brought forward

16-50 A	16-50 U	50-60 A	50-60 U	60+	Aff	Cert	T	R	N	I
44	2	4	1	8			1	4	2	2
56	7		5	16			3	2	2	
50	10	2	2	5			4	2		
61	10			12			1			

Total Number:

16-50 A	16-50 U	50-60 A	50-60 U	60+	Aff	Cert	T	R	N	I
219	22	6	9	48	9	6	10	9	7	2

1777 MILITARY CENSUS

HOPKINTON, RHODE ISLAND

Page 1 (Reverse)

Those Who are in the Service:

Covil Larkin	George Popple	Nathan Champlin
Sam^{ll} Champlin	Paul Clerke	Joseph Congdon
Ebenezer Crandall	Nathan Closen	John Button
William Button	John Smith	Joseph Tanner
William Tanner	Ephraim Hall J^n	John MacLoud
Asa Hill	Isaiah Button	Roysal Smith

South Kingston April 19th 1777
In Obedince to the order of the Genaral Assembly I have taken the Number of
the Inhabitince of the Town of Hopkinton from 16 years old and upward and finde
219 from 16 to 50 able to Bare arms from 16 to 50 onable 22 from 50 to 60 able
to Bare arms 6 onable 9 from 60 and upwards 48 those that have taken the af-
formation 9 those that have Sertificates from the friends Meeting 6 Traineant
Persons 10 Residence 9 Negros 7 Indian 2 all which is Submitted to the Honorable Assembly By your Hon^{ll} Ser^t Thomas Wells

Kings County Ss April 19th 1777 Personally appeared the above named Thomas Wells
and on Oath declared that he had justly and truly
made out the aforegoing lists of all male Persons
of Sixteen Years of age and upwards in the town
of Hopkinton according to the best of his knowledge Before me
Wm Greene Just Sup^r C^t

Page 2

Levy Crandall,	
Joseph Weight	two 16-50 A
John Braman,	
Samuel Foster	two 60+
David Maps	T-Warwick
Ebenezer Lanpher	16-50 A
Daniel Lester,	
William Sandors	two 60+
William Sandors J^r,	
Uriah Sandors	two 16-50 A
Henry Sandors,	
Nickles Vincent	" "
Joseph Pettis,	
Peter Wilber	" "
John Brown	16-50 U
Sam^{ll} Reyondls [sic]	
Joseph Sandors	two 16-50 A
William Burdick &	
Edward	two 60+
Weight Burdick,	
Pery Burdick	two 16-50 A
Benjamin Crandall	16-50 A

Page 2 (cont.)

Stephen Kinyon,	
John Barber	two 16-50 A
Phelix Merril,	
Henry Meriat	" "
Jesse Burdick,	
James Lewis	" "
Daniel Button,	
Jonathan Forster	" "
Stephen Maxson,	
Matthew Maxson	" "
Peleg Maxson & Mathew	" "
George & Nathan Maxson	" "
John Ma[r]shel	16-50 A
Jesse Clerk,	
John Cottrell J^n	two 16-50 A
Luke Burdick	16-50 U
Hubrart Burdick	60+
Nathaniel Burdick	16-50 A
Able Burdick,	
Libeus Burdick	two 16-50 A
Rufus Burdick	16-50 A
Peter Burdick & Joseph	two 60+

1777 MILITARY CENSUS

HOPKINTON, RHODE ISLAND

Page 2 (cont.)

Joseph Burdick J^r &	
William B.	two 16-50 A
Parker Burdick	
& Paul Bu.	" "
Elnathan Burdick,	
Asa Ealestone	" "
Amos Palmer & Amos J^n	" "
Asil Palmer,	
Stephen Palmer	" "
Thomas Cottrell	16-50 A
John Weight,	
Matthew Wells	two 16-50 A
Elisha Wells,	
Elias Wells	" "
Daniel Peckham	60+
William Barber	16-50 A
Joseph Barber	"
John Philipes	"
Benjamin Maxson &	
Phinehas	two 16-50 A
Zaccheus Maxson,	
Stephen Bur^{dk}	" "
John Cottrell	60+
Libeus Cottrell,	
Sam^{ll} Button	two 16-50 A
Joshua Button,	
Daniel Lester	" "
Richard Robins	60+

Totals:

61	16-50 A	2	16-50 U
12	60+	1	T

Page 3

John Lawton,	
Theodaty Popple	two 16-50 A
William Thurston,	
Ross Coon	" "
Negro Scass & Will	
Negro man	" N
James Wells &	
James Wells Jn^r	" 16-50 A
Joshua Collins	16-50 A
Samuel Collins	16-50 U
Nathan Collins,	
Jabish Collins	two 16-50 A

Daniel Peckham J^r,	one 16-50 A
Sam^{ll} Witter	" 16-50 U
Joseph Witter,	
John Witter	two 16-50 A
Rowse Babcock	
Joseph Witter Jn^r	two 16-50 A
David Derry	T-Stonington
Thompson Wells	16-50 U
William Cole	16-50 A
Sam^{ll} Lewis,	
Amos Coon	two 16-50 A
John Gardner J^r	16-50 A
William Popple	"
Lebous Sweet	"
John Hall, John Coon	two 16-50 U
William Basset	R-Charlestown
Benjamin Kinyon	16-50 A
Niles Davis	R-Westerly
Simeon Babcock	50-60 U
Jason Babcock,	
Joseph Crandal	two 16-50 A
Joseph Langworthy	16-50 A
Sam^{ll} Langworthy	"
Stephen Crandall	"
James Kinyon,	
Peleg Burdick	two 16-50 U
Oliver Babcock	16-50 A
Robert Burdick,	
Thomas Coon	two 16-50 A
Nathan Burdick,	one 16-50 A
Adam Burdick	one 50-60 U
James Wells, Wm Wordin	
Roger Wells	three 60+
Mical West	16-50 A
Sam^{ll} Maxson J^r	"
Joseph Clerk,	
Thomas Stutson	two T
Joshua Wells 2^d,	
Barker Wells	two 16-50 A
Henry Adams	T-Charlestown
Elias Coon,	
Sam^{ll} Coon	two 16-50 A
William Coon,	
Fones Gardner	" "
John Maxson	50-60 A
John Maxson Jn^r	16-50 A

1777 MILITARY CENSUS

HOPKINTON, RHODE ISLAND

Page 3 (cont.)

Maxson Lewis	16-50 U
Sam[ll] Babcock,	
Hezekiah Babcock	two 16-50 A
Nathan Porter,	
Josiah Witter	" "
William Witter,	
Abel Tanner	" "
Jacob Hall	60+
James Braman,	
James Braman J[r]	two 16-50 A
John Popple	50-60 A
John Millard	60+
Elijah Millard	16-50 A
Gardner Thurston,	
Covel Larkin	two 16-50 A
Jeffery Champlin	16-50 A
Caleb Potter	"

Totals:

50	16-50 A	18	16-50 U
2	50-60 A	2	50-60 U
5	60+	4	T
2	R	2	N

Page 4

Benjamin Langworthy	16-50 A
Briant Cartwright,	
Isarel Stiels	two 60+
Briant Cartwright Jn[r]	16-50 A
Peter Kinyon	50-60 U
Ichabud Proser,	
Thomas Brombley	two 50-60 U
Stephen Potter &	
Elisha Coon	two 16-50 U
John Satterly &	
Caleb Ney	two 60+
Daniel Coon &	
Pasivil Allen	two 60+
Caleb Church,	
Gideon Allen	two 16-50 A
John Satterly J[r],	
Gideon Satterly	two 16-50 A
David Crandall &	
David Crum	" "
Thomas & Henry	
Brightman	" "
Stephen Potter Jn[r],	
Nathaniel Palmer	" "

Page 4 (cont.)

Lawton Palmer,	
John Larkin	two 16-50 A
Timothy Larkin &	one 16-50 A
John Larkin Jn[r]	one 16-50 U
Joseph Maxson &	
Wil[m] Coon	two 16-50 A
Caleb Ney J[n] &	
Amos Rogers	two 16-50 A
Elisha Stilmon	50-60 U
Stilmons Two Sons &	
Stephen Clerk	three 16-50 A
Jonathan Coon,	
David Coon	two 16-50 A
Joshua Coon, Asa Coon	" "
Cary Rogers, Joshua Ney	" "
Francis West, Wil[m] West	" "
Nathan Tanner,	
Joshua Tanner	" "
William Tanner,	
Sam[ll] Stilmon	" "
Ebenezer Lane,	
Amos Lewis	two 60+
Daniel Captener,	
Nicklis Barber	two 16-50 A
Daniel Knowles & his	
brother	" "
Benjamin Colegrove,	
David Button	" "
Sam[ll] Button &	
Joshua Lanpher	two 60+
Rufus Button,	
Elijah Burdick	two 16-50 U
Jonathan West,	
Paul Lewis	two 16-50 A
Jeremiah Crandall,	
Jonathan Cran[ll]	two R-Westerly
Ebenezer Hill	one 16-50 A
Josiah Hill J[r]	" "
John Collins,	two
John Wever	T-Stonington
John Wever J[r],	
Lodwick Wever	two T
Joshua Rathbun	50-60 U
Aron Rathbun	16-50 U
Randall Lewis,	
Green Lewis	two 16-50 A
John Stanbury,	
John Stanbury J[n]	" "

1777 MILITARY CENSUS

HOPKINTON, RHODE ISLAND

Page 4 (cont.)

Peter Kinyon J^n,	
Francis Robinson	two 16-50 A
Siras Button,	
William Thorn	two 60+
Nathaniel Kinyon	16-50 U
Wells Kinyon,	
Joshua Lanpher Jn^r	two 16-50 A
Zeffeniah Brown,	
Joseph Braman	" "
John Burdick J^n & his	
brother	" "
Jonathan Rogers,	
Edward Robinson	two 60+
Henry Brightman	60+
Benjamin Clerke	T-Westerly
William Neadom	60+

Totals:

56	16-50 A	7	16-50 U
5	50-60 U	16	60+
3	T	2	R

Page 5

Samuel Maxson	60+
Elisha Maxson	16-50 U
Amos Maxson	50-60 U
Silvenus Maxson	16-50 A
Jesse Maxson	"
John Crandall	"
William Davis	R-Westerly
Joshua Wells	16-50 A
Perry Edwards	"
Thomas Wells 2^d	"
Thomas Wells	50-60 A
Henry Wells	16-50 A
Thomas Wells J^n	"
Amos Wells	"
Randall Wells	"
Edward Wells	50-60 A
John Covey	60+
Clerk Reynolds	16-50 A
Asa Miner	R-Stonin[g]town
Phinehas Miner	16-50 A
Zaccheus Reynolds Jn^r	"
Zaccheus Reynolds	60+
Joseph Cole	60+
Sands Cole	16-50 A
Isaiah Maxson	50-60 A

Page 5 (cont.)

Clerke Maxson	16-50 A
Perry Maxson	"
Paul Maxson	"
William Maxson J^r	"
Edward Chever	T-Boston
Amos Langworthy	16-50 A
Amos Pattison &	
Ephreham Rogers	two 16-50 A
John Robinson J^r &	
Mark Lewis	" "
Richmond Reynolds &	
Simeon Reynold	" "
Joseph Statton	R-Groton
Moses Statton	R-Groton
Gideon Wilber &	
Oliver Davis	two 16-50 A
Negro Jim & Jahal	two N
Henry Clerke &	
Willit Clarke	two 16-50 A
Clerk Wilber &	
William Tanner	" "
Josiah Hill,	
John Tanner	two 60+
Phinehas Edwards	16-50 A
Jonathan Wells	60+
Elnathan Wells &	
Jonathan Wells J^r	two 16-50 A
Elias Lewis	16-50 A
John Popple J^n	50-60 A
Oliver White	50-60 A
Oliver White Jr	16-50 A
Christopher White	"
Oliver White 2^d	"
William White	16-50 U
Asa Burdick &	
Joseph Thurston	two 16-50 A
Hubart Burdick,	
George Thurston	two 60+
George Thurston Jn	16-50 A
Joseph Lawton,	
Joseph Lawton Jr	two 16-50 A
Indian Amos & Joseph	two I

Totals:

44	16-50 A	2	16-50 U
4	50-60 A	1	50-60 U
8	60+	1	T
4	R	2	I

1777 MILITARY CENSUS

JAMESTOWN, RHODE ISLAND

Page 1

Residents of N. Kingstown:
Edward Carr Jun[r]   16-50 A
John Weeden son of
   Daniel Jun[r]   "
Samuel Carr Jun[r]   "
William Weeden   "
Benjamin Underwood   "
Daniel Carr   "
William Smith   "
Benjamin Tewel   "
Samuel Tewel   "   N 1

Resident of Exeter:
Benedict Robinson   16-50 A

Residents of N. Kingstown:
James Greenman   16-50 U
Samuel Slocum   16-50 A
Peleg Carr   "
Elisha Tew   "

Residents of Exeter:
James Carr J[r]   "
Robert Carr   "
John Carr   "
Benjamin Remington   "   N 1
Oliver Remington   16-50 A
Peter Remington   "

Residents N. Kingstown:
John Cranston   16-50 A
Jonathan Fowler   "

Residents S. Kingstown:
John Franklin   16-50 A
Abel Franklin   "
Tiddeman Hull   "   I 1
William Slocum   16-50 A

Residents E. Greenwich:
Stephen Remington   "
Gershom Remington Jr. "
John Howland   "   N 1
Jonathan Greenold   16-50 A
Tiddeman Remington   "
Robert Greenold   "

Resident Warwick:
John Weeden   "

Page 1 (cont.)

Totals:
   32 16-50 A   1 16-50 U
    3 N   1 I

Page 2

George Smith   16-50 U R-Exeter
Isaac Howland   16-50 A N 1
Paine Hammond   16-50 A
Nathaniel Hammond   16-50 A
William Batty   16-50 A N 1
Peleg Slocum   16-50 A
Clarke Fowler   "
Samuel Fowler   "
Christopher Fowler   "
Josiah Fowler   "
Samuel Eldred   "
Jonathan Greene   Cert
David Greene   "
Joseph Greene Jr.   "
John Tew   16-50 A
deserted Isaac Carr   "
Nicholas Carr   "
Phillip Ackland   "   R-Newport
Benjamin Tayer   "   R   "
John Tayer   "   R   "
Daniel Carpenter J[r] "   R-S.Kings-
                                 town
Daniel Weeden Jun.   Aff   N 1
George Tew   50-60 U N 2
John Gardner   "   N 2
                               R-Exeter
Ebenezer Smith   "   R   "
John Eldred   60+   N 3
Josiah Arnold   60+   R-E.Green-
                                 wich
                               N 1
Joseph Underwood   60+   R-N.Kings-
                                 town
Daniel Underwood   60+   R   "
James Carr   60+   R-Exeter

Totals:
   17 16-50 A   1 16-50 U
    3 50-60 U   5 60+
    1 Aff   3 Cert
   11 N

1777 MILITARY CENSUS
JAMESTOWN, RHODE ISLAND

Page 3			Page 3 (cont.)		
John Eldred Jr.	16-50 A		Samuel Carr	50-60 U	N 1
Peleg Eldred	"	R-E.Green-wich			R-N.Kingstown
Gershom Remington	60+		Benjamin Carr	50-60 U	
Daniel Weeden	60+		Edward Carr	"	N 1
Joseph Greene	Cert				R-N.Kingstown

Totals:	16-50 A	16-50 U	50-60 A	50-60 U	60+	Aff	Cert	N	I
) No. 3	2			3	2		1	2	
from) No. 2	17	1		3	5	1	3	11	
) No. 1	32	1						3	1
	51	2		6	7	1	4	16	1

43 Males of the town of Jamestown)	
in the Different Towns in the State)	Total 88

I the Subscriber being appointed by the Hon[ll] General Assembly, at their Session held at South Kingstown on the fourth Monday in March, A.D. 1777, to Number all the Male Persons in the town of Jamestown, from Sixteen years of age & upwards, whether Residents, Transient or those having Certificates from the friends Meeting, or taken the affirmation, have in Obedience to Said appointment, Carefully Performed that Service and find of those from 16 to 50 able to bear arms, 51. From D[o] [ditto] to D[o] unable 2. from 50 to 60 able to bear arms, none. from D[o] to D[o] unable 6. from 60 and upwards 7. taken the affirmation 1. Certificates 4. Transient none. Resident persons 6. Negroes 16 and Indians 1. The same, as set down in the preceding Collums, exclusive of the Six Residents, is Considered as belonging to Said Town of Jamestown, and Submitted by your Honours most humble Serv[t].

April 18th 1777 there appears to be but 32 from 16 to 50 of the town of Jamestown able to bear arms. The whole of the Rest being their or in some other town unknown.

Kings County April 18th 1777

The above Subscriber personally Appeared and Made Oath to truth of the Aforegoing list Before me

W[m] Green C Jus[t] Sup[r] C[t].

JOHNSTON, RHODE ISLAND

Page 1		Page 1 (cont.)	
William Angell	16-50 A	Eleazer Arnold	16-50 A
Daniel Angell	"	Jonathan Arnold	60+
Caleb Alverson	"	Andrew Aldrich	16-50 A
John Alverson	"	Richard Aldrich	"
William Alverson	"	Prince Angell (negro)	N
Isaac Arnold	"	Joseph Borden Jun	16-50 A
William Antram	50-60 A	Richard Borden	"
Jonathan Arnold Jun	16-50 A	Joseph Borden	60+

1777 MILITARY CENSUS

JOHNSTON, RHODE ISLAND

Page 1 (cont.)

Roger Burllinggame	16-50 A	R-Cranston
Abram Belknap	16-50 A	
Jacob Belknap	"	
John Brown Jun	50-60 A	
Charles Brown	16-50 A	
Chad Brown	"	
John Brown	60+	
Obadiah Brown	50-60 A	
Reuben Brown	16-50 A	
William Baxter	"	R-Newport
Abram Borden	"	
Nathaniel Baley	"	R-Providence
Gideon Brown	"	
Prime Brown negro	N	

Totals:
22 16-50 A   3 50-60 A
 3 60+   [3 R]
 1 N [sic]

Page 2

Edmond Brown	16-50 A	
Oliver Borden	"	
David Brown	50-60 A	
William Borden	16-50 A	
Thomas Borden	60+	
John Carey	16-50 A	
Richard Clemence	60+	
Thomas Carey	16-50 A	R-Providence
Joseph Corp	"	R-E.Greenwich
James Colvin	"	R-Coventry
John Clifford	"	R-Providence
Jeffery Cuchop	I	
Stephen Crosby	16-50 A	R-Newport
James Converss	"	R-So.Kingstown
Benj^a Carpenter	"	
Israel Carpenter	50-60 U	
Nicholas Carpenter	16-50 A	
Zebedee Clemence	50-60 A	
Thomas Clemence	"	
Benj^a Coman	60+	
Solomon Daley	16-50 A	R-Smithfield

Page 2 (cont.)

Nathaniel Day	16-50 A	
John Dyer	"	
James Dyer	"	
Oliver Dyer	"	
Stephen Dyer	"	
Reuben Daley	"	R-Smithfield
Richard Eddy	"	
David Freeman	"	R-Cranston
John Fenner	"	
George Fenner	"	

Totals:
23 16-50 A   3 50-60 A
 1 50-60 U   3 60+
 1 I   [9 R]

Page 3

Seth Fenner	16-50 A	
John Fenner Jun	"	
Thomas Field	50-60 A	R-Providence
Stephen Field	16-50 A	R- "
Joseph Fisk Jun	16-50 A	
Edward Fenner	"	
Antram Fenner	"	
Arthur Fenner	50-60 A	
Pardon Fenner	16-50 A	
Richard Fenner	50-60 A	
James Fenner	16-50 A	
Richard Fenner Jun	"	
Rhodes Fenner	"	
Arnold Fenner	"	
Joseph Fisk	60+	
Joseph Fisk 3^d	[no listing]	
Joshua Greene	16-50 A	
Samuel Greene	"	
Henry Harris	60+	
Caleb Harris	16-50 A	
Josiah Harris	"	
Mingo Hawkins	N	
Rufus Hawkins	60+	
Rufus Hawkins Jun	16-50 A	
Christopher Harris	60+	
Andrew Harris	16-50 A	
Christopher Harris Jun	"	
William Harris	"	
Benj^a Harris	"	

1777 MILITARY CENSUS

JOHNSTON, RHODE ISLAND

Page 3 (cont.)

Thomas Harris	60+	
Stephen Hammon	16-50 A	
Tobe Harris	N	
Josiah King	60+	
Wm Borden King	16-50 A	

Totals:
22 16-50 A   3 50-60 A
6 60+   2 N
[2 R]

Page 4

Joel Keech	16-50 A	
Benjamin King	"	R-Glocester
Nicholas King	"	R- "
Esaias King	60+	
Isaiah King	16-50 A	
Samuel Kilton	"	
Adam Kerr	"	R-Boston
Benoni Latham	"	R-Smith-field
Benj^a Larned	"	R-Killingly
William Latham	"	
Consider Luther	"	
Benj^a Luther	"	
Stephen Luther	"	
Israel Mathewson	60+	
Daniel Manton	16-50 A	
Edward Manton	"	
William Mathewson	"	
William Moorhead	"	
John Mathewson	60+	
Noah Mathewson	16-50 A	
Charles Mathewson	"	
Asa Mathewson	"	
Daniel Mathewson	16-50 U	
Barak McDonald	16-50 A	
John McDonald	"	
Saml McIntosh	"	
Thomas Man	"	
James Mathewson	"	
Emor Olney	"	
Ezekiel Olney	"	
Ephraim Pearce	"	
William Potter	16-50 U	
Jonathan Patt	16-50 A	
William Pain	"	
Benj^a Pain	"	

Page 4 (cont.)

Square Pain	16-50 U	
Simeon Potter	16-50 A	R-Glocester
William Parker	"	R-Scituate
Robert Potter	"	
Jeremiah Ceasor	N	
John Ceasor	N	

Totals:
33 16-50 A   3 16-50 U
3 60+   2 N
[7 R]

Page 5

William Sprague	16-50 A	R-East Hosock
John Sweet	50-60 A	
Philip Sweet	16-50 A	
James Sweet	"	
Volintine Sweet	"	
Samuel Saunders	50-60 U	R-Smith-field
Samuel Saunders Jun	16-50 A	R- "
John Saunders	"	R- "
Rufus Sprague	"	
Arthur Strivens	"	
Ebenezer Sprague	"	
Henry Strivens	"	
Rhodes Strivens	"	
Nicholas Strivens	16-50 U	
Peleg Rhodes	50-60 A	
William Rhodes	16-50 A	
Peleg Rhodes	"	
Jeremiah Rhodes	60+	
Joshua Remington	16-50 U	
Stephen Remington	16-50 A	
Joshua Remington Jun.	"	
James Randall	"	
Joseph Randall	"	
Caleb Randall	"	
Samuel Smith	60+	
Jeremiah Sheldon	60+	
Daniel Sprague	60+	
Daniel Sprague Jun.	16-50 A	
Benj^a Smith	"	R-Warwick
Samuel Sweet	"	
Joseph Ceasor	N	
John Thornton	16-50 A	
Elihu Thornton	60+	

1777 MILITARY CENSUS

JOHNSTON, RHODE ISLAND

Page 5 (cont.)

Daniel Thornton	16-50 A	
Ephraim Thornton	"	
Solomon Thornton Jun.	"	
Seth Tripp	"	

Totals:

27	16-50 A	2	16-50 U
2	50-60 A	1	50-60 U
5	60+	1	N
[5	R]		

Page 6

Edward Tripp	16-50 A	
Stephen Thornton	"	
Thomas Truman	"	R-Provi-dence
Solomon Thornton	"	
Christopher Thornton	"	
Noah Thornton	"	
Esek Thornton	"	
Joseph Thornton	"	
Richard Thornton	"	
Caleb Vinsent	"	
Nicholas Vinsent	"	
Pardon Vinsent	"	
Caleb Vinsent Jn	16-50 U	
Laben Vinsent	16-50 A	
Zachariah Whitaker	16-50 U	R-Rehoboth
Jonathan Wells	16-50 A	R-West Greenwich
William Warner	50-60 A	
Henry Warner	16-50 A	
Job Waterman	60+	
Daniel Waterman	16-50 A	
Benj^a Waterman 3^d	"	
David Waterman	"	
Saml Winsor	50-60 A	
Isaac Winsor	16-50 A	
James Winsor	"	
John Waterman	60+	
Job Waterman Jr.	16-50 A	
William Waterman	"	
Charles Waterman	"	
Laben Waterman	"	
Jeremiah Waterman	"	
Joseph Wilbour	"	R-Newport
John Waterman Jr.	"	
Edwd Waterman	"	
Joseph Waterman	50-60 A	

Page 6 (cont.)

Tim^o Williams	50-60 A	R-Provi-dence
Nich^o Williams	16-50 A	R- "
Tim^o Williams Jr.	"	R- "

Totals:

30	16-50 A	2	16-50 U
4	50-60 A	2	60+
[7	R]		

Page 7

Richard Waterman	60+	R-Cranston
Daniel Williams	60+	
William Williams	16-50 A	
Oliver Williams	"	
Benj^a Waterman	50-60 A	
Nathaniel Waterman	60+	R-Cranston
Nathaniel Waterman Jr	60+	
Robert Williams	60+	
Peleg Williams	50-60 A	
Elisha Williams	16-50 A	
Edward Williams	"	
Benj^a Waterman Jr.	"	
Joshua Kimball	"	
William Ladd	"	
Robert Harrison	"	T-Great Briton

Totals:

16-50 A	16-50 U	50-60 A	50-60 U
8	–	2	–
22	–	3	–
23	–	3	1
22	–	3	–
33	3	–	–
27	2	2	1
30	2	4	–
165	7	17	2

60+	R	N	I
5	[2]	–	–
3	–	1 [sic]	–
3	–	–	1
6	–	2	–
3	–	2	–
5	–	1	–
2	–	–	–
27	[2]	6 [sic]	1

1777 MILITARY CENSUS

JOHNSTON, RHODE ISLAND

Agreeable to the appointment of the Honble General Assembly I have taken a
List of the Male Persons in the Town of Johnston according to Act of Assembly
Johnston April 15, 1777   Richard Eddy

Providence ss in Johnston April 15, 1777
Richard Eddy Esq. Subscriber to the foregoing Lists personally appeared and
made Oath that the Above and Six preceding pages were Justly and truly taken
according to the best of his knowledge
             Before C" Harris Jus^t Peace

NORTH KINGSTOWN, RHODE ISLAND

Page 1

Beriah Brown	60+	1 N	
William Spencer	16-50 A		
William Albro	"		
Silvester Cheseborough	"		R-Connect- icutt
Isaac Vaughan	60+		
Joseph Case	60+	2 N	
Joseph Case Junr	16-50 A	1 N	
Samuel Brown	50-60 A		
Christopher Spencer	60+	1 N	
George Nichols	50-60 A		
Jonathan Nichols	16-50 A		
Gideon Ellis	"		
Thomas Nichols	60+		
Lebeus Northup	16-50 A		
William Briggs	"		
John Dyre	"		
Samuel Dyre	"		
Ishmael Spink	"		
Nicholas Spink	"		
Matthew Manchester	60+		R-Scituate
		1 N	
John Greene	16-50 A		
George Whightman	60+		
Holmes Whightman	16-50 A		
Judediah Stutson	50-60 A		
Thomas Allin	60+		
Thomas Allin Junr	50-60 A		
Jonathan Allin	"		
Christopher Allin	16-50 A		
Arthur Alesworth	50-60 A		
Dyre Alesworth	16-50 A		
Jeremiah Alesworth	"		
Josiah Spink	60+		
Caleb Hill	16-50 A	1 N	
Benj^a Tanner	"		

Page 1 (cont.)

Nathan Tanner	16-50 A		
Oliver Carpenter	"		
Jonathan Reynolds	"		
James Boone	[blank]		
James Chaffield	16-50 A		R-S.Kings- town
John Jeffers	"		R-Nova- scotia
William Grindman	60+		R-Jamestown
Peleg Carr	16-50 A		
Daniel Fones of Saml	"		

Page 2

Sylvester Gardner	16-50 A	1 N	
John Inyan	60+		R-Pourch- mouth
Matthew Allen	16-50 A		
Giles Olin	"		
Joseph Coggeshall	"		
John Cleavland	50-60 U		
George Hiams	16-50 A		
Sylvester Hiams	"		
George Thoms S^o John	"	1 N	
Jonathan Bly	"		
Zebulon Northup	"		
James Northup	"		
Samuel Rathburn	60+		
John Rathburn	16-50 A		
Roger Rathburn	"		
Anthony Rathburn	"		
John Havens	"		
Thomas Smith	60+		
Benjamin Worden	16-50 A		R-S^o Kings- town
William Barbour	"		

1777 MILITARY CENSUS

NORTH KINGSTOWN, RHODE ISLAND

Page 2 (cont.)			Page 3 (cont.)			
Thomas Whaley	50-60 U	R-S⁰ Kings-town	Israel Phillips	60+		
Joseph Congdon	60+		Samuel Nichols	50-60 A	R-Newport	
John Congdon of Jo^s	16-50 U		Samuel Nichols J^r	16-50 A	R-Newport	
Caleb Congdon	16-50 A		George W. Babcock	"		
George Congdon	"		George Fowler	60+		
Stuckely Congdon	"		Joseph Peirce	16-50 A		
Samuel Codner	"		Edward Dyre of Saml	50-60 A	R-West	
Abraham Greene	"				Greenwich	
Judediah Kingsley	"		John Richards	16-50 A	R-Newport	
Sawell Kingsley	50-60 U		Peter Coszens	50-60 A	R-	D⁰
Samuel Kingsley	16-50 A		Benjamin Coszens	16-50 A	R-	D⁰
Jonathan Kingsley	"		William Coszens	"	Aff	
Sawell Kingsley Junr	"				R-Newport	
Benjamin Jefferson	60+		John Coszens	"	R-	D⁰
Sweet Hitt	16-50 A		Leanard Coszens	"	R-	D⁰
Henry Shearman	50-60 A		James Durham	50-60 A	R-	D⁰
Benjamin Cole	50-60 U		Thomas Standley	"	R-	D⁰
Benjamin Cole Junr	16-50 A		Aaron Vaughan	16-50 A	R-Newport	
John Reynolds	60+		William Coszens Junr	"	R-Newport	
Josiah Arnold	16-50 A		Towndsend Goddard	"	R-	D⁰
Peleg Arnold	"		Samuel Sweet	50-60 A	R-	D⁰
Oliver Arnold	"		John Sweet	16-50 A	R-	D⁰
Edmond Arnold	"		Phillip Wilkinson	60+	R-	D⁰
Stukely Westgate	"				1 N	
William Hall Junr	"		Benjamin Fowler	16-50 A		
			William Havens	60+	1 N	

Page 3			Page 4			
Lodowick Updike	50-60 A	4 N	William Hall son John	50-60 A	Aff 1 N	
Daniel Updike	16-50 A		Slocum Hall	16-50 A		
Ephraim Harzard	"		Robart Havens	50-60 A		
William Allin	50-60 U	R-Newport	Samuel Slocum	16-50 A		
		1 N	Henry Wall	50-60 A	1 N	
Thomas Cranston J^r	16-50 A	R-Newport	Richard Updike	16-50 A		
Benedick Dayton	"		Richard Phillips	"		
Gilbert Cooper	"		Thomas Hill	16-50 U		
James Cooper	"		Nicholas Hart	50-60 U		
Nathan Cooper	16-50 U		Samuel Thomas Jr	16-50 A		
Silvester Havens	16-50 A		James Fowler	50-60 U		
Volintine Whightman	50-60 A		George Fowler J^r	16-50 A		
James Whitman	16-50 A		Phillip Card	50-60 A		
Oliver Whightman	"		William Card	16-50 A		
Updike Cooper	"		Charles Tillinghast	"		
Ebenezar Slocum	50-60 A		Joshua Peirce	50-60 A		
John Slocum	16-50 A		Job Corey	16-50 A		
John Mowrey	"		John Peirce	50-60 A		
Ebenezar Scranton	"	R-Newport	Edward Dyre Ju^r	50-60 A		

1777 MILITARY CENSUS

NORTH KINGSTOWN, RHODE ISLAND

Page 4 (cont.)   Page 5 (cont.)

Amherst Dyre	16-50 A			
Edward Lawton	"			
Nathan Allin	"			
Samuel Allin	"			
Silas Spink	"			
Sylvester Peirce	"			
Fedrick Whitman	"	)Excus^d from		
George Whightman ye 3^d	"	) Duty		
Stuckely Hill	"			
Caleb Hill J^r	"			
John Manchester	"	)		
Joseph Manchester	"	) R-Scituate		
Gideon Manchester	"	)		
Christopher Peirce	"			
John Shearman J^r	"			
Stephen Northup J^r	"			
Samuel Northup	"			
James Sweet	"			
Abraham Havens	"			

Page 5

Thomas Bissell	50-60 A		
Daniel Bissell	16-50 A		
Thomas Bissell Junr	"		
John Bissell	60+		
John Bissell Junr	16-50 A		
David Northup	"		
Peter Reynolds	"		
Christopher Allen	"		
John Duglass	"		
John Cole	60+		
John Cole Junr	16-50 A		
Samuel Cole	"		
Hutchinson Cole	"		
William Davis	60+	R-Exetor	
Joseph Northup	50-60 A		
Henry Northup	16-50 A		
Joseph Northup Junr	"		
William Northup	"		
Nicholas Northup	50-60 A		
Gideon Northup	16-50 A		
Jeremiah Haszard S^o Robt	"	1 N	
John Barbour	50-60 A	1 N	
Jeremiah Haszard s^o Jeffry	50-60 A	1 N	
William Cole	16-50 A		

Thomas Haszard of Jo^s of Jeffry	16-50 A		
Robart Haszard Junr	"		
David Greene	16-50 U	2 N	
Stephen Bouyes	) 50-60 A	R-England	
John Bouyes	) 16-50 A	R-England	
Stephen Bouyes Junr	) "	R-England	
John Congdon	"	4 N	
Samuel Place	"		
Samuel Place Junr	"		
Benjamin Gardner	"	3 N	
Francis Carpenter	"	2 N	
Caleb Cranston	"		
Robart Mowrey	"	1 N	
Caleb Allen	60+	3 N	
Joshua Allen	60+		
Benjamin Allen	60+		

Page 6

Jeremiah Vaughan	16-50 A		
Joshua Vaughan	"		
Gideon Devenport	"	1 N	
Rufus Sweet	"		
Joseph Taylor	50-60 A		
John Austin	60+		
Stephen Davis	16-50 A		
Jeremiah Smith	50-60 A		
Jeremiah Smith Ju^r	16-50 A		
William Taylor	"		
Pollipus Austin	"		
Pearcius Austin	"		
James Albro	"		
Eber Sweet	60+		
Stephen Sweet	16-50 A		
Job Sweet	50-60 A		
William Congdon	16-50 A		
William Congdon J^r	"		
Langutha Peirce	"	R-East Greenwich	
Jonathan Card	50-60 A		
William Card	16-50 A		
Jonathan Card Ju^r	"		
Lawrence Peirce	"	R-East Greenwich	
Ezekiel Gardner Ju^r	"	1 N	
Job Card	"		
Bowen Card	"		

1777 MILITARY CENSUS

NORTH KINGSTOWN, RHODE ISLAND

Page 6 (cont.)

Stephen Card	16-50 A		
Gideon Haszard	"		
Freborn Haszard	"		
Martin Read	16-50 U		
Robart Northup	50-60 U		
David Northup	16-50 A		
Nicholas Northup S^o			
Robt	"		
Benjamin Northup	16-50 U		
Nicholas Bragg	50-60 A	Cert	
		R-Coventry	
Peleg Bragg	16-50 A	R-Coventry	
Robart Haszard	60+	1 N	
Ezekiel Gardner	60+	2 N	
George Gardner	16-50 A		
Jeffery Gardner	"		
Oliver Gardner	"		
John Haszard	"	2 N	
George Duglass J^r	"		
James Duglass	50-60 A		
Charles Duglass	16-50 A		

Page 7

Francis Reynolds	16-50 A		
Jabez Reynolds	"		
William Satshell	"		
James Austin	"		
Jeremiah Hunt	"		
Ezekiel Hunt	"		
Samuel Hunt	60+		
Francis Tanner	16-50 A		
Adam Hunt	"		
John Reynolds	50-60 A		
John Tourje	16-50 A		
Benj^a Nichols	"		
James Fones	60+		
William Fones	50-60 U		
Havens Tennant	16-50 A		
John Carr	50-60 A	R-Jamestown	
Samuel Warner	50-60 A		
Peleg Cory	16-50 A		
Phillip Jenkens	50-60 A		
Edward Dyre	60+		
William Wall	16-50 A		
Paul Whightman	"		
Benjamin Reynolds	"	R-Exetor	
Peter Wright	"		

Page 7 (cont.)

James Havens	16-50 A		
William Havens Junr	"		
Nathaniel Clarke	"		
Samuel Watson Doct^r	"		
Nathaniel Berrey	60+		
Ephraim Mitchell	60+		
Ephraim Mitchell J^r	16-50 A		
Samuel Cooper	"		
Barnett Godfrey	"		
Caleb Godfrey	"		
Thomas Cobb	50-60 A		
William Slocum	16-50 A		
John Underwood	50-60 A		
James Reynolds	16-50 A		
Peleg Slocum	"		
Jeffry Davis	60+		
Joshua Davis	16-50 A		
William Davis of Benj^a	"		
Samuel Hunt Junr	"		
Nathaniel Tibbitts	"		

Page 8

Stephen Watson	16-50 A		
Caleb Watson	"		
Moses Slocum	"		
Stephen Northup	60+	R-Newport	
William Hammond	16-50 U	1 N	
Benjamin King	60+	R-Newport	
		1 N	
Joseph Hammond	16-50 A		
John Morey	"		
Charles Dyre	"		
Rowse Northup	"		
Stuckley Northup	"		
Daniel Northup	"		
Benjamin Allen	"		
William Duglass	"		
Nicholas Hart	50-60 A		
Charles Slocum [x'd out]		2 N	
James Sweet	60+		
Joseph Campbell	16-50 A	R-England	
		or Scotland	
Caleb Carr	[blank]		
John Whightman	16-50 A		
George Fowler Junr	"		
Thomas Clark	"		
Volintine Whightman J^r	"		

1777 MILITARY CENSUS

NORTH KINGSTOWN, RHODE ISLAND

Page 8 (cont.)

Rowse Helme	60+		
Daniel Hall	16-50 A	1 N	
Nicholas Spencer	"		
John Spink	"		
Ebenezar Peirce	[blank]		
Elisha Clarke	16-50 A		
Samuel Wilsson	"		
William Corey	"		
Joseph Corey	60+		
Jeremiah Fones	16-50 A		
Joseph Ward	"		
Richard Boone	"	1 N	
John Wells	60+		
Samuel Thomas	50-60 A		
George Thomas S⁰ Sam¹	16-50 U		
Simeon Fowler	50-60 A		
Isaac Fowler	16-50 A		
Samuel Boone	60+		
Benedick Eldred	60+		
Benjamin Davis	16-50 A		
Francis Bradfield	"		
James Gardner	50-60 A		

Page 9

Geoffry Allen	16-50 A		
Caleb Allen Junr	"		
Jeremiah Cranston	50-60 A	R-Newport	
John Northup	16-50 A	1 N	
John Northup Junr	"		
Thomas Haszard	50-60 A	2 N	
Jonathan Haszard	16-50 A		
Immanuel Northup	60+	2 N	
Thomas Hitt	16-50 A		
Ephraim Gardner	"		
Jeremiah Gardner	50-60 A	1 N	
Amos Gardner	16-50 A		
Augustus Mowrey	"		
William Mowrey	"		
Samuel Albro	"		
Isaac Nichols	"		
Ishael Williams	"		
Jones Smith	16-50 U		
Joseph Cole	16-50 A		
Peter Phillips	"		
Isaac Peirce	"	R-Jamestown	
Isaac Browning	"		
Samuel Browning	"		

Page 9 (cont.)

Benjamin Browning	16-50 A		
Stephen Congdon	"		
James Congdon	"		
William Shearman of W^m	50-60 U		
William Browning	16-50 A		
James Eldred	"		
Nathaniel Shearman	"		
James Rose	"		
John Shearman	60+		
William Shearman	60+		
Thomas Shearman	16-50 A		
Eber Shearman	50-60 A		
Silas Shearman	16-50 A		
Wm Shearman of Eb^r	"		
Samuel Arnold	"		
Moses Shearman	"		
Jeremiah Whaley	50-60 A	R-S⁰ Kingstown	
Richard Phillips	16-50 A		
Samuel Watson	60+		
Benjamin Watson	50-60 A		
Robert Watson	16-50 A		
Benj^a Watson Junr	"		

Page 10

Joseph Eldred	50-60 A		
Thomas Cutter	16-50 A	R-Newport	
Henry Eldred	"		
James Grindman	16-50 U	R-Jamestown	
William Hall S⁰ Benoni	16-50 A	R-Exeter	
Thomas Phillips	16-50 A	1 N	
John Brown	50-60 A		
John Brown Junr	16-50 A		
Benedick Brown	"		
Charles Brown	50-60 A		
Charles Brown Junr	16-50 A		
Fenex Brown	"		
Joshua Brown	"		
Christopher Brown	"		
Beriah Weight	"	R-Exeter	
Peleg Arnold	"	R-West Greenwich	
Jonathan Vaughan	"		
Elexander Huling S⁰ Sam	50-60 U		
E[torn]nezar Brown	50-60 A		
Richard Briggs	"		

1777 MILITARY CENSUS

NORTH KINGSTOWN, RHODE ISLAND

Page 10 (cont.)

Barzilla Duglass	16-50 A	
Sylvester Sweet	"	
Stuckley Brown	"	
Samuel Mitchell	"	
Daniel Sweet	50-60 A	
Charles Hunt	16-50 A	
William Hall S^o Robt	50-60 A	1 N
Samuel Gardner	16-50 A	
Jabez Chadsey	50-60 A	
William Reynolds	16-50 A	
Christopher Jenckens	"	
John Reynolds S^o Peter	50-60 A	
John Reynolds of John dec.	50-60 U	
Caleb Corey	50-60 A	
Nathaniel Carpenter	60+	
John Vaughan	16-50 A	
William Clarke	"	
Samuel Boone Junr	"	
Ephraim Smith	50-60 A	R-S^o Kingston
John Olin	60+	
Thomas Fowler	60+	
Henry Fowler	16-50 A	
John Haszard of Jer	"	
Stephen Arnold	"	1 N

Page 11

John Fones	16-50 A	
Caleb Corey Junr	"	
Joseph Battey	"	R-Newport
Robert Dunbarr	"	R- "
Gideon Sweet	"	
Thomas Duglass	"	
Thomas Cranston of Caleb	"	
William Northup of Rhob^t	"	
David Bates	"	
Jeremiah Cole	"	
George Northup	"	
Henry Shearman J^r	"	
Henry Reynolds of John	"	
James Reynolds	"	
Stafford Congdon	"	
Joseph Whaley	"	R-S^o Kingstown

Page 11 (cont.)

Joseph Mory	16-50 A	
Zebulon Gardner	"	
Caleb Arnold	"	
John Whaley	"	R-S.Kingstown
Thomas Hitt	"	
John Reynolds Junr	"	
Joseph Spancer Taylor	"	T-England
George Duglass	50-60 U	
Benajah Smith	16-50 A	
Daniel Chace	"	R-Portsmouth
Benjamin Albro	"	
Thomas Nichols Ju^r	"	
Rowland Hall	"	R-Exeter
Benjamin Reynolds	"	
Gardner Hall	"	
Robert Mowrey Ju^r	"	
Peter Tourje	"	
Benjamin Whitford	"	
Jonathan Slocum of W^m	"	
Joseph Lawton	"	
Jabez Chadsey Junr	"	
Benjamin Tuell	"	R-Newport
John Tennant	"	
Samuel Carr of John	"	
Thomas Whitford	"	
Joseph Hambleton	"	R-E^t Greenwich
Dublin Brenton	"	T-Newport 1 N
Tube Roms	"	T-Newport 1 N

Page 12

N^o:			
336	16-50 A	10	16-50 U
64	50-60 A	12	50-60 U
49	60+	1	Aff
1	Cert	4	T
54	R	60	N	1 I

Those who are Inlisted into the 15 m^o Service

Capt Samuel Phillips	1
Charles Dyre 2^d Leiu^t	1
Christopher Phillips Ensg	1
Carrismus Austin	1

1777 MILITARY CENSUS

NORTH KINGSTOWN, RHODE ISLAND

Page 12 (cont.)   Page 12 (cont.)

William Northup	1	Robart Hart	1
Samuel Northup	1	Nicholas Hart Jun[r]	1
John Bowler Jun[r]	1	Benoni Hunt	1
Benjamin Reynolds	1	Gideon Corey	1
Daniel Scranton	1		27
Daniel Wall	1	Those Who Belong to the Continental
Christopher Shearman	1	Batalions
Peter Reynolds	1	Cap[t] Thomas Cole	1
Daniel Reynolds	1	Leiu[t] Samuel Bissell	1
David Colvin	1	Robart Dickson	1
John Cobb Jun[r]	1	William Thomas	1
William Oakley	1	Christopher Fowler	1
Benjamin Congdon	1	Ebenezar Slocum Ju[r]	1
Robart Albro	1	James Nason	1
Thomas Shearman	1	John Gibbins	1
George Havens	1	Henry Freborn	1
Jonathan Godfrey	1	William Helme	1
Caleb Corey Jun[r]	1	Peleg Helme	1
Thomas Wall	1	James Phillips	1
			12

The Foregoing Contains a List of The Male Inhabitance and Residors in North
Kingstown, and Being Appointed By the Honb[l] the General Assembly for That
Purpose, do Submit the Same and am gent[ll] your Most Hhb[l] Serv[t]

Joseph Coggeshall

North Kingstown
April y[e] 17th 1777

Kings County ss at North Kingstown Afores[d] on the 19th day of April A.D. 1777
then personally appeared the Above Subscriber, Joseph Coggeshall, and made
Solemn Oath that the foregoing List hath been Justly and Truly made according
to the Best of his Knowledge Before Geo Thomas Justice

NORTH PROVIDENCE, RHODE ISLAND

Page 1   Page 1 (cont.)

Capt Ealeazer Jencks	16-50 A	James Angell	16-50 A
Left Samuell Olney	"	Cristopher Olney	"
Ensin Eseck Olney	"	Ebenezer Jenks Juner	"
Beniman Coman	"	Neamiah Smith	"
Jesse Whipple	"	Ruben King	"
Eseck Jencks	"	Philip Sweet	"
Ezra Healy	"	Elisha Angell	"
Eseck Angell	"	Uriah Hopkings	"
John Whipple	"	Thomas Hudson	"
Ethan Whipple	"	Andrew Brown	"
Ezekiel Whipple	"	Edward Smith	"
Benjamin Jencks	"	Peter Fen-h [?]	"
Gorge Jenks	"	Nathan Hamon	"

1777 MILITARY CENSUS

NORTH PROVIDENCE, RHODE ISLAND

Page 1 (cont.)

Benjiman Nichools	16-50 A	
Zakriah Williams	"	
Harman Richardson	"	
Constant Martain	"	T-Rehoboth
Gidan Olney Juner	"	
Abraham Haman	"	
Zebdee Williams	"	
Joy Lad	"	
Jeremiah Sayls	"	
John Pitcher	"	
Joseph Bagley	"	
Moses Jenks	"	
Levi Phillips	"	
Jeremiah Robartson	"	
William Shepard	"	
Nicholas Jenks	"	
Esek Eston	"	
Nemiah Olney	"	
Jabez Greene	"	
Ginis Davis	"	

Totals:
    46   16-50 A

Page 2

Chartered Company in North Providence

Cap Joseph Olney	50-60 A	
Lef Thomas Olney	16-50 A	
Ens Joseph Hawkings	"	
Cristphor Whipple	"	
Thomas Burgis	"	
Arnold Benshle	"	
William Dexter	"	
Jermiah Dexter	"	
John Comstock Juner	"	
John Randal	"	
James Angell	"	
Joseph Whipple Juner	"	
Peter Cupper	"	
Ens Silas Bunday	"	
Elezer Whipple	"	
Hezeciah Smith	"	
Capt Enock Angell	"	
Isaac Angell	"	
John Chlson	"	
Epenetus Olney	"	
Obedias Anis	"	R-Old Provi-dence

Page 2 (cont.)

Thimothy Tucker	16-50 A	
Rufus Angell	"	R-Smith-field
Jehu Pain	"	
John Jencks Durfey	"	

The Chartred Company

Nathaniel Walker	"	R-Attel-borough
~~Samuell Pitcher~~	"	"
Benjamin Martin	16-50 A	
Gideon Jenks	"	
John Trip	"	
Eleazur Sprague	"	
John Wartor	"	
George Pitcher	"	R-Attel-borough
Thomas Arnold	"	R-Smith-field
Benjamin Harris	50-60 A	
James Comstok a minister	Cert	
David Antony a frind	"	
John Comstock	Aff	
Oliver Angell	"	
Smith Brown	"	
Joseph Randall	"	
Elisha W[ior?]on Es-quire	"	

Totals:
    32   16-50 A   2   50-60 A
     1   60+   4   Aff
     2   Cert

Page 3

Esek Hopkings	50-60 A	
Benjamin Whipple	60+	
Nathaniel Day	60+	
Edward Tripp	60+	
Joseph Brown	60+	
John Olney	60+	
John Owen	60+	
Samuel Tucker	60+	
Abrham Readwod	60+	T-Rhod-iland
Ebenezar Jenks	60+	

1777 MILITARY CENSUS

NORTH PROVIDENCE, RHODE ISLAND

Page 3 (cont.)

Jonathan Jenks	60+	
Robard Yong	60+	
Hedibiah Angell	60+	
Benjamin Chaniel	16-50 U	T-Rodiland
1 Left Stephen Jenks	50-60 A	
2 Left Thomas Olney	"	
Ensin Charles Olney Juner	16-50 A	
Thomas Whipple	50-60 A	
James Packham	16-50 A	T-Road-iland
Jonathan Jenks	"	
Hope Angell	"	
William Bagley	"	
Iacbod Jenks	"	
Charles Olney	50-60 U	
Jonathan Whipple	50-60 A	
Benjman Whipple Juner	"	
Daniel Whipple	16-50 A	
Ephram Whipple	"	
Joseph Whipple	"	
John Inman	50-60 A	
Gideon Olney	"	
Abrham Olney	16-50 A	
Daniel Ruttenburgh	"	
William Philips	50-60 A	
Isaac Olney	16-50 A	
Jason Angell	"	lam[e]
Samuell Tucker lost one ey[e]	"	
Peter Pike	"	
Christopher Dexter	"	
Peter Randal	50-60 A	
Jerimiah Smith	16-50 A	lam[e]
Daniel Clark	"	
John Scott Juner	50-60 A	
Benjman Earl	16-50 A	
David Freeman	"	
Samuel Pitcher	"	
William Jenks	50-60 A	T-Attel-borough
Jabis Palmer	16-50 A	
Ezra Olney	"	
William White	50-60 A	
Hasakiah Hawkins	16-50 A	lam[e]
Jacub Wordrd	"	
Henery Randal	50-60 A	

Page 3 (cont.)

Josiah Owen	16-50 A	
Noah Mason	"	T-Old Providence
Jonathan Pike	50-60 A	
Benjman Shepard	16-50 A	

Totals:

28	16-50 A	1	16-50 U	
14	50-60 A	12	60+	

Page 4

Esek Hopkins two Negroes	2 N	
Andre Whipple	1 N	
Aron Frank	1 N	
Tom	1 N	T-Road-island
Prince	1 N	T-Road-island
Jam	1 N	T-Road-island
Prim Jenks	1 N	

Totals:

106	·16-50 A	1	16-50 U	
18	50-60 A	13	60+	
4	Aff	2	Cert	
8	N			

North Providence April 19th 1777
Whereas I the Subscriber was appointed
by the Honble General Assembly at their
last Session to Number all the Male
Inhabitants in the Town of North Providence from 16 years of Age and upwards
in Consequence of which appointment I
have proceeded upon the business and
herewith present the Preceeding Roll
which is Humbly Submitted by your Honors
Humble Servant

Joseph Olney

1777 MILITARY CENSUS

PROVIDENCE, RHODE ISLAND

Page 1

Honoble Nicholus Cook Esqr	50-60 U	
Nicholas Cook Juner	16-50 A	
Jesse Cook	"	
Daniel Cook	"	
Wisson Grinnold	"	
John Burrough	"	
Wm Burrough	Niher fit Nor willing	
Cor Jos Nightingall	16-50 A	
John Momford	"	
2 Negar Man	N	
John Tower	16-50 A	
W.m Fisk	"	
[blank] Glover	"	T-Boston
Samuel Brownwil	"	R-Newport
Robart Blinn	"	
Joshua Hackker	50-60 A	
1 Negar Man	N	
Nicholas Weever	16-50 A	R-Newport
James Berrey	"	
Jos Ingerham	"	
Edward Spolding	"	
William Card	"	R-Newport
John Tillinghast	"	
Daniel Colyer	"	
Silas Downer	16-50 U	
Jos Field	50-60 A	
Nathan Field	16-50 A	
Edward Field	"	
John Carpenter	"	
Philip Justes (CS)	"	
Daniel Buckling	"	
W.m Buckling	"	
1 Negar Man	N	
Garsham Carpenter	16-50 A	
Jos Tillinghast	"	
Richard Swan	50-60 U	R-Newport
John Peters	16-50 A	R-Newport
Elijah Abbet (CS)	"	R-Newport

Totals:

2	CS	29	16-50 A	1	16-50 U
3	N	2	50-60 A	2	50-60 U

Page 2

Henry Ward	16-50 U	R-Newport
John Brown	16-50 A	

Page 2 (cont.)

William Tillinghast	16-50 A	
Daniel Smith	"	
Elkanh Watson	"	
Pomp Brown	N	
Amboy Brown	N	
Arthar Fenner Esq	60+	
Arther Fenner Juner	16-50 A	
A Negar Man	N	
Jabesh Bowing Esqr	16-50 A	
A Negar Man	N	
Moses Brown	16-50 A	
Levi Arnold	"	
Daniel Aldridg	"	R-Smith-field
A Negar Man	N	
John Jenck Esqr	16-50 A	
Rufas Jencks	"	
Daniel Jencks	"	
2 Negar men	N	
Ephram Bowing Esqr	60+	
Pardon Bowing	16-50 A	
Ephram Bowing Jun (CS)	"	
A Negar man	N	
Willim Bowing	16-50 A	
Willm Whipple	"	R-Cumber-land
Willm Chace	"	
Samuel Chace Esqr	50-60 U	
Samuel Chace Juner	16-50 A	
[Doc.?] Malcom (SM)	"	
Samuel Clark	"	R-Newport
Nicholas Brown Esqr	16-50 U	
Rufas Hopkens	16-50 A	
Thomas Green Esqr	"	
Jos Green	"	
Daniel Tillinghast	"	
Jos Green	"	
Daniel Tillinghast Juner	"	
Gibbs Tillinghash	"	
Simeon Allen	16-50 U	

Totals:

1	CS	1	SM	27	16-50 A
3	16-50 U	1		1	50-60 U
2	60+	8	N		

Page 3

Mager Ebenezer Thompson	16-50 A

1777 MILITARY CENSUS

PROVIDENCE, RHODE ISLAND

Page 3 (cont.)

Cap Jonothan Russell	16-50 A	
Samuel Pool	60+	
John Pool	16-50 A	R-Boston
Jos Pool (SM)	"	
Thomas Russell	"	
Jonathan Hammon	50-60 A	
Uriah Wescott (SM)	16-50 A	
Jesse Wilmut (SM)	"	
Robart Hutson	"	
Benjn Hamman	"	
Jos Larrance	"	
John Larrance Juner	"	
Thomas Larrance	"	
John Lar[t?]al	"	
David Howel	"	
John Howel	"	R-Jerses
1 Negar Man	N	
William Barker	Cert	
Abraham Barker	16-50 A	
Isaac Barker	"	
Charles Holdring	"	
James Dud Rulf?	"	
Caleb Ormsbary	"	
Jacob Orberson	"	
Lues Thomas	"	
John Granger	"	
Elihu Robbeson	"	
Christopher Robboson	" (SM)	
Peleg Brown	"	
Nehemiah Allen	"	
Nathan Warterman	"	
William Holride	"	
Jos Rogers	"	R-Newport
1 Negar Man	N	
Caleb Fuller	16-50 A	

Totals:
    4 SM   31 16-50 A
    1 50-60 A 1 60+
    1 Cert   2 N

Page 4

Edward Knoles	16-50 A
Abnor Laylon	"
William Martin	"
Wallard Sothard	"
Timothy Shelding Juner	"

Page 4 (cont.)

Timothy Fuller	16-50 U	
Esmarillon Fuller	"	
John Warters (CS)	16-50 A	
William Middelton (CS)	"	
Benjm Cussons	50-60 U	
Benjm Cossons Juner	16-50 A	
John Cossons	"	
Seth Luther	60+	
Bright Luther	16-50 A	
Caleb Bowing	"	
Ammasa Gray	"	
John Jenckens	"	
Jeremiah f. Jenckens	"	
Charles Esterbroocks	50-60 U	
Simeon Martin	16-50 A	
William Wheat	"	
Ezra Hubbord	"	
John Fitton	"	
William Donnoson (SM)	"	
Amos Horton	16-50 U	
Robart Lennard	16-50 U	
James Sabin	16-50 A	
Jacob Whitman	50-60 U	
William Bradford	16-50 A	
Josiah Miller	"	
Wilm Coller	"	
Abijah Ford (CS)	"	
Jos Donnoson	"	
David Pain	"	
John Dog MacDogle	"	
John P Jones	"	
Thomas Jones	"	
Wilm Jones	"	
Wilm Proud	50-60 U	
Samuel Proud	16-50 A	
Isaac Proud	"	
John Dunwell	"	
Archable Steward	"	
Cornileas Cooper	"	

Totals:
    3 CS 1 SM 35 16-50 A
    4 16-50 U   4 50-60 U
    1 60+

Page 5

Georg Taylor Esqr	60+

1777 MILITARY CENSUS

PROVIDENCE, RHODE ISLAND

Page 5 (cont.)

James Wardel	16-50 A	
Mical Medcalf	16-50 U	
Whipple Crow	16-50 A	
Azariah Whipple	"	
Jos Olney	60+	
George Olney	16-50 A	
Peter Olney	"	
Jeremiah Olney (CS)	"	
Til Merreck Olney	"	
one Negar Man	N	
Samuel Dun	50-60 U	
Samuel Dun Juner	16-50 A	
Samuel Smith	"	
Samuel Allen	"	
Benj^m Marthes	"	T-Rehobeth
Robart Sterry	60+	
Georg Brown	16-50 A	
Thomas Page	"	
John Read	"	
Jos Hews Juner	"	
Georg Tain	16-50 U	
John Cooper (CS)	16-50 A	
David Burr	50-60 A	
David Burr Juner	16-50 A	
Joshua Wilbar	"	
Peter Files	"	
William Whippe	60+	
Edward Taylor	16-50 A	
Benj^m Taylor	"	
Ebenezer Averell	"	
Noah Smith	"	
James Currey	"	
Elias Collinder	"	
Coomer Hayl	"	
Ebenezer Fuller	16-50 U	R-Newport

Totals:
  2 CS   26 16-50 A   3 16-50 U
          1 50-60 A   1 50-60 U
          5 60+   1 N

Page 6

Henry Tillinghast	16-50 A	
A Negar Man	N	
Nicholas Tillinghast	16-50 U	unwilling
Parres Tillinghast	16-50 A	
Jonathan Fillips	60+	
A Negar Man	N	

Page 6 (cont.)

William Grinlod	16-50 A	R-Newport
Hon.Stephen Hopkens	60+	
2 Negar men	N	
Thomas Stoddard	16-50 A	
Mical Dorronce	"	
~~Dennes Tayler~~	"	
Benjn Clap		
Isaac Clap	"	
Benjn Seamans	"	
Benjn Johnson	"	
Stepen Johnson (CS)	"	
Henry Starling	16-50 U	
Jos. Brown	16-50 A	
Georg Benson	"	
Calven Holoway	16-50 U	
Paul Two Esq	50-60 U	
William Compton	60+	
Daniel Larrance (CS)	16-50 A	
~~Samuel Momford~~	"	
Frances [sic] Braton		R-Newport
Jeremiah Hawkens	50-60 A	
Antone Kinnecut	I	
John Corlile	16-50 A	
Thomas Corlile (SM)	"	
John Young	"	
Jos Crofford	"	
Daniel Stilwel	"	
Barnan Dun	"	
Benjn Davis	"	
Jonathan Slone	"	
Thomas Burket	50-60 U	

Totals:
  2 CS   1 SM   22 16-50 A
  3 16-50 U   1 50-60 A
  2 50-60 U   3 60+
  3 N   1 I

Page 7

Samuel Coy	16-50 A
Isaac Corey	60+
Nich^s Power	16-50 A
Ephram Carpenter	50-60 A
3 Negar Men	N
Stephen Hartshorn	16-50 A
Edward Hunt	16-50 U
Partdrick Dwier	16-50 A
James Mitchel	"
Jeremiah Jencks Jun	"
Georg Whitehorn	"

1777 MILITARY CENSUS

PROVIDENCE, RHODE ISLAND

Page 7 (cont.)

Jos Shelding	16-50 A	
Wil^m Cossons	"	
John Gainor	"	R-Newport
Allen Brown	50-60 A	
Wil^m Foster (CS)	16-50 A	
Mical Field	50-60 A	
John Jones	60+	
John Pitts	50-60 A	
Edward White	16-50 A	T-Attle-bourh
8 Negar at the Pamacity works		
Wil^m Stuard	16-50 A	
Jos Stuard	"	
Samuel Coddoth	"	T-Smith-field
Thomas Bennet	16-50 A	
Jabesh Wescott	60+	
Benjaiah Lewes	16-50 A	
James Arnold	"	
Soloman Drown Esq	60+	
Somoman Drown Juner (SM)	16-50 A	
Wil^m Drown	"	
John Wescott	50-60 A	
John Wescott Junr	16-50 A	
Georg Beveley	"	
Ford Wescott	"	
Barnabas Allen	"	

Totals:
   1 CS   1 SM   24 16-50 A
   5 50-60 A   4 60+
  11 N

Page 8

John Larrance	60+	
David Larrance	16-50 A	
Welcom Arnold	"	
Olney Winsey	"	
Isaac Bartley	"	
Nathan Angel	50-60 A	
Samuel Angel (SM)	16-50 A	
Daniel Spensor	"	
William Lea	"	
Isreal Low	"	
Aaroren Man	"	
James Green	50-60 A	

Page 8 (cont.)

John Morley Green	16-50 A	
Rufas Warterman	"	
Job Stone	"	
Thomas Waate	"	
John Frey	"	
Benj^m Frey	"	
George Stratton	"	T-Boston
Aaron Right	"	
James Hill	"	
Jos Russell	"	
William Russell	"	
Jos D Russell	"	
William Russell Juner	"	1 N
1 Negar Man	N	
Ambres Page Esqr	50-60 A	
Benj^m Page (SM)	16-50 A	
in the Nave		
Job Page	"	
William Hoppins	"	
1 Negar Man	N	
Nathan Green	16-50 A	
John Updike	"	
John Carter	"	
John Dabney	"	
Bennett Wheeler	"	T-Halafax
Daniel Bowing	"	
A Negar Man	N	T-Newport

Totals:
   1 SM   31 15-60 A   3 50-60 A
   1 60+   3 N

Page 9

Arther Burket	16-50 A	
Charles Boman	"	
Paul Allen	"	
Jos Allen	"	
Simon Smith	"	
Jonathan Jenkins	50-60 A	
John B. Hopkins (CS)	16-50 A	Cont. Fleet
Benj^m Green	"	
Jos Thornton	"	
John Saben	"	
Jonathan Clark	"	T-Nan-tucket
William Wall (SM)	"	
1 Negar Man	N	

1777 MILITARY CENSUS
PROVIDENCE, RHODE ISLAND

Page 9 (cont)

Giles Peckham	16-50 A	
Aaron Peckham	"	
Jonathan Peckham	"	
Silas Peckham	"	

Totals:
2	SM	28	16-50 A		
2	50-60 A	1	60+	5 N	

Page 10

John Croos	16-50 A	
Ickerbord Brown	"	
Georg Brown Esqr	60+	
Nathan Brown Juner	16-50 A	
Joshua Ashton	60+	
Timothy Sabing	50-60 A	
Daniel Thornton	16-50 U	
William Ashton	50-60 A	
Christopher Arnold	"	
Christopher Arnold Juner	16-50 A	
Christopher Shelding	"	
~~Samuel Warnar~~	~~50-60 A~~	
Samuel Warnar Juner	16-50 A	
Samuel Godfrey	"	
Parden Shelding	"	
Andrew Cole	"	
William Daggett	"	
Russell Brayley	"	
Richard Swan	"	R-Newport
~~Jack Ear Negar Man~~	~~N~~	
a Negar Man (SM)	N	
Daniel Parce	16-50 A	
Jos Arnold	50-60 A	
Jonathan Hill	16-50 A	
John Thompson	"	
Remmenton Shelding	"	
Isrel Shelding	"	
Isaac Filler	"	R-Newport
William Tillinghas son of Willm So Deaf He is Not fit for a Soger		
Natiors? Pitts	16-50 A	
Nathaniel Viel	50-60 U	R-Newport
John Davis	16-50 A	
Jos Davis	"	

Page 10 (cont)

Totals:
1	SM	21	16-50 A		
1	16-50 U	4	50-60 A		
1	50-60 U	2	60+	1	N

Page 11

Jos Sampson	16-50 A	
Edward Allen	"	
Samuel Jackson	"	
Comfort Bardne	"	
John Russell	"	
John Innes Clark	"	
John Morrey	"	
1 Negar Man	N	
John Smith	16-50 A	
John Beveley	"	
Laben Beveley	"	
Amos Throp	"	
Stephen Kilton	"	
Benj^m Coshing	60+	
Benj^m Coshing Juner	16-50 A	(CS)
Sandres Pitman	"	
A Negâr Man	N	
Benj^m Hunt	16-50 A	
Dirias Antram	"	
John Fostor Esq	50-60 A	
Richard Olney	60+	
A Negar Man	N	T-Rehoboth
Stepen Harres	16-50 A	
One Negar Man	N	
Joseph Jacobs	16-50 A	
Abr^m P. Mindes	"	
Calab Green	Cert	
Christopher Fry	16-50 A	
Thomas Green	"	R-Newport
Eseck Brown	"	
Zachariah Allen	"	
Philip Allen	"	
Elishar Brown Juner	"	
William Thurbor	"	
William Capron	"	
Ruben Anthony	"	R-Conatiut
Benj^m Bowing	16-50 U	

Totals:
1	CS	28	16-50 A

1777 MILITARY CENSUS
PROVIDENCE, RHODE ISLAND

Page 11 (cont)

Totals (cont):

1	16-50 U	1 50-60 A	
2	60+	1 Cert	4 N

Page 12

~~Nathaniel Packard~~	~~16-50 A~~	
Rodes Packard (SM)	16-50 A	
Samuel Packard	"	
James Somnord	"	T-Boston
Daniel Simons	"	
Benj^m Marshel	60+	
Benj^m Marshel Juner	16-50 A	
Recompence Heley	"	
Simeon Olney	"	
David Arnold	"	
Gideon Crofford	60+	
Gideon Crofford Juner	16-50 A	
John Crofford	16-50 A	
Arther Crofford	"	
A Bimilick Rigs (SM)	"	
Charles Smith	"	
Jeremiah Stone	"	
One Negar Man	N	
Samuel Fripe	16-50 A	
Benj^m Allen	"	
Jos Omsbary	"	
William Umprey (CS)	"	
Nathaniel Sandres	"	
Jos Burk	"	
Levi Hall	"	
After Fripp	"	
Nathan Fisher	"	T-Killinghat
Caleb Teal	"	
Esaw Thayer	"	
Charles Keen	"	
Ezikiah Keen	"	T-Duckberrey
Joel Ide	"	T-Attlbary
Ray Ward	"	
One Negar Man	N	
Jos Parker	16-50 A	
One Negar Man	N	
Timothy Sheldon	60+	

Totals:

1	CS	2	SM	30	16-50 A
3	60+	3	N		

Page 13

Lawton Ingram	16-50 A	
John Salsbary	16-50 U	
Archable Salsbory	16-50 A	
Daniel Brown	"	
Thomas MacClish	"	T-Rehobeth
Ephram Wheton	50-60 U	
William Wheton	16-50 A	
James Wheton		
son Decon	"	
Benj^m Wheton	"	
James Burr	"	
William Cesar	I	
Thomas Miller	16-50 A	
Thomas Miller Juner	"	
Mamaduke Warterman	"	
one Negar Man	N	
Jos Smitton	50-60 U	
Robart Dickkey	60+	
Isreal Brown	16-50 A	R-Newport
Nathaniel Jenck	"	
Jonathan Jencks	"	R-Smithfield
Jabesh Whipple	"	
William Morres	"	
Isaac Brown	"	
Jonathan Knoles	"	
John P. Knoles	"	
John Apling	"	
Benjn Apling	"	
William Apling	"	
Thomas Apling	"	
John Nash Juner	"	
Richard Fuller	16-50 U	
William Brown (CS)	"	
Antone Kinnecut	I	
Alfred Arnold	16-50 A	
Timothy Mayson	"	
Aaron Mason	"	
Jos Stanton	"	R-Charlestown
Thomas Luther	"	
John Luther	"	

Totals:

1	CS	31	16-50 A	
2	16-50 U	2	50-60 U	
1	60+	1	N	2 I

1777 MILITARY CENSUS
PROVIDENCE, RHODE ISLAND

Page 14

Daniel Shelding	16-50 A	
Nathaniel Wheton	"	
Seth Wheton	"	
Jeremiah Laton	"	R-Newport
William Smith	50-60 A	
James Hedding	16-50 A	T-Marraland
William Smith, Coper	"	
Joshua Burr	"	
Soloman Bradford	16-50 U	
Uriah Thayer	16-50 A	
Benj[m] Comstock	"	
William Seamans	"	
John Lues (SM)	"	
Wil[m] Tylar	"	
Wil[m] Tylar Juner	"	
Samuel Yong	"	
Melser Packard	"	
Arch Yates	"	
W.m. Sanford Brown	"	T-Swanzey
Benj[n] Still	"	
Jon[a] Arnold (SM)	"	
Step. Harding (SM)	"	
Martin Seamans	"	
Garner Luther (SM)	"	
Benj[m] Spooner (SM)	"	
Tennes Ryley	"	
Samuel Wescott	"	
John Demount	"	
Abnor Thayer	"	
Samuel Martin	"	
Job Smith	"	
William Braton	"	
Benj[m] Alger	"	
Edward Thurbor	"	
Ellick Shelding	"	
Samuel Hill	"	
John Godfrey	"	

Totals:
    5   SM   36 16-50 A
    1   16-50 U   1 50-60 A

Page 15

Benjm Man Esqr	16-50 U	
Gideon Young	50-60 U	
Richard Sisson	"	

Page 15 (cont)

George Brown Juner	16-50 A	
Wil[m] Rodes	"	
Finias Frasher	"	
David Arnold (SM)	"	
Jabesh Donneson	"	R-Newport
Gideon Manchester	50-60 U	
Jos Manchester	16-50 A	
Thomas Manchester	"	
Cyrus Manchester (SM)	"	
Caleb Goodfrey	"	
Job Sweten	50-60 A	
Allen Peck	16-50 A	
Jos Kook	"	
Robart Taylar	"	
John Taylar	"	
Jos Potter	60+	
Phinias Potter	16-50 A	
Jos Potter Juner	"	
Wil[m] Jeames	60+	R-Newport
Samuel James	16-50 A	R-Newport
Wil[m] James Juner	"	
Lues Bosworth	"	
Wil[m] Chickley	16-50 U	
one Negar Man	N	
Gideon Tanner	16-50 A	
James Hammon	"	
Antony Mory (SM)	"	R-Newport
Thomas Rone	"	
Zachary Eddy	"	
James Field	50-60 A	
James Field Juner	16-50 A	
Edward Field (CS)	"	
Ford Wescott	"	

Totals:
    1   CS   3   SM   26 16-50 A
    2   16-50 U   2   50-60 A
    3   50-60 U   2   60+   1 N

Page 16

Jos Wodford	16-50 A	
Silas Whelar	"	T-Conckard
Charles Boller	"	
Daniel Solovan	"	
James Burk	"	T-Nantuckket
Ferrel Ryley	"	
Henry Ryce [or Pryce]	"	

1777 MILITARY CENSUS
PROVIDENCE, RHODE ISLAND

Page 16 (cont)

Samuel Bugbee	16-50 A	
Thomas Linsey	"	
Peleg Hull	"	R-Newport
Samuel Hamlin	16-50 U	
Garsham Jones	16-50 A	
Grindal Rawson	50-60 U	
Wemath Ham	60+	
Levi Ham	16-50 A	
John Larsher	50-60 A	
Josiah Green	16-50 A	
Wil^m Bartan (SM)	"	
Seth Bartan	"	
Jos Martin	"	
Sweet Luther	"	
Stepen Thurbar	"	
Abial Smith	16-50 U	
Samuel Black	"	
John Kilton	16-50 A	
Zepheniah Andres	"	
David Martin	"	
Jos Kinnecut	"	
Georg Thayer	60+	
Simeon Thayer (CS)	16-50 A	
Jabesh Wesott Juner	"	(SM)
James Whetan	"	
Nathaniel Daynay	"	
Hazikiah Dayton	"	R-Newport
Samuel Butler	50-60 U	
Samuel Butler Juner	16-50 U	
Peter Tayler	16-50 A	
John Sothard	"	
Wil^m Tylar	"	
Pepprel Tyler	"	
John Adye	"	

Totals:
    1 CS   2 SM   32 16-50 A
    4 16-50 U   1 50-60 A
    2 50-60 U   2 60+

Page 17

John Umphrey	16-50 A	
Jos Whittemore	16-50 U	
Thomas Cain	16-50 A	R-Newport
Wil^m Wheaton	"	
Umphrey Parmar	"	
William Allen	"	

Page 17 (cont)

Lues Peck	16-50 A	
Elezer Harding	50-60 U	
Theodore Foster	16-50 A	
Wil^m Ayr Peck	16-50 U	
Wil^m Mumford	"	
John Jenckins	16-50 A	
Wil^m Mallam	"	
Wil^m Creed	"	
Ephram Peabody	"	
Ephram Walker	"	
Wil^m Walker	"	
Obediah Planting	50-60 U	
Amas Attwel Esqr	16-50 A	
Thomas Melolney	"	
John Runnols	50-60 U	
Grindal Runnols	16-50 A	
Benj^m Runnols	"	
John Runnols Juner	"	
Wil^m Bager (SM)	"	
Isreal Pearce	"	
John Jeames	"	R-Newport
Benj^m Creapman	"	
James Black	"	
Daniel Jackson	"	
Benoni Pearce	"	
Wamoth Ham	16-50 U	
Wil^m Ham	16-50 A	
Jotham Ham	"	
Joshua Lindley	"	
Benj^m Shelding	"	
Thomas Harding	60+	

Totals:
    1 SM   29 16-50 A
    4 16-50 U   3 50-60 U   1 60+

Page 18

Jonathan Olney	60+	
Christopher Olney	16-50 A	
Warterman William	"	
John ol Warterman	"	
John Wels	"	R-Gloshertor
Zachary Maddeson	"	
Benj^m Smith	"	
James Boyd	"	R-Cranston
John White	"	
1 Negar Man	N	

1777 MILITARY CENSUS
PROVIDENCE, RHODE ISLAND

Page 18 (cont)

James Angel	50-60 U	
John Angel	16-50 A	
Jos. Angel (CS)	"	
Trimmen Angel	"	
Soloman Rotenbar	60+	
Thomas Rotenbar	16-50 A	
?Comford Whiton	"	
Prince Keen	"	
Benj^m Keen	"	
Samuel Thurber	60+	
Samuel Thurber Junr	50-60 A	
Squier Thurbor	16-50 A	
Samuel Turbor 3	"	
Edward Thurbor Junr	"	
Martin Thurbor	"	
Jos. Tillinghast		
son of Jonath	"	
Daniel Cohoon	"	
Robert Mickers	"	
Obidiah Sprage	50-60 U	
Ebenezer Burrell	16-50 A	R-Newport
Jos. Burrell	16-50 U	R-Newport
Jos. Burrell Juner	16-50 A	R-Newport
Levi Burr	"	
Peleg Shaw	"	
William Page (SM)	"	
William Stevens	"	
Edward Price (SM)	"	R-Newport
Robort Corey	"	
Andrew Comstock	"	
Samuel Bastow	"	
David Britton	16-50 U	R-Smithfield
Nehemiah Sweet	16-50 A	
Benj^m hide	"	

Totals:

1	CS	2 SM	34	16-50 A
2	16-50 U	1	50-60 A	
2	50-60 U	3	60+	1 N

Page 19

Andrew Williams	16-50 A
Allexander Sampson	"
Samuel Sampson	16-50 U
Stase Sampson	16-50 A
Benj^m Robason	60+
John Atwood	16-50 A

Page 19 (cont)

Allexander Sampson Juner	16-50 A	
Wil^m Spenser	16-50 A	
Warterman Carpenter	16-50 U	
Timothy Carpenter	16-50 A	
John Shanne	"	
Jos. Fuller	"	
Caleb Fuller	"	
Elihu Peck	"	
James Weeden	"	T-Newport
Samuel Weeden	"	T-Newport
James Manro	"	
Morey Potter	"	
Ebenezer Hill	"	
Jos. Snow Juner	"	
Jos. Clark Esqr	50-60 U	R-Newport
Robart Layton	16-50 A	R-Newport
one Negar Man	N	
Samuel Spooner	16-50 A	
Wil^m Grafton	"	
Jos. Grafton	"	
Nathan Warnar	"	
Jos. Willon	"	
Silas Talbut	"	
John Mumford	"	

Totals:

25	16-50 A	2	16-50 U		
1	50-60 U	1	60+	1 N	

Page 20

James Snow	16-50 A
Daniel Snow	50-60 A
James Snow Juner	16-50 A
Daniel Snow Juner	"
James Potter	"
Soloman Sears	"
Peter Ritto	50-60 U
one Indian	I
Benj^m Gladding	16-50 A
John Howland	"
Nathan Frothingham	"
Richard Sever	60+
Obed Sever	16-50 A
Ebenezer Peck	"
Wil^m Hoyl	"
John Colwell	"
Richard Whitehorn	60+ R-Newport

1777 MILITARY CENSUS
PROVIDENCE, RHODE ISLAND

Page 20 (cont)

Richard Hoyl	16-50 A	
Antony Wescott	[blank]	
Barnabas Chace	50-60 U	
Nathan Brown Sener	60+	
Nathan Arnold	16-50 A	
Daniel fenner	60+	
David Tifft	50-60 A	
David Tifft Juner	16-50 A	
Ebenezer White	"	
Charles Lee	"	
Ollever Carpenter	"	
Benj^m Randal	[blank]	
Jos. Williams	16-50 A	
Jeremiah Williams	"	
Georg Potter	"	

Totals:

21 16-50 A   2 50-60 A
2 50-60 U   4 60+   2 I [sic]

Page 21

Samuel Snow (SM)	16-50 A	
Robart Ellet (SM)	"	R-Newport
John Carpenter	"	
Whitterur	"	
Nathaniel Viel	"	R-Newport
Daniel Tifft	"	
Elij^h Babbet (SM)	"	
John old Ham	"	R-Newport
John Wiley (CS)	"	
Robart Wiley (CS)	"	
Samuel Wiley (CS)	"	
John Wiley Juner (CS)	"	
Isaac Jacobs (SM)	"	
Samuel Jacobs	"	
Stutley Williams	"	
Jos. Manning	"	
Amas Chace	"	
Elij^h Waker (SM)	"	
John McNickels	"	
Bersiller Ritchman	50-60 U	
Ebenezer Ritchman	16-50 A	
Charles Stephan	"	
Thomas Peek	"	
David Smith	"	
Joshua Smith	"	
Nathan Potter	"	
John Pettes	"	

Page 21 (cont)

Joseph Clevelnd	16-50 A	
Zepheniah Brown	"	
Jos. Smith	"	
Edward Hawkins	"	
Isaac Corey	60+	
Samuel Coshing	16-50 A	
Ruben Potter	"	
1 Negar Man	N	
Wil^m Compton	60+	

Totals:

4 CS   5 SM   32 16-50 A
1 50-60 U   2 60+   1 N

Page 22

Elijah Shepperson	16-50 A	
Walker Harding	"	
Wil^m Billens	"	R-Newport
Honry Horthman	"	R-Newport
Jeremiah McCoy	"	T-Belong no where
Benj^m Eddy	"	
Jos. Eddy	"	
Jeremiah Eddy	"	
John Hoppin	60+	
Levi Hoppen	16-50 A	
Simmeon Hoppen	"	
Nicholas Clark	16-50 U	
Hopsid Mackneal	16-50 A	
Benj^m West	16-50 U	
Gabrel Allen (SM)	16-50 A	
Jonathan Elles	"	
Job Danford	"	
Jonathan Woodbery	"	
Ghilip [sic] Peckham	"	R-Newport
Henry Peckham	"	R-Newport
James Burrel	"	
Daniel Hutson	"	R-Newport
Timothy Gladding	"	
Nathaniel Dexter	"	
Loudan Lippet	"	
John Gibbs	"	
John Bowers	"	
Timothy Browning	"	
Ruben Potter	"	
Elishar Cocksel	"	R-Newport
Asa Frankling	"	
John Field	"	

1777 MILITARY CENSUS
PROVIDENCE, RHODE ISLAND

Page 22 (cont)

Totals:
| 1 | SM | 29 | 15-60 A |
| 2 | 16-50 U | 1 | 60+ |

Page 23

Elijah Bacon	16-50 A	
Jos. Hoyl	"	
Daniel Pettet	"	
John Wood	"	R-Newport
one Negar Man	N	
Robart Newel	16-50 A	
Jehu Smith	"	
Archable Solsbory	"	
John Ward	"	
Thomas Pitman	"	
Jos. Hawkens	"	
John Armes	60+	
Simon Dival	50-60 U	
one Indian Man	I	
2 Negars	N	

Page 23 (cont)

Samuel Turbar		
son of Sam[l]	16-50 A	
Cap[t] Wil[m] Allen (CS)	"	
John Chace	"	
John Field, Decon	50-60 U	
Lemuel Feald	16-50 A	
Dexter Brown	"	
one Negar Man	N	
Cor[l] William Brown	60+	
1 Negar Man	N	
Phinias Brown	50-60 A	
Selvester Brown	16-50 A	
Richard Brown	60+	
Wil[m] Lancksford	16-50 A	
Isaac Field	"	
Sipperan Stevey (CS)	"	

Totals:
2	CS	19	16-50 A		
1	50-60 A	2	50-60 U		
3	60+	1	I	5	N

Providence April 17 1777
A List of all the Male Persons in The Town of Providence From 16 years of age and upwards - and of Negars & Indians and Those that have Listed in the Conanantal Armev and Those who have Listed in the 15 Months Servis That are inhabetannce of This Town That is To Say -----

In the Con[t] Armey	)	11
In the 15 Month Ser[s]	)	16

The Hole Number of whites from 16 To 50 is 646 able To Bare armes
Now Residing in this Town - Belonging to   64
This and the Nabering States is included   11 Con[t] Armey
in the 646   16 15 Months Servis
There Remains in This Town from 16 to 50   ——
able to Bare arms   555

Totals:
646 16-50 A 35 16-50 U 28 50-60 A 29 50-60 U 45 60+ 2 C
The 64 I have Mentioned beLongs Hear - T & R   54 N 6 I
Som Total 845 NB all the Negars & Indians are able To Bear Arms

Providence April 1777 The State of Rhod Island Dr To Dowing the above Servis, For Taking the Number of Male Inhabitance from 16 years of age and upwards in the Town of Providence--------------------£2=8-0
Examined Nath[l] Mumford Martin Seamans

Providence Ss In Providence April 18th AD 1777 Martin Seamans, who hath Subscribed the above and annexed List in his own proper Person came and made Solemn Oath, that the said List hath been by him justly and truly made, according to the best of his Knowledge. Before me - John Foster, Jus. Peace

Richmond

1777 MILITARY CENSUS
RICHMOND, RHODE ISLAND

Page 1

Simeon Clarke Jun[r]	16-50 A	
Thomas James	"	
Smiten Potter	"	
Richard Bailey	60+	
Richard Bailey Ju[n]	16-50 A	
Charke [sic] Bailey	"	
Ebenezar Hall	Aff	
William Potter Jun[r]	60+	
Robert Potter	16-50 A	
Samuel Stanton	"	
George Webb	"	
John Webb	"	
George Webb Jun[r]	"	
Joshua Webb	"	
John Webb Jun[r]	"	
Elias Dewey	"	T-Middletown
		in Connecticut
[Samuel] Tefft	60+	
William Potter	60+	
Samuel Wells	16-50 A	
George Hollway	"	
Ezekiel Bently	60+	
Jonathan Tindal	1 Mollatto	
David Moore	50-60 A	
Silas Moore	16-50 A	
James James	60+	
William James	16-50 A	
James James Ju[r]	Aff	
Stephen Willcox	50-60 U	
Benjamin Baker Jn[r]	16-50 A	R-South
		Kingston
Joshua Barber	"	R-South
		Kingston
George James	"	
Jonathan James	Aff	
Randal James	16-50 A	
Simeon Clarke	60+	
Asa Clarke	16-50 A	
William Willcox	"	
Thomas Clarke	60+	
Moses Clarke	16-50 A	
Pain Waite	"	R-Hopkinton
Thomas Hill	"	R-Pourtsmouth
Samuel Barber	16-50 U	
Bartholomew Phillips	16-50 A	
1 Cesar	N	

Page 1 (cont)

Samuel Kinyon	16-50 A	
Arnold Clarke	"	

Totals:

29	16-50 A	1	16-50 U	
1	50-60 A	1	50-60 U	
7	60+	3	Aff	

Page 2

Hezekiah Tefft	16-50 A	
Noel Allen	"	R-Pourtsmouth
Ezekiel Tefft	"	
Thomas Records	"	R-South
		Kingston
William Strange	"	
Robert James	"	
Edward Willcox	60+	
Peleg Willcox	16-50 A	
Stephen Willcox J[n]	"	
Sheffield Willcox	"	
Peleg Thomas	16-50 U	
Benadit Kinyon	16-50 A	
Benjamin James	"	
Daniel Dye	"	
John Dye	Cert	
Samuel Dye	"	
William Potter	60+	
Gideon Mosier	16-50 A	
James Brown	50-60 U	
Thomas Brown	16-50 A	
Elisha Babcock		
son Elisth	"	
Benjamin Babcock	"	
Samuel Cory	50-60 U	
Jonathan James Jr	16-50 A	
Jeremiah Vallet	50-60 U	R-North
		Kingston
John Vallet	16-50 A	R-North
		Kingston
Edward James	50-60 A	
Ezekiel James	16-50 A	
David Moore Jn[r]	"	
John Potter	"	R-Exeter
James Reynolds	16-50 U	R-in Kings
		County
Joseph Hoxsie	16-50 A	

1777 MILITARY CENSUS
RICHMOND, RHODE ISLAND

Page 2 (cont)

Gideon Hoxsie	16-50 A		
William Hoxsie	"		
William Reynolds	50-60 A		
William Reynolds J^r	16-50 A		
Robert Reynolds	"		
Job Hoxsie	"		
Elijah Hoxsie	"		
Rodman Sisson	Aff		
Caleb Young	16-50 A		
Robert Moore	60+		
George Moore	16-50 A		
David Potter	50-60 A		

Totals:

30	16-50 A	2	16-50 U	
4	50-60 A	2	50-60 U	
3	60+	1	Aff	
2	Cert			

Page 3

Benjamin Hoxsie	16-50 A	
Solomon Kinyon	Cert	R-Hopkinton
Jeremiah Tefft	16-50 A	
Zebulon Weaver	Cert	R-Hopkinton
Stephen Hoxsie	60+	
John Hoxsie	Cert	
Edward Hoxsie	"	
Joseph Austin	50-60 A	
Joseph Austin Jr.	16-50 A	
Jeremiah Austin	"	
David Austin	"	R-West Greenwich
Waite Rogers	Aff	
Robert Pettys	16-50 A	
James Potter	"	
David Nichols	60+	
Elisha Babcock	50-60 U	
Will	N	
Jesse Babcock	16-50 A	
William Austin	"	
Isaac Clarke	16-50 U	R-Charlestown
Joshua Clarke	16-50 A	
Peter Clarke	"	
William Clarke	60+	
Robert Clarke	60+	
Weeden Clarke	16-50 A	
James Clarke	"	
Remington Clarke	"	

Page 3 (cont)

Elias Clarke	16-50 A	
Jonathan Boss	"	
Henry Greene	"	R-Exeter
Thomas Potter	50-60 U	
Thomas Potter Jr.	16-50 A	
Peleg Potter	"	
Pain Potter	"	
Gideon Potter	"	
Joseph Clarke	60+	
Christopher Clarke	16-50 A	
James Smith	"	R-Exeter
John Clarke	"	
Joshua Clarke Esqr	"	
John Clarke	"	R-Newport
John Wilbore	50-60 A	R-Exeter
Benjamin Wilbore	16-50 A	R-Exeter
Jonathan Maxson	"	

Totals:

28	16-50 A	1	16-50 U			
2	50-60 A	2	50-60 U			
5	60+	1	Aff	4	Cert	

Page 4

Income Potter	16-50 A	
Phillip Potter	"	
Jeremiah Hoxsie	"	
William Kinyon	"	
Jeremiah Pendleton	"	
Thurston Kinyon	"	
David Kinyon	"	
Edward Perry	"	
Benjamin Perry	"	
Daniel Stedman	"	R-South Kingston
Benjamin Card	16-50 U	
Phillip Kinyon	"	
Israel Lewis	16-50 A	
Thos Kinyon son David	"	
Thomas Kinyon	60+	
Oliver Kinyon	16-50 A	
Joseph Woodmansee Jn^r	"	
Joseph Deake	Aff	
Barnabas Hoxsie	Cert	
Sylvester Kinyon	60+	
John Fenner	16-50 A	
James Woodmansee	"	

1777 MILITARY CENSUS
RICHMOND, RHODE ISLAND

Page 4 (cont)

Benjamin Enoss	16-50 U	
Joseph Enoss	16-50 A	
Edmund Burdick	50-60 A	
John Enoss	60+	
Phillip Griffith	16-50 A	
John Baggs	50-60 U	
John Baggs Un^r	16-50 A	
David Larkin	16-50 U	
John Larkin	16-50 A	
David Larkin Jn^r	"	
Oliver Larkin	"	
Jesse Larkin	"	
Elisha Hall	60+	
Job Hall	16-50 A	
John Griffith	60+	
Nicholas Larkin	60+	
Elisha Larkin	16-50 A	R-Hopkinton
Edward Larkin	16-50 U	
Job Waite	16-50 A	R-Hopkinton
Lester Lillibridge	"	
Solomon Hoxsie	60+	
Peter Hoxsie	Cert	

Totals:
27	16-50 A	5	16-50 U		
1	50-60 A	1	50-60 U		
7	60+	1	Aff	2	Cert

Page 5

David Remington	16-50 A	R-Tivertown
Andrew Stafford	"	
Nathaniel Church	"	T-Uncertain where he belongs 1 N - Jack
Robert Stanton	"	
Ichabod Peterson	"	
William Tefft	"	
David Tefft	"	
Pardon Tefft	"	
Stephen Larkin	50-60 U	
George Ney	16-50 A	
Joseph Woodmansee	50-60 A	
David Woodmansee	16-50 A	
Peter Wilbore	"	
James Webster	60+	
Stephen Webster	16-50 A	
John Webster 3^d	"	
Daniel Webster	"	
James Webster Jn^r	"	

Page 5 (cont)

John Webster	60+	
William Webster	16-50 A	
Thomas Webster	16-50 U	
John Webster Jn^r	16-50 A	
Thomas Webster son John	"	
Taber Tefft	"	
Walter Clarke	"	
Perry Watson	"	
John Knowles	Cert	
William Knowles	"	
John Knowles Jn^r	"	
Jonathan Knowles	16-50 A	
Ezekiel Shearman	50-60 U	R-Exeter
Robert Knowles	16-50 U	
John Lewis	16-50 A	R-Hopkinton
Peter Boss	"	
Joseph Boss	"	
Dyre Burdick	"	R-Hopkinton
Samuel Knowles	Aff	
John Records	50-60 U	R-South Kingstown
Ezekiel Barber	60+	
Benjamin Barber	16-50 A	
Ezekiel Barber Jn^r	16-50 U	
John Woodmansee	16-50 A	
Nicholas Hollway	60+	
Sylvester Fowler	16-50 A	R-Jamestown
Robert Rogers	50-60 U	
Stephen Rogers	16-50 A	
William Lee	16-50 U	
Eber Mosier	16-50 A	

Totals:
31	16-50 A	4	16-50 U		
1	50-60 A	4	50-60 U		
4	60+	1	Aff	3	Cert

[on the side is the following but apparently not in the total count]
Caleb Barber	50-60 U	
David Willcox	16-50	
John Pendleton	"	Ordained Minister
Charles Kelly	"	Taken at Fort Washington, and a Prisoner upon Parole

1777 MILITARY CENSUS
RICHMOND, RHODE ISLAND

Page 6

Samuel Larkin	16-50 A - R-Hopkinton
John Bently	60+	
William Bently		
son John	16-50 A	
Thomas Lillibridge Jn^r	"	
George Lewis	60+	
Benjamin Lewis	16-50 A	
William Sheldon Jn^r	"	
William Sheldon	50-60 U	
Oliver Colegrove	16-50 A	
Nathan Kinyon	"	
Gardner Kinyon	"	
Benjamin Baker	60+	R-South Kingston
Elijah Baker	16-50 A	R-South Kingston
Josiah Baker	"	R-South Kingston
Latham Johnston	"	
Jonathan Johnston	"	
Lot Larkham	"	
William Herrington	16-50 U	
Stephen Grinnold	16-50 A	R-Charlestown
John Foster	"	
James Pettys	"	
Thomas Weaver	[blank]	R-Bristol
John Kinyon	50-60 U	
Jarvis Kinyon	16-50 A	
Thomas Kinyon		
son John	"	
Samuel Morey	"	
Joshua Griffith	"	
Samuel Worden	"	
Jonathan Potter	50-60 A	
Jonathan Potter Jn^r	16-50 A	

Page 6 (cont)

Elisha Potter	16-50 A	
Joseph Tefft	60+	
Samuel Tefft Jn^r	16-50 A	
Jonathan Palman	"	
Remington Bidgood	"	R-Hopkinton
Thomas Rogers	"	
John Worden Jn^r	"	R-Hopkinton
Thomas Kinyon Junr	Aff	
Thomas Lillibridge	16-50 A	
Edward Lillibridge	Aff	
John Foster Junr	Cert	
Jirrah Mumford	16-50 A	
Joseph Tefft Junr	"	
Thomas Tefft	"	
Benjamin Tefft	"	
Newman Herring	"	
Jedediah Collins	"	R-Hopkinton
Samuel Clarke	"	

Totals:

36	16-50 A	1	16-50 U
1	50-60 A	2	50-60 U
4	60+	2	Aff	1	Cert

Totals: [all pages]

182	16-50 A	16	16-50 U
10	50-60 A	11	50-60 U
30	60+	9	Aff
12	Cert	4	N

[Signed] Caleb Barber

Kings County to wit)
Richmond   ) Be it remembred that on the 17th Day of April AD 1777
                    Caleb Barber, personally appeared and made Solemn Oath
                    that the annexed Lists was taken justly and truly, accord-
                    ing to the best of his knowledge

          Before   Edward Perry Justice of the Peace

Scituate

1777 MILITARY CENSUS
SCITUATE, RHODE ISLAND

Page 1

Stephen Shelden	16-50 A
William Howard	"
James Wells	"
Daniel Howard	"
Silas Burlingame	"
James Phillips	"
John Hammon	"
Comfort Cook	"
Benjamin Fry	"
Francis Fuller	"
Abraham Walker	"
Benjamin Brownel	"
Peter King	"
Samuel Tillinghast	"
Petter Parker	"
Samuel Pirkens Jun	"
James Mackoon	"
Noah Simons	"
Thomas Hammon	"
William Sheldan	"
Calab Parker	"
William Cook	"
James Brown	"
Samuel Cranson	"
John Cranson	"
Peleg Cranson	"
Elias Pirkens	"
Benj: Hill	"
George Walker	"
Jobe parce	"
Amasee Brown	"
Stephen Brown	"
Daniel Wood	"
Elisha Brown	"
Jonah Young	"
Asaph Young	"
John Wells	"
Stephen Foster, Jr.	"
Joab Young	16-50 U
Daniel Judrack[?]	16-50 A R-Resides here

Totals:
39 16-50 A   1 16-50 U
1 R

Page 2

Joseph Kimbell   16-50 A

Page 2 (cont)

Gideon Cornell	16-50 A	
Bartrom Round	"	
Lemuel Slack	"	
William Eddy	"	
Caleb Westcut	"	
Abnor Burlingham	"	
Owen Arnold	"	R-Providence Residing
Joseph Slack	"	
William Brownel	"	R-Dartmouth Residing
William Seamons Jr	"	
Joseph Medbury	"	
Asa Sheldon	"	
[D]avid Potter	"	
William hines	"	
Benjagah Bozworth	"	
Robert Potter	"	R-North Kingstown Residing here
Timothy hopkins Jr	"	
Noah Aldrich	"	
Ebnezer Bullock	"	
Simon Davis Jr.	"	
John Salsbury	"	
William ford, Jr	"	
hanry herris	"	
Joseph Salsbury	"	
Ezekiel Sheldon	"	
Oliver hopkins	"	
James hines	"	
Elcony Eddy	"	
John Sheldon	"	
Daniel Cole	50-60 U	
Joseph Manchester	"	
Peleg Westcot	16-50 A	
John Batty	50-60 A	
Benjn Wight	"	
John Harris	Cert	

Totals:
31 16-50 A   2 50-60 A
2 50-60 U   1 Cert   3 R

Page 3

Peleg Fisk	16-50 A
John Rice	"

1777 MILITARY CENSUS
SCITUATE, RHODE ISLAND

Page 3 (cont)

Peleg Peck	16-50	A
Jacob Parker	50-60	A
James Brown	"	
John Parker	16-50	A
Elisha Bowen	50-60	A
Arom Dorr	50-60	U
Job Shearman	16-50	A
Robert Davis	50-60	A
John Randall	"	
Henry Wheeler	"	
Ezekiel Phillips	16-50	A
Robert Potter	50-60	A
James Rounds	"	
Uriah Franklin	50-60	U
Peleg Cranston	50-60	A
Elias Collins	16-50	A
Timothy Hopkins	50-60	A
Simon Davis	50-60	U
John Tayler	50-60	A
Joseph Davis	16-50	A
Nath[n] Bates	50-60	A
Christopher Bullock	50-60	U
Jonath[n] Pray	"	
Tho[s] Bishop	16-50	A
Henry Easton	50-60	A
Andrew Angell	16-50	A
John Pearce	50-60	A
Hugh Pray	50-60	U
Tho[s] Aylsworth	50-60	A
Nath[l] Herindeen	"	
James Hammond	"	
Joseph Collins	16-50	A

Totals:
  11 16-50 A   17 50-60 A
   6 50-60 U

Page 4

William Gallop	16-50	A
Joseph Place	"	
Samuel Foster	"	
Jonathan Herindon	"	
John Howard	"	
Stutely Whitford	"	
Matten Luther	"	
Jerimiah Willcox	"	
John Bennet	"	

Page 4 (cont)

Alexander Dorance	16-50	A
Ruphes Herindan	"	
Thomas Place	"	
Ruben Weever	"	
Christopher Whitford	"	
Joseph Holden	"	
Ruben Blancher	"	
asher Bennet	"	
Joseph Place	"	
Randol Herindon	"	
Nathen Bennet Jun	"	
Daniel Herindon	"	
Peleg Alesworth	"	
William Herindon	"	
Laben Bennet	"	
Jacob Sherman	"	
Jonathan Sole	"	
Stephen Deruse	"	
Samuel Tylar	"	
David Raymack	"	
Thomas Harington	"	
James Clark	"	
Matthew Bennet	"	
Stukely Stafford	"	
Josiah Herindon 3d	"	
Nathaniel Herindon	"	
Abraham Willcoxs	"	
Alexander Canaday	"	
Silas Herindon	"	
Ruphes Place	"	
Joseph Gallop	"	
Matthew Herindon	"	
Abial Tripp	"	

Totals:
  42 16-50 A

Page 5

David Smith	16-50	A
Job Fisk Jr	"	
Thomas West	"	
Thomas Mathewson Jr	"	
Stephen Leach Jr	"	
John West	"	
Charles West	"	
Nathan Walker	"	
Abraham Phillips	"	

1777 MILITARY CENSUS
SCITUATE, RHODE ISLAND

Page 5 (cont)

Jonathan hopkins	16-50 A
Christopher howard	"
John Seamons 3^d	"
Jeremiah Colegrove	"
Zebedee hopkins	"
Laben hopkins	"
Isriel Shippee	"
Abnor pratt	"
George Stone	"
Pardon Angell	"
John Atwood	"
Daniel Seamons	"
Jonathan Salsbury	"
Thomas Bickford	"
Stephen Whitman	"
Seth Peckum	"
Benj Tayler Jr	"
David Kimbell	"
Oliver Carver	"
hope Smith	"
Edward Phillips	"
Thomas Eddy	"
Winsor Potter	"
Nathaniel Cornell	"
Peleg hopkins	"
John El[i]ot	"

Totals:
   35 16-50 A   1 R

Page 6

Samuel Smith	50-60 A
Ezekel Hopkins	"
Beriah Willis	16-50 A
Samuel Dorance	"
John Fisk	50-60 A
Hannon Hopkens	16-50 A
James aldrich	"
Stephen Colegrove	50-60 A
Stephen Smith	"
Richard angel	50-60 U
Stephen Leach	50-60 A
Jonathan Turtelott	"
Joseph Rounds	"
Squire Bucklin	"

R-Resides here
an able
Country man

Page 6 (cont)

Joseph Weatherhad	50-60 A	
W^m taler	"	
David Blackmar	16-50 A	
James Allen	"	R-Portsmouth
Jacob Philips	"	
Joseph Carver	50-60 A	
Thos Hill	"	
Peleg Round	"	
John Weaver	16-50 A	
Gid^n Burlingame	50-60 A	
John Pratt	16-50 A	
Nathl Lovell	"	
Job Wilber	"	
John Pain	"	
Bernett Wood	50-60 A	
Caleb Fisk	16-50 A	
Bays Machester	50-60 A	
Peleg Cole	"	
Benjn Pettice	50-60 U	
Philip Parker	16-50 A	
W^m ford	50-60 A	
Jemes fenner	16-50 A	R-Jonson

Totals:
   15 16-50 A   19 50-60 A
    2 50-60 U   2 R

Page 7

Joseph Bickford	60+
Samuel Mery	60+
David Aldrag	60+
William Salsbary	60+
Fisher Potter	60+
Thomas Smith	60+
Stephen Smith	50-60 A
George Baker	"
Charls Hopkins	"
Isaac Medbury	16-50 A
Job Cole	"
Charls Walker	50-60 A
George Wilbour	"
Zepheniah Wright	16-50 A.
James Simons	"
Jesse Angell	"
Joshua King	"
Stephen Kimbell	"
John Edwards	50-60 A

1777 MILITARY CENSUS
SCITUATE, RHODE ISLAND

Page 7 (cont)

John Seamons	16-50 A	
Petter Cook	50-60 A	
Thomas Harris	Cert	
John Walker	"	
Elihu Bowen	"	
Ezral Potter	"	
Samuel Howland	"	
Ruben Hopkens	60+	
Frances Fuller	60+	
Nathan pero	16-50 A N	
William pero	" N	
Jubetor Randal	" N	
William Prosper	" N	
Volentine allen	" N	
Noha Batty	" N	
Peter Prophett	" N	
Shuble Round	" N	
Benjamin Boss	50-60 A T-Resides here	
Benjamin Boss Junr	16-50 A T- " "	
Comer Smith	"	

Totals:

18	16-50 A	8	50-60 A	
8	60+	5	Cert	
1	T [sic]	8	N	

Page 8

Peter parker	60+	
Richard Colwel	60+	
Paul parker	16-50 U	
John phillops	60+	
Job Randal	60+	
John Simons	60+	
Timothy myls	60+	R-North providence
Amos Herndon	60+	
Josias Hernton	60+	
Jonathan Hernton	60+	
Thomas Bennet	60+	
Samuel pirkens	60+	
Jerimiah Angel	60+	
Job Shipey	60+	
Hew Cole	60+	
Daniel Hopkens	60+	
Joseph Tucker	60+	
John Younge	60+	
Joseph Hopkens	60+	

Page 8 (cont)

Jeremiah Rounds	16-50 A	
Jonathan Fuller	60+	
Nathen Youngs	50-60 A	
Joseph guile	60+	
Christopher Smith	60+	
Josias Bennet	50-60 A	
Abial Trep	50-60 U	
Jonathan Knight	60+	
Thomas Eldred	16-50 A	
Benjamin Wells	60+	
Judah Brown	60+	
John Barding	60+	
Joseph parker	50-60 U	
John tyler	60+	
Enick place	60+	
Richard michel	16-50 A	R-Resides here from E Greenwich
Frances [sic] Bennet	"	
John Sherman	"	
Stephen place	"	
Palmer Threp	"	

Totals:

7	16-50 A	2	16-50 U	
2	50-60 A	2	50-60 U	
27	60+	2	R	

Page 9

Jeremiah Davis	16-50 A	
Isaac Hopkins	"	
Oziel Hopkins	"	
Phillop Walker	"	
Calob Seamons	"	
Isaac Payn	"	
Samuel Cole	16-50 U	
Amos Hammond	16-50 A	
Benjamin Whitman	"	
Squire Bucklon Junr	"	
George Westcot	"	
Nathaniel Horton	"	
Abner Hopkens	"	
Stephen Davel	"	
Stephen Goodspeed	"	
David pray	"	
Richard Cole	"	
Nehemiah arnold	"	
Joseph Salsbury	"	

1777 MILITARY CENSUS
SCITUATE, RHODE ISLAND

Page 9 (cont)

Robert Hills	16-50 A
Ephraim Salsbury	"
Phillop yaw	"
Gideon Dextor	"
William Colwell	"
Charls potter	"
Jonathan Fuller	"
Thomas fenner	"
Calob Hill	"
Eddy Cole	"
John Cole	"
amos Williams	"
Abner Smith	"
William Randall	"
Robert Whitman Junr	16-50 U
Benjamin Whitman	16-50 A
Enoch Hopkins	"
Padden Hopkins	"
Sisson Cole	"
Daniel Colwell	"
John Pray	"
Job Sheppee	"

Totals:
39 16-50 A   2   16-50 U

Page 10

Royal Hopkins	16-50 A
Thomas Simans	"
Jams Cole	"
William Round	"
Abel Hopkins	"
Phillip Franklin	"
Samuel Salsbury	"
?eben Hopkins	"
Solomon Shippe	"
Jonathan pray Junr	"
Joshua Jones	"
John Smith	"
Jonah Hopkins	"
Jacob Walker	"
Robart Davis Junr	"
Jotham Round	"
Levi Round	16-50 U
Levi Wade	16-50 A
Jacob pray	"
Comfort Weatherhead	"

Page 10 (cont)

Phillop Salsbury	16-50 A
Ruben Colegrove	"
Theophilus Esten	"
Ezekel Lewis	"
John Round	
son of James	"
Squier Bucklin	"
John Eddy	"
Jeptha Hopkins	"
Joseph Auston	"
Ruben Hins	"
John Round	
son of peleg	"
Stephen Davis	
son of Robert	"
Gidean Hammond	"
Joseph pray	"
Joel Hopkins	"
Simeon Seamans	"
Samuel Smith Junr	"
Anthony Brown	"
Josep Hopkins Juner	"
Abraham Jones	"
Nathan Goodspeed	"
Barnet hopkins	"
Pardon Dolbee	"
Nathan Wood	"

Totals:
43 16-50 A   1   16-50 U

Page 11

John Sheldon	16-50 A	R-Residing Pourtsmouth
Jonathan Semans	"	
Phillip Mathewson	"	
Elisha Barns	50-60 A	
Jerimah Hopkens	16-50 A	
Nathaniel Manchester	50-60 U	
Rufus Hopkens	50-60 A	
Isaac Midbury	"	
Daniel Bennet	"	
John Herindoon	"	
Nathan Bennet	"	
Caleb Steere	16-50 A	
Christopher Relph	50-60 A	
Royal Mathewson	"	

1777 MILITARY CENSUS
SCITUATE, RHODE ISLAND

Page 11 (cont)

Oliver Westcot	50-60	A
John Round	"	
Richard Smith	16-50	A
Jonah Hopkens	50-60	A
Benjamin Bozworth	"	
Joseph Remington	"	
John Martain	"	
Nehemiah angell	16-50	A
John andrews	"	
John Stafford	50-60	U
John Blackmore	50-60	A
Nemiah Randal	16-50	A
John Vaghane	50-60	A
Benijar? place	16-50	A
Stephen Herndon	"	
William Seamans	50-60	U
Peabody Cole	16-50	A
Thomas Mathewson	"	
John Wight	50-60	A
Jams andrews	"	
William Cory	16-50	A
Nichols Hopkins	50-60	A
Christopher Potter	16-50	A
George Taylor	"	
Jabez Bowen	50-60	A
Josiah Herindeen	16-50	A
Cyril Carpenter	"	
Philemon Hins	"	
Thomas Sallasbury	"	

Totals:
  29 16-50 A   20 50-60 A
   3 50-60 U   1 R

Page 12

William West	16-50	A
Ezekel Cornwel	"	
John Colwell	"	
Joseph Knigt	"	
Samuel Wilbour	"	
Thomas Field	"	
William Potter	"	
John Battey	"	
Joshua Battey	"	
Benjaman Wood	"	
Mycal Phillops	"	
Ezekel Broock	"	

Page 12 (cont)

Ezekel Broock Junr	16-50	A	
Benadick Whipple	"		
John Edwards Junr	"		
Joseph angel	"		
Abel angel	"		
John Guile	"		
David Cory	"		
Joseph Bennet	"		
Knight Wilbour	"		
John Carpendar	"		R-Cranson
John Cory	"		
Richard Knight	"		
Richard Colwell	"		
John Wilbour	16-50	U	
Olaver Wilbour	16-50	A	
Joseph Wilbour	"		
Nicholas Edwards Junr	"		
Cristopher Edwards	"		
Abnar Wilbour	"		
Jerimiah Stone	"		
Job Randal Junr	"		
David franklan	"		
Hoza Bennet	"		
Isaac Horten	"		
Benjamin Horten	"		
Stephen Young	"		
Stephen Young Junr	"		
William Young	60+		
William Cory	60+		
Thomas parker	16-50	A	
John Wood	"		
Phillop Brown	"		

Totals:
  41 16-50 A   1 16-50 U
   2 60+   1 R

Page 13

Epheram Hernton	16-50	A
Rhodes fry	"	
James Howard	"	
Peleg Cole	"	
Monassa Bloys	"	
Peleg ?Fray	"	
Thomas Parce	"	
Thomas Brown	"	
Daniel Hopkens	"	

1777 MILITARY CENSUS
SCITUATE, RHODE ISLAND

Page 13 (cont)

Comfort Carpinter	16-50 A	
William Parker	"	
Simeon potter	"	
James Simons	"	
Job alsbary	"	R-Dartmouth
Epheram Hopkens	"	
Constant Cook	"	
John Phillops	"	
Charls Brown	"	
James Rice	"	
Fleet Brown	"	
Joseph Howard	16-50 U	
Samuel albro	16-50 A	
Gideon Sherman	"	R-Dartmouth
Gorton Talman	"	R-Dartmouth
William Tyler Juner	50-60 A	
Stephen Foster	60+	
George Dorance	60+	
John Dorance	60+	
Mickel Dollef	50-60 U	
James Dorance	60+	
Othenial Presson	60+	
Benjamin Fisk	60+	
Daniel fisk	60+	
Thomas Relph	60+	
Hugh Relph	60+	
John Colven	60+	
Job fisk	60+	
John Bats	60+	
Benjamen pettes	[blank]	R-Resides here
Samuel parce	"	R-Dartmouth
Samuel fenner	16-50 A	
Daniel fisk Juner	"	
Joseph Remington	"	
Thomas feld	60+	

Totals:
    26 16-50 A   1 50-60 A
    1 50-60 U 13 60+
    [5 R]   [1 16-50 U]

Page 14

Salvenas Sole	16-50 A
Josiah Foster	"
Besjah Shearman	"
Daniel Weaver	"
John Pirkens	"

Page 14 (cont)

John Herindon Jun	16-50 A	
Jencks Herindon	"	
John Tyeler Jun	"	
John parker	"	
William Blancher	"	
Jonathan Fuller Jun	"	
Rows Place	"	
John Collens	"	
Nathaniel gallop	"	
Edward Hammon	"	
Constant Weaver	"	
Thomas Foster	"	
Thomas Howard	"	
Simeon Herindon	"	
George Dorance	"	
Ruben Read	"	
James Tyter	"	
David Sole	"	
Isaac Blancher	"	
Enoc place	"	
Benjamin Bennet	"	
Samuel Hammon	"	
Joel Young	"	
Ephram Williams	"	
Petter parce	"	
Rows potter	"	
John Swain	"	R-Resides here
John Phillops Jun	"	
Samuel King	"	
William Eldred	"	
Samuel Eldrad	"	
Samuel Jencks	"	
Joseph Young	"	
Thomas Hill Junr	"	
John Hill	"	
William Vaughan	"	
John Vaughan	"	

Totals:
    42 16-50 A   1 R

Page 15

Cornelius Wollen	16-50 A
Jonathan Hopkens	"
Jerimiah Pray	"
Ebenezer Cole	"
William pray	"

1777 MILITARY CENSUS
SCITUATE, RHODE ISLAND

Page 15 (cont)

Christopher Colwell	16-50 A
Elisha King	"
Joseph Tucker Junr	"
John Walker	"
Peregreen Smith	"
Nicolous Brownen	"
Joel Daves	16-50 U
William Walker	16-50 A
William yaw	"
Jerimiah Davis	"
Peleg Round	"
William Davis	"
Nehemiah Hill	16-50 U
Calab Siamans	"
John Horton	60+
Samuel Salsbury	60+
Phillop franklen	60+
William Hins	60+ Resides here
Jerimiah Weatherhad	60+
John Colwell	60+
John Smith	60+
Bonony Williams	60+
Benjamin Wilkerson	60+
Thomas Hopkens	60+
Henray Hill	16-50 A
Palmer Fanner	"
Nathan Smith	"
Gidan Asting	"
Pasca Asting	"
Isak Asting	"
David Phillops	"
Thomas Wilbour	"
Simeon Wilbour	"
James parker	"
William parker	"
Antony parker	"
Frances [sic] parker	"
William Edwards	50-60 U
Stephen Edwards	16-50 A

Totals:
    30 16-50 A   3 16-50 U
     1 50-60 U   10 60+   1 R

Page 16

Benjamin Slack	16-50 A
John Potter	"

Page 16 (cont)

Daved Tailor	16-50 A
William West Junr	"
George Howland	"
William Colgrove	"
Asael Harris	"
Calab Viel	"
Amariah Blackmore	"
Thomas taylor	"
Aaron Aldrich	"
Elisha Estes	"
Benjamin Angel	"
Royal Matthewson Jun	"
Jonathan Matthewson	"
Samuel Angel	"
James luther	"
Bejamin Williams	"
Resolved Matthewson	"
Caleb arnold	"
Abraham Burllinggame	"
Edward Howland	"
Thomas Salsbury	"
Richard Tayler	"
Joseph Wilkinson	"
Ebenezar Bardain	"
Oliver arnold	"
Abraham Angel	"
Oliver Cornell	"
Jeremiah Williams	"
Jeremiah Andrew	"
John Jencks Hilton?	"
Benjamin Collens	"
Aaron Colven	"
Robart Knight	"
Ruben Bats	"
James Andrew junr	"
Hugh Relph Junr	"
Alexander Lovell	"
Joseph Collens	"
John Baker	"
Thomas Collens	"
Israel Phillops	"
Job pratt	"
Henery Collens	"
Thomas Field the 3d	"
Michael McDonald	"
Samuel Tift	"
David Knight	"

88

Scituate

1777 MILITARY CENSUS
SCITUATE, RHODE ISLAND

Page 16 (cont)

Joseph Dow	16-50 A
Moses Potter	"
Elizur Collens 3^d	"
Joseph Brigs	"

Totals:
53 16-50 A

Page 17

Gilbert Salsburry	16-50 A
Benjamin Kimbel	"
Christopher Smith	"
Christopher Potter	"
James Cole	"
John Westcot	"
William Collgrove	"
Clark Smith	"
Charles Harris	"
Ezekel Hopkens	"
Benjamin Bowen	"
Obediah Cole	"
Jeriah Hopkins	"
Samuel Whitan	"
Richard Waterman	"
Obediah Walker	"
Gedion Harris	"
Lot Crosbe	"
Ephram Williams	"
Sprag Potter	"
Elisha aldrich	"
Ebenezer Handy	"
William aldrich	"
Potter Hopkens	"
Nehemiah Randal	"
John parker	"
Squier Williams	"
Hezekiah Whelan	"
Asa Turtalot	"
Samuel Spicer	"
Stephen Harres	"
Knight Tayler	"
Peleg fuller	"
Theofelas Blackmore	"
William Daves	"
Jesse Bowen	"
Ruben Brown	"
Solmon Carver	"

Page 17 (cont)

Stephen peckcom	16-50 A
Elisha Potter	"
Thomas Mory	"
Samuel Brown	"
James Wheler?	"
Nathan Ralph	"
Jonathan Knight	"
Daniel Baker	"
David White	"
Angel Swet [Sweet]	"
Thomas potter	"
John Wight junr	"
Thomas Ralph junr	"
Benony Colven	"
Oliver Lech	"
William Barns	"
Constant Graves	"
Azariah Thrasher	"
William Batty	"

Totals:
57 16-50 A

Page 16 upside down, right hand column

Those Names are from Sixteen to fifty able to bare arms

William Roberts	16-50 A
Nathaniel Phillips	"
John Andrew	"
Squire Jilson	"
Zebedee Snow	"
Robert Knight Jun	"
John Manchester	"
George King	"
Francis Fuller	"
Benajah Baker	"
William Stafford	"
Oliver Fisk	"
Resolved Matteson	"
Eleazar Wight	"
Freeborn Brayton	"
Charles Knight	"
Thomas Walton	"
Rufus Knight	"
Amasa Pratt	"
Nathan Franklen	"
Obadiah Relph	"

1777 MILITARY CENSUS
SCITUATE, RHODE ISLAND

Page 16 upside down (cont)

Matthew Colvin	16-50 A
Collin Roberts	"
Moses Colven	"
Abraham Yaw	"
Peter Wight	"
Edward Randall	"
Thomas Potter Juner	"
Abraham Morgan	"
Jonathan Remington	"
Abel Collins	"
Joseph Bennet	"
Amos Silvester	"
John Fisk? son of Job	"
Aaron Wight	"
Curnel Potter	"
Enoch Brownel	"
William Salsbury Junr	"
Moses Fish	"
Israel Knight	"

Totals:
  40 16-50 A

Page 17 upside down, right hand column

Those Names hereunder mentioned are from
Sixteen to fifty able to Bear Arms

Jabez Relph	16-50 A
John Potter	"
John ?Guile	"
Samuel Henry	"
Nicholas Thomas	"
William Biddlecome	"
Reuben Randall	"
William Fairbanks	"
Richard Fords	"
Edward Dorr	"
William Fisk	"
Edward Sarles	"
James Wood	"
Oliver Bates	"
James Fuller	"
Uriah Franklen junr	"
John Franklen	"
Elisha Franklen	"
Squire Franklen	"
Joshua Franklen	"
Benjaman Whitman	"

Page 17 upside down (cont)

David Knight	16-50 A
Richard Knight	"
Samuel Wight	"
Joseph Wight	"
Stukely Harington	"
Thomas Robarts junr	"

Totals:
  27 16-50 A

Those Names under here are listed for
fifteen months

William Tayler	(SM)
Jonthan Briggs	(SM)
Nathaniel Tayler	(SM)
Levy parce	(SM)
William Edwards	(SM)
James Williams ?Cpt	(SM)

Page 31 [sic]

From 16 to 50 able to Bear Arms	617
From 16 to 50 unable to bear Arms	10
From 50 to 60 able to bear Arms	69
From 50 to 60 unable to bear Arms	16
From 60 and upwards	60
Those who have taken the affirmation	none
Those who have Certificates from the Friends Meeting	6
Transient Persons	2
Residents	18
Negro's	8
Indians	None
	806

Scituate April 17th 1777
Whereas I the Subscriber was by the Honble
Genl Assembly appointed to take an Account
of all the Male Inhabitants in the Town of
Scituate from 16 years and upwards, agreeble
thereunto I have numbered the Male inhabit-
ants in Town according to the preceeding
Roll which is Submitted by yr Honor Humble
Servant

Scituate April ye 17 Day AD 1777
This Day Personally appeared Benjamin Hill
of Scituate and Made Oath that he had to

Smithfield

1777 MILITARY CENSUS
SCITUATE, RHODE ISLAND

the Best of his Knowleg and Judgment Truly Performed the trust Reposed in Him
by Mr Christophor Potter one of the Deputies for Said Town to Number all the
Male Persons From Sixteene years of age and upwards in Said Town

Before Me

Thomas Hill Just of Peace

SMITHFIELD, RHODE ISLAND

Page 1

Elisha Mowry	50-60 U	
Stephen Mowry	16-50 A	
Elijah Comstock	16-50 U	
Joseph Chillson	50-60 U	
Rueben Aldrich	50-60 A	
Jacob Arnold	16-50 A	
Caleb Arnold	16-50 U	
Israel Aldrich	"	
Joseph Comstock	Cert	
James Morton	16-50 U	
Thomas Morton	16-50 A	
Philip Mowry J^r	"	
David Mowry	"	
Ananias Mowry J^r	Cert	
Gideon Mowry	16-50 A	
Stephen Mowry J^r	"	
Ezekiel Mowry	50-60 A	
Esek Sayles	16-50 U	
Petor Tiffle	50-60 U	
John Tiffle	16-50 U	
Rufus Tiffle	16-50 A	
Ebenezer Cass	50-60 A	
Moses Man	16-50 U	
John Rogers (CS)	[blank]	
David Aldrich	16-50 U	
Samuel Winsor	60+	
Joseph Carpenter	60+	
Nathan Barnes	60+	
Philip Smith	60+	
Jonthan Smith	60+	
Richard Smith	50-60 A	
Ebenezer Herndeen	60+	
Uriah Mowry	60+	
Othnial Mathewson	60+	
Ananias Mowry	60+	
James Appleby	60+	
Joseph Spauldin	50-60 A	
John Dexter	60+	
Abad Wilkinson	16-50 U	

Page 1 (cont.)

Thos Lapham	60+	
Daniel Phillips	60+	
John Man	60+	
Benjamin Pain	60+	
John Ballou	60+	
Thos Shippe	60+	
Joseph Herndeen	60+	
Nathaniel Bucklin	60+	
David Harris	60+	R-Providence
Joseph Harris	16-50 A	
Saml Rodman	Cert	R-Newport
Wm Gulley	16-50 A	
Oliver Arnold	"	
John Jenckes J^r	"	
Abrum Benj^a Angell J^r	"	

Totals:

13	16-50 A	9	16-50 U	
5	50-60 A	3	50-60 U	
20	60+	3	Cert	

Page 2

Adam Harkness	Cert	
Adam Harkness Jr	"	
Hezadiah Comstock	60+	
William Sprague	60+	
Jonathan Read	Cert	
Samuel Cruff	50-60 A	
Joseph [Sh?]elley	50-60 U	
Samuel Buxton	16-50 A	
Joseph Buffum	Cert	
Benjamin Buffum	50-60 A	
Caleb Buxton	16-50 A	
Nathaniel Staples	60+	
Jonathan Southwick	60+	
Edmund Arnold	60+	
Seth Arnold	60+	
Philip Loga	50-60 U	
Israel Wilkinson	60+	

1777 MILITARY CENSUS
SMITHFIELD, RHODE ISLAND

Page 2 (cont.)

John Pope	[blank]	R-Boston
John Sayles Junr	50-60 A	
John Sayles 4th	16-50 A	
Robert Harkness	"	
James Harkness	"	
Daniel Comstock	"	
Jacob Comstock	"	
William Buffum	Cert	
David Buffum	"	
Asa Smith	16-50 A T	
James Buffum	16-50 U	
Caleb Buxton	"	
Aaron Buxton	"	
James Buxton	16-50 A	
Samuel Buxton	"	
Benj^a Buffum	[blank]	
John Read	Cert	
Elisha Thornton	"	
Jonathan Cook	16-50 U	
Benj^a Cook	"	
Job Handy	50-60 A	
Enoch Sprague	16-50 A	
Ezekiel Comstock	Cert	
George Comstock	"	
George Southwick	[blank]	
Zaceus Southwick	16-50 A	
George Arnold	Cert	
Elisha Arnold	50-60 A	
Israel Mowry	16-50 A	
Robert Wilkinson	"	
Israel Wilkinson J^r	"	
David Wilkinson	"	
Caleb Aldrich	50-60 A	
William Arnold	16-50 A	
Namon Aldrich	"	
John Garish	" T	

Totals:

20	16-50 A	6	16-50 U
6	50-60 A	2	50-60 U
7	60+	11	Cert
2	T	1	R

Page 3

Daniel Mowry 4th	16-50 A
Philip Sweet	"
Abner Bishop	"
Samuel Bartlet	"

Page 3 (cont.)

Benoni Bishop	(CS)	16-50 A	
Stukley Inman	(CS)	"	
Benjamin Smith	(CS)	"	
Reuben Smith	(CS)	"	
John Smith Junr		"	
Noah Farnum		"	
Samuel Aldrich Junr		50-60 A	
Amos Keech		60+	
Seth Baker		16-50 A	R-Cranston
Benjamin Crosbee		"	R-Worcester
Elisha Mowry Junr		"	R-Glocester
James Rogers		"	
Job Mowry Junr		"	
Thomas Appleby		"	
Joseph Basset		"	R-Glocester
William Arnold		"	
Othaniel Young		"	
Samuel Keech		"	
John Steere Junr		"	
Jabez Wing		Cert	
Joshop Wing		"	
Benjamin Wing		"	
Sylvanus Mowry		16-50 A	
Benjamin Henry		"	
Charles Hawkins		"	
Jeseniar Barnard		"	R-Killingly
Israel Tucker		"	
John Barnes		50-60 A	
Arther Latham		16-50 A	
Stephen Angell		"	
Joseph Spraugue		"	
Daniel Mowry 3rd		"	
Joseph Latham		"	
John Hawkins		"	
Jesse Joslen		"	R-Killingly
Zenas Winsor		"	
Samuel Shippe Junr		"	
George Mowry		"	
Daniel Mowry		60+	
Joseph Mowry		60+	
Robert Staples		60+	
Thomas Steere		Cert	

Totals:

36	16-50 A	2	50-60 A
4	60+	4	Cert
[6	R]		

1777 MILITARY CENSUS
SMITHFIELD, RHODE ISLAND

Page 4

John Phillips	16-50 A
John Wilkinson	"
Benj^a Medbry	"
Charles Angell	"
Christopher Brown	"
Jos. Whipple	"
Wm Benchly	"
Saml Tucker	"
James Olney	"
Gideon Angell J^r	"
Gideon Angell	"
Jon^a Newell	Aff
James Mussy	"
Stephen Handrek	"
Danl Sayles	"
Daniel Steed	"
Solomon Angell	"
Eph^m Comstock	"
Stephen Woodward	16-50 U
John Coe	"
Ozial Sayles	"
Nathl Woodward	"
Stephen Whipple	16-50 A
Thos Jenckes	"
Sylvanus Bucklin	"
Isaac Arnold	"
Abram Arnold	"
Jer^e Arnold	"
Saml Cook	"
Joseph Cook	Aff
Israel Harris	"
Jeremiah Harris	"
Preserved Harris	"
Jabez Harris	[blank]
Jon^a Dexter	Aff
Jon^a Pain	"
Jer^e Smith	[blank]
David Harris J^r	Aff
Benj^a Newell	"
Obed Pain	"
Saml Arnold	Cert
Jon^a Arnold Jun	"
Ozial Wilkinson	"
Thomas Lapham J^r	"
George Hazard	" R-South Kingstown
Augustus Lapham	"

Page 4 (cont.)

Rufus Smith	Cert
Benj^a Wing	"
Aza Arnold	"
John Arnold	"
Benj^a Smith	"
Benj^a Arnold	"
Jon^a Harris	"
Jacob Smith	"
Jon^a Arnold	60+
Obediah Olney	60+
Richard Harris	60+
Joshua Arnold	50-60 A

Totals:
   24 16-50 A   4 16-50 U
    1 50-60 A   3 60+
   10 Aff   14 Cert
   [1 R]

Page 5

John Comstock	50-60 A
Peleg Newfield	I
Elisha Newfield	I
Oliver Man	50-60 A
Isaac Indian	I
Jonathan Comstock	16-50 A
?Hosea Mowry	N
Uriah Arnold	50-60 A
Peso Mowry	N
David Eddy	16-50 A
Tom Arnold	N
Ebenezer Trask	16-50 A
Peso Sly	N
Simeon Ballou	16-50 A
James Brayton	N
Thomas Sayles	16-50 A
?Chrmy Waterman	N
David Aldrich J^r	16-50 A
James Arnold	N
Naham Aldrich	16-50 A
Prince Aldrich	N
Eli Read	16-50 A
Newport Comstock	N
Samuel White	16-50 A
Daniel Arnold J^r	"
David Aldrich	"
Samuel Aldrich ye 5th	"

1777 MILITARY CENSUS
SMITHFIELD, RHODE ISLAND

Page 5 (cont.)

Stephen Eddy	16-50 A	
John Smith,	"	
~~Thomas Sayles Junr~~	"	
Daniel Smith Junr	"	
Thomas Smith Junr	"	
Daniel Smith	50-60 A	
~~Amos Backer~~	16-50 A	
John Comstock Junr	16-50 A	
Esek Mowry	"	
Abial Mowry	"	
Uriah Mowry Junr	"	
Stukley Sayles	"	
Elconey? Spears (CS)	"	
Barnard Chace	"	
Joshua Sheriff	"	
Nehemiah Sprague	"	
John Mowry	"	
John Sayles	60+	
Richard Sayles	60+	
Elias Sprauque	16-50 A	
Aaron Loja	"	
Ezekiel Arnold	"	
John Pain	"	
Joel Aldrich	"	
Peleg Arnold	"	
Rufus Phillips	"	
Jesse Arnold	:	
Jacob Marsh	"	R-Killingly
Thomas Aldrich	"	
Joseph Man	"	
Daniel Arnold	"	

Totals:
    40 16-50 A   4 50-60 A
     2 60+   9 N
    [3 I]   [1 R]

Page 6

Benjamin Ballou	16-50 A	
Rufus Streeter	"	R-Cumber-land
Nathaniel Bucklen Jr	"	
Simeon Wilkinson	"	
Abner Thompson	"	
Abraham Smith	"	
Joshua Jenckes	"	
Abisha Carpenter Reniff	"	R-Cumber-land
Simon Aldrich	"	

Page 6 (cont.)

John Wilkinson Junr	16-50 A	
Saml Dexter	"	
Richd Ballou	"	
Jos. Wilkinson	"	
Simon Whipple	"	
Thaducy Williams	"	R-Fair-field
Nathaniel Dexter	"	
Amriah Yeats	"	R-Ux-bridge
Nathaniel Spauldin	"	
Joshua Phillips	"	
Daniel Sayles	"	
?Moris Tucker	"	
Levi Young	"	
Charles Caperin	"	R-Cumber-land
Aholiab Spauldin	"	
Nathl [?Arnold]	"	
Levi Brown	"	
Edward Thomson	"	
Daniel Brayton	"	
Benj^a Razy	"	R-Cumber-land
Joseph Benchley	"	
Abra^m Angell	"	
Isaac Brayton	"	
Christopher Arnold	"	
Silas Arnold	"	
Zebedee Arnold	"	
Joseph Chillson J^r	"	
Ezekiel Angell J^r	"	
Cornelas Young	"	
Eber Angell	"	
Benjamin Angell	"	
Elisha Olney	"	
Jeremiah Olney	"	
George Jenckes	"	
David Young	"	
Eleazar Brown	"	
Abra^m Keech	"	
Jenckes Brown	"	
John Angell	"	
Thomas Woodward	60+	
Benj^a Ballard	60+	

Totals:
    48 16-50 A   2 60+   [6 R]

1777 MILITARY CENSUS
SMITHFIELD, RHODE ISLAND

Page 7

Stephen Balloue	16-50 A	
Fenner Angell	"	
Daniel Sweet	"	
Joseph Mathewson	"	
Esek Smith	"	
Charles Sweet	"	
Jonathan Miles	"	R-Pumfort
Abel Mowry	"	
Jesse Foster	"	R-Providence
Daniel Field	"	R-North Providence
Samuel Homes	"	R-Scituate
John M^c^emarer	"	R-Ireland
Amos Man	"	R-Wrentham
Caleb Aldrich	"	
Sylvanus Mathewson	"	R-Glocester
James Bowen	"	R-Glocester
William Aldrich	"	
Resolved Smith Jun	"	
Jonthan Angell	"	
Benjamin Brown	"	
Abel Man	"	
Thomas Right	"	T
John Steere	"	
Isaac Hix	"	R-Glocester
Thomas Smith	"	R-Glocester
Aaron Herndeen	"	
John Appleby	"	
Benjamin Sheldon	"	
John Aldrich	"	
Samuel Hopkins	"	R-North Providence
Jeremiah Burllingham	"	R-Killingly
Eleazer Mowry	"	
Daniel Man	"	
Ezekiel Herndeen	"	
Charles Sayles	"	
Joseph Aldrich	"	
Jacob Gorff	"	
Seth Baker Junr	"	R-Cranstown
John Carpenter	"	R-Providence
Samuel How	"	
Sylvanus Sayles J^r^	"	
Zebedee Appleby	"	
Resolved Smith	"	
Joseph Inman	"	
Jonthan hite	"	T
Joseph Herndeen	"	

Page 7 (cont.)

Benjamin Aldrich	16-50 A	
Oliver Dyer	"	R-Cranstown

Totals:
48 16-50 A   [2 T]   [15 R]

Page 8

Oliver Read	16-50 A	
Elijah Arnold	"	
Joeb Cruff	"	
John Goldthwaite	"	
John Buxston	"	
Elisha Inman	"	
Joseph Buffum Junr	"	
Moses Buffum	"	
Stephen Comstock	"	
David Man	"	
John Man Junr	50-60 A	
Mikel Cook	16-50 A	
Ebenezer Staples	"	
Andrew Man Junr	"	
Richard Thornton	"	R-Johnston
James Tiffte	"	
Robert Tiffte	"	
Gidion Bishop	"	
Daniel Mathewson	"	
Israel Man	"	
Laben Comstock	"	
Jonathan Elett	"	
William Read	"	
Voice Kimble	"	R-Glocester
Thomas Elett	"	
David Gaskell	"	R-Cumberland
Barok White	"	R-Mendon
Samuel Thomston	"	
Aaron Read	"	
Paul Aldrich	"	
Thomas Arnold	"	
Augustus Aldrich	"	
Mikeeage Killey	"	
James Smith	"	
Jesse [Smith]	"	
?Emer Smith	"	
Richard Aldrich	"	
Pallatric Macentire	"	R-Wrentham
Joseph Aldrich J^r^		
Stephen Aldrich	"	
Stephen Whiteman	"	

1777 MILITARY CENSUS
SMITHFIELD, RHODE ISLAND

Page 8 (cont.)   Page 9 (cont.)

William Wright   16-50 A   Samuel Smith   16-50 A
John Smith ye 3rd   "   Stephen Phillips   "
Joshua Angell   "   Nathan Coman   "
Allen Mosher   "   Stephen Brayton   "
Oliver Smith   "   David Shippe   "
Benajah Sweet   "   Joseph Coman   "
                                       Jesse Jencks   "
Totals: Robert Harris   "
  46 16-50 A   1 50-60 A   [5 R]   Gideon Phillips   "
                                       Daniel Angell   "
Page 9   Ahab Jenckes   "
                                       Stephen Gulley   "
Nicholas [ink blot]   16-50 A   Joshua Whitnee   "
David Al ["   "]   "   Abial Crossman   "
Charles Bennet   "   Jethro Aldrich   "
John Ballou Jun   "   Isaac Bucklen   "
James Arnold   "   Gideon Dexter   "
Stephen Arnold J^r   "
Christopher Jencks   "   Totals:
Isaac Harris   "   54 16-50 A   [2 R]
David Benchley   "
Moses Ballou   "   Page 10
Stephen Harris   "
Nathan Harris   "   Samford Rose   16-50 A R-Newport
Abial Brown   "   R-Cumberland Jacob Shippe   "
Benj^a Whipple   "   Enoch Arnold   "
Nathan Medbury   "   David Bowen   "
Aaron Clark   "   Benj^a Ballard   "
Jesse Harris   "   Joseph Jenckes J^r   "
Edmund Herendeen   "   John Jenckes   "
John Whiteman   "   Job Arnold   "
William Aldrich   "   Samuel Bagley   "
Simeon Arnold   "   Luke Arnold   "
Israel Arnold   "   Benj^a Medbery Jr   "
Aaron Ballou   "   John Sheldon   "
Smith Sayles   "   Waterman Dexter   "
Jon^a Phillips   "   Thomas Bates   "   R-Scituate
David Jenckes   "   Abial Baker   "
Abram Shippe   "   Andrew Brown   "
?ila Pain   "   Jer^e Bucklen   "
John Shippee Jun   "   Benj^a Bagley   "
James Harris   "   Danl Phillips Jr   "
William Wilbour   "   Danl Woodward   (CS)   "
John Shippee   "   Oliver Kimpton   "
Solomon Barrow   "   R-Attleborough Jac[ob] [Je]nckes   "
Joseph Kimpton   "   Jer^e Scott   "
Thomas Newman   "   Saml Day   "
John Sayles 3rd   "   George Streeter   "
Abram Herndeen   "   Richd Sayles 3rd   "

1777 MILITARY CENSUS
SMITHFIELD, RHODE ISLAND

Page 10 (cont.)

Name		Age
Dan[l] Sheldon	(SM)	16-50 A
Solomon Shippe	(CS)	"
Sam[l] Whippe	(SM)	"
David Sayles	(CS)	"
And[w] Dexter	(SM)	"
Sam[l] Hills		"
James Sheldon		50-60 A
Ichabod Comstock		16-50 A
Joseph Jenckes		"
John Whipple		50-60 A
W[m] Whipple		"
John Man 3rd		16-50 A
Jon[a] Gulley		"

Page 10 (cont.)

Name	Age
Gideon Sayles	16-50 A
Jon[a] Sayles	Aff
Rich[d] Sayles Jun	16-50 A
Uriah Alverson	"
Sam[l] Shippe	[blank]
George Baker	16-50 A
Abner Harris	"
Rich[d] Harris Jun	"
Dan[l] Wilbour	"
Mannassa Kimpton	50-60 A
Henry Jenckes	16-50 A
Knight Dexter	"

Totals:
45 16-50 A   4 50-60 A
 1 Aff   [2 R]

On reverse side of Page 9:

From 16 to 50 Years able to bear Arms	From 16 to 50 Years unable to Bear Arms	From 50 to 60 Years able to bear Arms	From 50 to 60 Years unable to bear Arms	From 60 Years upwards	Those who have taken the Aff	Those who have Certificates from the Friends Meet.	Transient Persons	Residents	Negro's	Indians	
13	9	5	3	20		3					Bro't from 1st Page
20	6	6	2	7	11		1				2d "
36	0	2	0	4		4	0	[6]			3d "
24	4	1	0	3	10	14	0	[1]			4 "
40	0	4	0	2	0	0	0	[1]	9	3	5 "
48	0	0	0	2	0	0	0	[6]	0	0	6 "
48	0	0	0	0	0	0	0	[15]	0	0	7 "
46	0	1	0	0	0	0	0	[5]	0	0	8 "
54	0	0	0	0	0	0	0	[2]	0	0	9 "
45	0	4	0	0	1	0	0	[2]	0	0	10 "
374	19	23	5	38	11	32	0	[36]	9	3	Total

pursuant To an act of The Gen[l] Assembly pass[d] at Their Second Session in March 1777
I have Numbered The Male persons in the Town of Smithfield according to s[d] act
which are as above written: April 17th 1777. Witness Dan[l] Mowry Jun[r]

The State of Rhode Island pd to Daniel Mowry J[r] dr
To My above Service..............£3:12:0
                    Error Excepted p[r]   Dan[l] Mowry Jun[r]

1777 MILITARY CENSUS
SMITHFIELD, RHODE ISLAND

Reverse page 9 (cont.)

The above Service 7 days -- ? -- £3:3
Examined Nathl Mumford

On reverse side of Page 10:

Kings County, Southkingstown April 18th 1777
Daniel Mory of Smithfield Personally appeared & on his Solemn Oath declared that
he hath Justly and Truly made the aforegoing List of all the Male Persons, of
Sixteen Years of Age & Upwards in the Town of Smithfield according to the best
of his Knowledge
Before   Iman Case Just. Common Pleas

SOUTH KINGSTOWN, RHODE ISLAND

Page 1

Joseph Torrey	60+
John Torrey	16-50 A
Oliver Torrey	"
Wm Willson Polock	"
Jacob Taylor	N
Thomas Brown	60+
Joseph Brown	N
Newbury Brown	N
Jeremiah Brown	60+
Moses Brown	N
John Shearman	16-50 A
Elijah Mayes	"
Thomas Hazard of Robt	16-50 U
Robert Hazard	16-50 A
Thomas Hazard of s^d Thos	"
John Watson Junr	"
William Dyre	60+
Prince Dyre	N
Prince Dyre	N
William Dyre Junr	16-50 A
James Congdon (of Jos)	"
And^w Nichols	60+
Benjamin Brown	16-50 A
Zephaniah Brown	50-60 U
Henry Gardner (of Henry)	16-50 A
Chris^o Brown	"
Jer Brown Jr	16-50 U
William Brown	16-50 A

Page 1 (cont)

James Burk	16-50 A R-Newport
And^w Nichols Junr	16-50 U
John Fowler	16-50 A
Chris^o Fowler	60+
John Fowler	16-50 A
Oliver Tennant	50-60 U
Oliver Tennant Junr	16-50 A
Joseph Hull	"
James Helme	60+
Powel Helme	16-50 A
Rowse J Helme	"
James Helme J^r	"
Samuel Helme	16-50 U
Gabriel Helme	"
Rochiel Helme	N
Prince Helme	N
James Helme	N
Ray Sands	16-50 A
John Nichols	Aff

Totals:
23	16-50 A	5	16-50 U
2	50-60 U	7	60+
1	Aff	9	N

Page 2

Joseph Knowles Junr	16-50 A
Jeremiah Niles	60+
Pompy Niles	N
Tony Niles	N
Philip Niles	N
Prince Hull	N

1777 MILITARY CENSUS
SOUTH KINGSTOWN, RHODE ISLAND

Page 2 (cont)

London Hull	N	
Port Hull	N	
John Castoff	16-50 A	
James Robinson	"	R-Newport
Cudjo Robinson	N	R-Newport
John Dockray	16-50 U	
John Dockray Jun[r]	Cert	
Thomas Braman	16-50 A	
Christ[o] Robinson	16-50 U	
Christ[o] Robinson Jun[r]	16-50 A	
Joseph Goulding	N	
Henry Greene	16-50 U	
Peter Peckham	N	R-Charleston
Jack Rodman	N	
William Sands	N	
Jonath[n] Carpenter	16-50 A	
Stephen Potter	"	
Jon[a] Lock	"	
Moses Parr	"	
Silvester Northup	50-60 U	
Joseph Collins	Cert	
Silas Niles	16-50 A	
Jabez Niles	N	
Quash Niles	N	
Mingo Niles	N	
Joseph Hazard	16-50 U	
Peter Hazard	N	
Step[n] Hazard	50-60 A	
Mingo Robinson	N	
Jo. Hazard	N	
Benj[a] Stanton	16-50 A	
Samuel Hazard	16-50 U	
Jack Hazard	N	
William Holway	16-50 A	
George Holway	N	
Caleb Hazard	16-50 U	
Caleb Hazard Jun[r]	16-50 A	
Newport Hazard	N	
Robert Champlin	16-50 A	
Moses Barber	16-50 U	
Lodowick Shearman	16-50 A	

Totals:
```
15  16-50 A    7  16-50 U
 1  50-60 A    1  50-60 U
 1  60+        2  Cert
20  N
```

Page 3

Joseph Billington	60+	
Bristol Hull	N	R-Jamestown
Ossin Remington	N	R-Jamestown
~~Joseph Billington Jun[r]~~		
Thomas Sweet	16-50 A	
Thomas Sweet Jun[r]	"	
William Tourje	"	R-North Kingston
Thomas Tourje	50-60 U	
Job Card	60+	
William Card	16-50 A	
Shadreck Card	"	
Elisha Card	"	
James Card	"	
Gideon Cross	16-50 U	
Job Watson	16-50 A	
Daniel Shearman J[r]	"	
Step[n] Heffernan	"	
Harry Perry	N	
James Perry	50-60 U	
James Perry Jun[r]	16-50 A	
William Perry	"	
Tom Perry	N	
Jonathan Perry	16-50 U	
Samuel Perry	"	
Boston Perry	N	
Stephen Chapel	16-50 U	
Samuel Segar	16-50 A	
David Dikes	"	R-Newport
George Thomas	"	R-Exeter
Charles Hull	60+	
Peter Perry	N	
Abraham Card	N	
Abraham Dungo	N	
William Hull	16-50 A	
James Hull	"	
Silvester Hull	"	
Tom Hull	N	
William Knowles	50-60 U	
Henry Knowles	16-50 A	
Port Hull	N	
Simeon Tucker	16-50 A	R-Charlestown
James Harvey	"	R-Charleston
Jabez Clarke	"	R-Charleston
Ichabod Potter	16-50 U	R-Charleston
Clarke Burdick	16-50 A	R-Westerly
William Browning	16-50 U	

1777 MILITARY CENSUS
SOUTH KINGSTOWN, RHODE ISLAND

Page 3 (cont)

Totals:
   23 16-50 A   6 16-50 U
    3 50-60 U   3 60+
   10 N

Page 4

James Whitehorn	16-50 A	
Robert Albro	"	
Joseph Shearman	"	
Nathan Cottril	"	
Thomas Cottril	"	
Samuel Hopkins	"	
Clarke Hopkins	"	
William Hopkins	"	
Tim^o Peckham		
Blacksmith	16-50 U	
Barber Peckham	16-50 A	
Tim^o Peckham		
(of sd Tim^o)	16-50 U	
Stephen Peckham	16-50 A	
Daniel Shearman	60+	
John Shelden	60+	
Jonathan Shelden	16-50 A	
David Sprague	60+	R-North Kingston
John Browne	16-50 A	R-Connecti-cutt
Samuel Hoxsie	"	
Philip Boss	"	
Thomas Hopkins	60+	
John Albro	60+	
Gardner Wm Mumford	16-50 A	
Stephen Cottril	60+	
Step^n Cottril Junr	16-50 A	
David Cottril	"	
Benj^a Greene	"	
Samuel Whaley	60+	
Samuel Whaley Junr	16-50 A	
John Whaley	"	
Thomas Whaley	"	
Robert Knowles		
(of Joseph)	Cert	
James Barber	16-50 U	
Wm Barber	16-50 A	
Nathanel Perkins	16-50 U	
Ezra Glason	16-50 A	R-Massachu-setts Bay

Page 4 (cont)

William Perkins	16-50 A	
Quash Hawkins	N	
John Earle Junr	50-60 A	

Totals:
   24 16-50 A   4 16-50 U
    1 50-60 A   7 60+
    1 Cert   1 N

Page 5

Christ^o Gardner	16-50 A	
Cuff Gardner	N	
Prince Gardner	N	
Christ^o Gardner Junr	16-50 A	
Wm Champlin	"	
John Rose	60+	
John Rose jun^r	16-50 A	
John Congdon	"	R-North Kingston
Cesar Rose	N	
Tilford Rose	N	
Tony Rose	N	
Ned Rose	N	
Jeffry Watson Junr	16-50 U	
Ezekiel Watson	16-50 A	
Jeffry Watson ye 3^d	"	
James Watson	N	
Cesar Watson	N	
James Guy	N	
Joseph Briggs	16-50 A	R-Newport
James Tefft	"	
William Chace	16-50 U	
Prince Watson	N	
Philip Shearman	60+	
Daniel Billington	60+	
Abijah Babcock	16-50 A	
Jacob Boss	"	
James Pearce	"	
James Shearman	50-60 U	
Thomas Shearman	16-50 U	
Cuff Shearman	N	
Henry Case	16-50 A	
Pelethiah Henry's	N	
Enoch Hazard	16-50 U	
Michael Dye	16-50 A	
Thos Hazard	50-60 U	
	N	
Henry Marchant	16-50 A	

1777 MILITARY CENSUS
SOUTH KINGSTOWN, RHODE ISLAND

Page 5 (cont)

Ebenezer Pemberton	16-50 A	R-Newport
Samuel Underwood	"	
Primas Serring	N	R-Newport
Samuel Wickham	16-50 A	R-Newport
Mark Wickham	N	R-Newport
Gideon Clarke	16-50 U	
Jemmy Clarke	N	
Josias Tanner	16-50 A	
Benja Shelden	16-50 U	
Robert Brown	"	

Totals:
```
20  16-50 A    6  16-50 U
 2  50-60 U    3  60+
16  N         [6  R]
```

Page 6

Peter Smith	16-50 A	
Jona Shearman	60+	
Robt Shearman	16-50 A	
Cuff Shearman	N	
Thomas Potter Junr	16-50 A	
Geo. Champlin	"	R-Newport
Cudd Champlin	N	R-Newport
Daniel Gardner	16-50 A	R-Newport
Prince Gardner	N	R-Newport
Abel Cottril	16-50 A	
John Cranston	"	R-Newport
Thomas Reynolds	"	
Joseph Perkins	"	
Sands Perkins	"	
Benja Deake	"	R-Richmond
Willm Cottril	"	
John Weeden	"	
John Perry	"	R-Newport
George Spooner	"	R-Newport
Mason Spooner	N	R-Newport
Richard Chapel	16-50 A	
Allen James	"	R-Newport
Samuel Potter	16-50 U	
Edward Hazard	"	R-Newport
Tony Hazard	N	R-Newport
George Tefft	16-50 A	
William Champlin	"	R-Exeter
John Weight	"	
Paul Babcock	"	
John Cottril	"	
Lemuel Tisdale	16-50 U	

Page 6 (cont)

Caleb Wescotte	16-50 A	
Nathl Helme	16-50 U	
Benja Perry	16-50 A	
Quash Perry	N	
Narragansett Perry	N	
Chriso Champlin	16-50 U	R-Newport
Sharper Champlin	N	R-Newport
David Douglass	16-50 A	
Niles Helme	"	R-North Kingston
Elisha Reynolds	60+	
Henry Reynolds	16-50 A	

Totals:
```
27  16-50 A    5  16-50 U
 2  60+        8  N
[16  R]
```

Page 7

Thomas Draper	60+	
Amos Draper	16-50 A	
James Draper	"	
James West	50-60 A	
Samuel Rogers	16-50 U	
Nathan Peterson	"	
Thomas Hopkins Junr	16-50 A	
James Baker	16-50 U	
Mattw Robinson	60+	
Cuff Robinson	N	
Cato Robinson	N	
Peter Robinson	N	
Simeon Babcock	16-50 U	
Stephen Babcock	16-50 A	
Samuel Babcock Jr	"	
Amos Robinson	I	
Jeffry Watson	60+	
Elisha Watson	16-50 A	
Wm Watson	"	
John Watson (of Jeffry)	"	
Jack Watson	N	
Primas Watson	N	
John Gardner	60+	
Allen Gardner	16-50 A	
William Enos	"	
Richard Gardner	"	
Titus Gardner	N	
Thomas Hammond	16-50 A	R-Newport

1777 MILITARY CENSUS
SOUTH KINGSTOWN, RHODE ISLAND

Page 7 (cont)

John Dunkin	16-50 A	R-Newport
James Gardner	N	
William Gardner	60+	
Gideon Gardner	16-50 A	
Philip Gardner	"	
Nathan Gardner	16-50 U	
Nathan Gardner Jun[r]	16-50 A	
Jeffry Gardner	N	
Dick Gardner	N	
Adam Gardner	N	
Henry Mellard	16-50 A	R-London
Henry Gardner	60+	
Frederick Gardner	16-50 A	
Jack Gardner	N	
Mint Gardner	N	

Totals:
18	16-50 A	5	16-50 U
1	50-60 A	6	60+
12	N	1	I [3 R]

Page 8

William Case	60+	
Tom Reynolds	N	
Mingo Reynolds	N	
Samson Reynolds	N	
Jeremiah Sheffield	16-50 A	
William Case Clarke	"	R-Newport
Will[m] Hookey	"	R-Newport
James Potter	"	R-Newport
Caleb Tefft	"	
Tennant Tefft	60+	
Henry Fisher	50-60 U	
Benj[a] Peckham	60+	
Josephus Peckham	16-50 U	
W[m] Peckham	"	
Carder Peckham	"	
John Pain Peckham	16-50 A	
John Holway	"	R-Richmond
Job Babcock	"	
Job Casson	"	R-Newport
Job Babcock Taylor	16-50 U	
Champlin Babcock	16-50 A	
Nathan Taylor	"	R-Charleston
Isaac Tanner	"	
Amos Robinson	N	
Thomas Peter	N	
Benj[a] Shearman Shelden	16-50 A	

Page 8 (cont)

Tho[s] Champlin	16-50 A	
Hazard Champlin	"	
John Earl	16-50 U	
Samuel Babcock	50-60 U	
Samuel Whitehorn	16-50 A	
John Babcock	16-50 U	
Stephen James	16-50 A	R-Exeter
James Erving	"	R-Newport
Benj[a] Weight	50-60 A	
Holden Eldred	16-50 A	
Tho[s] Eldred	"	
Andrew Belfor	50-60 U	R-Newport
David Shearman	16-50 A	
Marshal Downing	"	
Sam[l] Fearweather	16-50 U	
George Fearweather	N	
Cuff Peckham	N	

Totals:
22	16-50 A	7	16-50 U
1	50-60 A	3	50-60 U
3	60+	7	N
[9	R]		

Page 9

Benjamin Rodman	16-50 U	
Jack Rodman	N	
William Potter	16-50 U	
Tho[s] Haszard	60+	
W[m] Robinson Potter	16-50 A	
Tony Potter	N	
Cesar Potter	N	
Mingo Potter	N	
Zealous Potter	N	
Pero Potter	N	
Samson Gardner	N	
George Brown	16-50 A	
Rowland Brown	"	
Glasgo Browne	N	
Sambo Browne	N	
Joshua Browne	N	
Dan[l] Shearman (of Philip)	16-50 A	
John Thurston	"	R-Newport
Samuel Oatley	50-60 U	
Step[n] Champlin	16-50 A	
Dick Champlin	"	
July Champlin	N	

1777 MILITARY CENSUS
SOUTH KINGSTOWN, RHODE ISLAND

Page 9 (cont)

Jack Champlin	N
Benedict Oatley	16-50 U
Joseph Oatley	16-50 A
Ephraim Carpenter	"
Gregory Cooke	"
Saml Jackwise	"
James Chapel	50-60 A
William Chapel	16-50 A
Thomas Chapel	"
Clarke Gardner	"
Thos Gardner	"
Jno Gardner	
(of Clarke)	"
Abijah Babcock	"
John Gardner	
(Bostone Neck)	"
John Smith	50-60 U
Thomas Smith	16-50 U
John Smith Junr	16-50 A
Amos Smith	N
Primas Smith	N
Cuff Smith	N

Totals:
```
18  16-50 A    4  16-50 U
 1  50-60 A    2  50-60 U
 1  60+       16  N        [1 R]
```

Page 10

Daniel Ginne J^r	16-50 U	R-Newport
Daniel Tefft ye 3^d	16-50 A	
Ebenezer Tefft	50-60 U	
Solomon Tefft	16-50 A	
Jeremiah Albro	"	
Thos Steadman	"	
Wm Steadman	"	
Briant Milleman	"	
Daniel Carpenter	60+	
Stephen Haszard		
(of Thos dec.)	16-50 A	
James Carpenter	"	
George Armstrong	"	
Cud Carpenter	N	
Jemmy Carpenter	N	
Wm Clarke	16-50 A	
Stepⁿ Clarke	"	
Pikas Austin	"	
Samuel Gavit	16-50 U	

Page 10 (cont)

Silvester Robinson	16-50 U	
James Robinson Junr	Cert	
Israel Robinson	N	
Quam Carr	N	
John Robinson	N	
Samuel Congdon	16-50 A	
Joseph Congdon Junr	"	
Dick Congdon	N	
George Hazard		
(Point Judith)	16-50 U	
Pero Hazard	N	
Josias Clarke	16-50 A	R-Charleston
Benj^a Clarke	"	R-Charleston
Nathaniel Mumford	"	
Ray Mumford	"	
Jack Mumford	"	
Thos Champlin	"	
Samuel Rodman	60+	
Thos Rodman	60+	
Robert Rodman J^r	16-50 A	
Daniel Rodman	"	
William Rodman	"	
Cuff Rodman	N	
Eli Rodman	N	
Cesar Niles	N	
Tom Niles	N	
Isaac Rodman	N	

Totals:
```
23  16-50 A    4  16-50 U
 1  50-60 U    4  60+
 1  Cert      12  N        [3  R]
```

Page 11

Michael Armstrong	50-60 U	
Jack Babcock	N	
Cudjoe Babcock	N	
Edward Armstrong	16-50 A	
Benajah Carpenter	"	
Daniel Hill	50-60 U	
Henry Hill	16-50 A	
David Babcock Junr	"	
David Babcock 3^d	16-50 U	
Nathaniel Lock	"	
Mevis Coon	N	
George Hazard	50-60 U	R-Newport
Arnold Hazard	16-50 A	R-Newport
Geo. Wanton Hazard	"	R-Newport

1777 MILITARY CENSUS
SOUTH KINGSTOWN, RHODE ISLAND

Page 11 (cont)

Troy Hazard	N	R-Newport
Paris Gardner	16-50 A	
Simon Smith	60+	R-Richmond
Adam Gould	60+	
John Gould	16-50 A	
Nicholas Gould	"	
Samuel Curtis	16-50 U	
Jonathan Gardner	16-50 A	
Samuel Hall	60+	
John Braman Jr	16-50 A	
Thos Hawkins	16-50 U	
William Underwood	50-60 U	
Joseph Underwood	16-50 A	
Paul Mumford	16-50 U	
Samuel Tefft	60+	
Samuel Tefft Junr	16-50 A	
Oliver Tefft	"	
Joshua Greene	60+	
Thoms Carpenter	60+	
Joseph Carpenter	16-50 A	
Oliver Armstrong	"	
Caleb Chapel	"	
Gardner Tefft	"	
Daniel Tefft	60+	
Joseph Jaquays	16-50 A	
Stepn Tefft	50-60 U	
Jona Jaquais	16-50 A	
Gideon Fowler	50-60 A	
Abel Fowler	16-50 A	
Daniel Ginned	60+	
Edward Lock	16-50 A	

Totals:
22	16-50 A	5	16-50 U
1	50-60 A	5	50-60 U
8	60+	4	N [6 R]

Page 12

William Willcox	16-50 A
Dick Brown	N
Prince Brown	N
James Brown	N
Silvestr Willcox	16-50 A
Pero Willcox	N
Robert Kinyon	16-50 A
Samuel Kinyon	"
Jeremiah Babcock	"
Freman Perry	16-50 U

Page 12 (cont)

Raymond Perry	16-50 A	
Richard Bush	60+	R-Jameston
Richard Bush Junr	16-50 A	R-Jamestown
Nathan Nash	60+	
Ichabod West	50-60 U	
John Cross	16-50 U	
Nathan Sheffield	"	
West Cross	N	
Seth Eldred	60+	
James Eldred	16-50 A	
Samuel Eldred	"	
Jack Hazard	N	
Thomas Armstrong	16-50 A	
Peleg Peckham	Cert	
Caleb Carpenter	Cert	
Silvester Hazard	16-50 U	
Timothy Lock	60+	
Chriso Hazard	16-50 A	
Joseph Congdon	60+	
Richard Ward	16-50 U	R-Newport
William Congdon	60+	
Silas Greenman	16-50 A	
Gideon Greenman	"	
John Greenman	"	
Timothy Peckham	16-50 U	
Carder Hazard	"	
Peter Hazard	"	
Jacob Hazard	N	
Bristol Congdon	N	
Quaco Hazard	N	
Pharoah Hazard	N	
John Hawkins	16-50 A	
Wm Congdon Junr	Cert	
John Congdon	Cert	
Charles Congdon	16-50 A	
Edward Hull	16-50 U	R-Jamestown

Totals:
16	16-50 A	9	16-50 U
1	50-60 U	6	60+
4	Cert	10	N [4 R]

Page 13

John Willson	16-50 U	
John Willson Junr	16-50 A	
John Pitman	"	R-Newport
Valentine Ridge	"	R-Boston
Benedict Helme	50-60 U	

1777 MILITARY CENSUS
SOUTH KINGSTOWN, RHODE ISLAND

Page 13 (cont)				Page 14		
John Potter	60+			Ephraim Smith	60+	
John Potter Junr	16-50 A			Ephraim Smith Junr	16-50 A	
Samuel Potter	"			Ebenezer Smith	"	
George Potter	"			Scranton Chapel	"	
Henry Potter	"			Benja Barker	"	R-Newport
Geo. Potter Taylor	"			William Slocum	"	R-Jameston
John West	16-50 U	R-Newport		Rowland Robinson	16-50 U	
John Gorton	Aff			William Robinson	16-50 A	
Daniel Babcock	16-50 U			Amos Gardner	16-50 U	
Daniel Clarke	16-50 A			Amos Gardner Jr	16-50 A	
Josias Arnold	I			John Gardner (of Amos)	"	
Elijah Champlin	16-50 A			James Gardner " "	"	
Elijah Champlin Junr	"			London Gardner	N	
Jeffry Champlin				John Watson	60+	
(of Elijah)	"			Walter Watson	16-50 A	
Samuel Young	"	R-Newport		Sipeo Watson	N	
Ichabod Clarke	"			Edward Watson	N	
Lyman Clarke	"			John Gardner	16-50 A	
Thomas Sanford	"	R-Newport		Oliver Tenant Junr	"	
Paul Ely	"	R-Newport		Bristol Gardner	N	
Joseph Gould	"	R-Middle-		Cesar Gardner	N	
		town		Sambo Gardner	N	
Solomon Lemonere	16-50 U	R-London		Caleb Gardner	60+	
Thos Carpenter Junr	16-50 A			Caleb Gardner Junr	16-50 A	
Weight Saunders	"	R-Westerly		Edward Willcox	"	R-Richmond
Nathan West	"	R-Newport		Robert Rodman	50-60 U	
William West Junr	"	R-Newport		Chas Gardner	N	
Joseph Segar Junr	"			Cuff Gardner	N	
Abiel Shearman	"			George Dyre	N	
Robert Browning	"			Stepn Gardner	N	
Joseph Segar	50-60 U			Immanuel Case	16-50 U	
John Segar	16-50 A			Peter Case	N	
Thomas Segar	"			Prince Case	N	
Daniel Williams	16-50 U			Robert Potter	16-50 A	
John Braman	16-50 A			Ezra Eldred	"	
Daniel Willcox	50-60 U	R-Jameston		Stepn Potter	N	
John Driskill	16-50 A	R-Ireland		Nicholas Gardner	16-50 A	
Joshua Williams	"			Primas Gardner	N	
McCoon Williams	"			Rowse Potter		
Henry Hooper	16-50 U			(of Robt)	16-50 A	
Joseph Hull	60+			Solomon Shearman	"	R-North
Joseph Knowles	16-50 U					Kingston
Robert Knowles	16-50 A			George Gardner	60+	
				Newbury Gardner	N	

Totals:

32	16-50 A	7	16-50 U	
3	50-60 U	2	60+	
1	Aff	1	I	[13 R]

Will Gardner   N
Elijah Heffernan   60+
Jeffry Champlin   16-50 U

1777 MILITARY CENSUS
SOUTH KINGSTOWN, RHODE ISLAND

Page 14 (cont)

Newport Champlin   N
Thomas Hazard Potter   16-50 A

Totals:
    20 16-50 A   4 16-50 U
    1   50-60 U   5 60+
    17 N   [4 R]

Page 15

Robert Knowles   50-60 U
Lewd Sands   N
Bandon Case   N
Jeremiah Knowles   16-50 A
James Knowles   "
Palmer Shelden   "
Godfrey Hazard   "
Mumford Hazard   "
Peleg Gardner   "   R-North
                                 Kingston
Robert Hazard (of Rich.)"
Benj^a Hazard   "
Peter Hazard   N
Nathaniel Cottril   16-50 A
Coggeshal Greene   "
Thomas Potter   60+
Rowse Potter (of Thos)16-50 A
Saml Potter   " " "
Jonathan Card   "
Samuel Card   "
Henry Card   "
Cyrus Babcock   "
Ephraim Babcock   "
Wm Browning J^r   "
Chris^o Browning   "
Step^n Browning   "
Wilkinson Browning   16-50 U

Page 15 (cont)

Nathan Bull   16-50 U R-Newport
Joseph Browning   16-50 A
Chris^o Bennit   16-50 U R-Newport
Philip Durfy   "   R-Newport
John Browning   16-50 A
Frank Browning   N
William Holt   16-50 A R-Newport
William Tew   "   R-Newport
Samuel Sheffield   "
David Willcox   "   R-Westerly
Benj^a Saunders   "   R-Westerly
James Allen   16-50 U
Daniel Tefft   60+
David Babcock   60+
Gideon Babcock   16-50 A
Asa Babcock   "
Bristol Babcock   N
Cesar Babcock   N

Totals:
    29 16-50 A   5 16-50 U
    1   50-60 U   3 60+
    6   N   [8 R]

Page 16

George Babcock J^r   (SM)
Robert Congdon   (SM)
Joseph Billington J^r   (SM)
Edward Anthony J^r   (SM)
    Mustee
Nathaniel Hawkins   (SM)
Edward Harvey   (CS)
Cuff Peckham   (CS)
    Mustee
James Parker   (SM)

South Kingstown April 18th 1777
        Benjamin Peckham of said Town Personally
appeared & on his Solemn Oath declared that he hath justly and truly made the
aforegoing List of all the Male Persons, of Sixteen Years of age & upwards in
said Town of South Kingston according to the best of his knowledge (and he
further Declares that in his Opinion that of the Negroes inserted in said
Lists, There is 85 who are able to bear Arms & 133 who are not able to bear
Arms.) Before
        Iman^l Case Justice Common Pleas

In all: 305 16-50 A 83 16-50 U   6 50-60 A 25 50-60 U 60 60+
           2 Aff   8 Cert   218 N   2 I   2 CS   6 SM

1777 MILITARY CENSUS
TIVERTON, RHODE ISLAND

Page 1

Almy John	50-60	U
Almy Gideon	16-50	U
Almy Joseph	16-50	A
Almy John son of Gid[n]	"	
Almy William	"	
Seabury Sion	60+	
Seabury Joseph	16-50	U
Seabury Philip	16-50	A
William Soule	60+	
Nathan Pettey	60+	
John Coggeshall	60+	
Richard Gifford	50-60	U
Joseph Taber	"	
Thomas Taber	"	
Joseph Crandell	"	
Joseph Remington	" R-Portsmouth	
George Cook	"	
Abial Cook	"	
Olphre King	16-50	U
John Willke	"	
Thomas Cory	60+	
Job Negus	60+	
Weaver Osband	16-50	A
John Cook	"	
Thomas Clossen	"	
Michael Macomber	"	
Rufus Tripp	"	
Daniel Pettey	"	
Stephen Tallman	"	
Richard Lake	"	
Thomas Cory Jn[r]	"	
Gilbert Devol	"	
Paul Cook	"	
William Woddle Jn[r]	"	
Peleg Manchester	"	
Walter Perry	"	
Joseph Sherman	"	
David Eddy	"	
Stephen Slocum	"	
Benjamin Borden	"	
Eseck Clossen	"	

Totals:
   23 16-50 A   4 16-50 U
    8 50-60 U   6 60+

Page 1 Reverse

Negroes

Abraham Cook	50-60	U
London Durfee	50-60	A
Boston Durfee	16-50	A
Prince Durfee	"	
Jack Durfee	"	
London Pearse	60+	
Jack Cook	60+	
Peter Barker	60+	
Domini Spencer	60+	
William Wanton	50-60	A
Solomon Wanton	16-50	A
Jeremiah Wanton	"	
Prince Durfee y[e] 2[d]	"	
Jack Almy	50-60	A
Cato Slocum	"	
Forten Slocum	"	

Mustees:

Richard Amos	16-50	A
Thomas Leazer	"	
Solomon David	"	
Solomon David y[e] 2[d]	"	
Daniel Cook	"	

Total: 21

Page 2

Thomas Cook	60+
John Dennis	60+
Giles Brownell	60+
Cornelius Soule	60+
Jonathan Soule	60+
Abial Tripp	60+
Christopher Manchester	60+
Benjamin Chase	60+
Abner Chase	60+
Smiton Hart	60+
Thomas Manchester	60+
Jonathan Grinnel	60+
David Round	60+
Benjamin King	60+
Benjamin Sawdy	60+
Benjamin Macomber	60+
Robert Bennet	60+
Thomas Shrieve	60+
Thomas Fish	60+
Stephen Cook	60+
Joshua Dwelly	60+

1777 MILITARY CENSUS
TIVERTON, RHODE ISLAND

Page 2 (cont)

William Cory	60+
Benjamin Durfee	60+
Samuel Durfee	60+
David Durfee	60+
Ebenezer Slocum	60+
John Negus	60+
Benjamin Hambly	60+
Peter Tallman	60+
John Bowen	60+
Samuel Borden	60+
John Borden	60+
Joseph Cook	60+
Samuel Hicks	60+
Jonathan Devol	60+
Thomas Taber	60+
Annaniah Gifford	60+
Benjamin Jenks	60+
Caleb Cory	60+
Giles Slocum	60+ R-Portsmouth
Roger Cory	60+
John Cook	60+
John Jennings	60+
Silvenius Westgate	50-60 U
John Taber	"
Oliver Cook	"

Totals:
    3 50-60 U   43 60+

Page 3

Joseph Fish	16-50 A
John Hicks	"
Earl Durfee	"
Benjamin Manchester	"
Job Sowle	"
Peleg Earl	"
James Tallman	"
Robert Burrington	"
Samuel Sherman	"
Peleg Sanford	"
Giles Manchester	"
John Shrieve	"
John Stafford	"
Joseph Borden	Aff
Daniel Dwelly	16-50 A
Philip Manchester	"
Joseph Hicks	Aff
Stafford Borden	16-50 A

Page 3 (cont)

Joshua Stafford	Aff
Abraham Burrington	Aff
Benjamin Durfee	16-50 A
Woodman Billings	"
John Manchester	"
David Sherman	"
James Durfee	"
Gideon Borden	"
John Freeman	"
William Gifford	"
Edward Borden	"
Gershom Woddle Jn^r	"
John Perry ye 2^d	"
John Bower Jn^r	"
Godfrey Bennet	"
William Cook	16-50 U
Daniel Cory	16-50 A
John Durfee	"
George Howland	"
Samuel Sherman	"
Aaron Borden	"
William Cory	"
Daniel Coggishall	"
Dwelly Coggishall	"
Thomas Cook	Aff

Totals:
    37 16-50 A   1 16-50 U   5 Aff

Page 4

Peter Simmons	16-50 A
Pardon Davis	"
Thomas Negus	"
Moses Simmons	"
Thomas Simmons	"
Peleg Simmons Jn^r	"
Joseph Simmons	"
Ephraim Sanford	"
William Hart	"
Eber Hart	"
Peleg Simmons	60+
Constant Hart	Aff
Peleg Hart	16-50 A
Moses Taber	"
Eber Crandall	"
John Waite	50-60 A
James Lake	"
George Peckham	"

1777 MILITARY CENSUS
TIVERTON, RHODE ISLAND

Page 4 (cont)   Page 5 (cont)

Enos Peckham	50-60 A			William Osband	16-50 A	
Enos Peckham Jn^r	16-50 A			William Borden	"	
Job Peckham	"			Benjamin Negus	16-50 U	
Ephrajm Macomber	16-50 U			Elijah Slocum	16-50 A	
Jonathan Gibbs	16-50 A	R-Newport		Israel Perry	"	
Giles Gibbs	"	R-Newport		Gideon Grinnell	"	
Benjamin Fish	"			Joseph Bennet	"	
Pardon Taber	"			Gideon Gray	"	
John Fish	"			Joseph Woddle	"	
Zuriel Fish	"			William Fish	"	
Robert Fish	16-50 U			Samuel Lamunyon	16-50 U	
Samuel Sawdy	16-50 A			Elihu Gifford	16-50 A	
John Tripp	"			William Cory	"	
Joseph Witherly	[blank]			Giles Lake	"	
Ephrajm Davenport	16-50 A			Abner Durfee	"	
Joseph Pitman	50-60 A			Christopher Borden	"	
George Wood	16-50 A			John Jolatt	"	
Paul Mosher	Aff			James Warren	"	
Obadiah Mosher	Aff			Robert Negus	16-50 U	
Samuel Hicks	Aff			Edward Manchester	16-50 A	
Elihu Hicks	Aff			John Westgate	"	
Joseph Sanford	16-50 A			John Manchester	"	
Earl Taber	"			John Frances	"	
Lemuel Baley	"			William Manchester	"	
John Sawyer	60+			Isaac Pettey	"	
William Baley	16-50 A			Godfrey Perry	"	
Oliver Baley	50-60 A			Jared Sherman	"	
Lemuel Taber	16-50 A			Gideon Durfee	"	
				Thomas Thurston	"	

Totals: William Durfee   "
   30 16-50 A   2 16-50 U
    6 50-60 A   2 60+   6 Aff   Totals:
                                                    42 16-50 A   3 16-50 U
Page 5

John Sherman	16-50 A	R-Portsmouth	Page 6	
Richard Thomas	"	R-Portsmouth	Cap^tn Ebenezer	
William Anthony	"	R-Portsmouth	Slocum Jn^r	16-50 A
William Cook	"	R-Portsmouth	Daniel Devol	"
John Earl	"	R-Portsmouth	Jacob Sowle	"
John Langutha	"	R-Newport	Daniel Grinnell	"
Thomas Nicher	"	R-Newport	Nathaniel Grinnell	"
John Philips	"	R-Newport	Pardon Taber	"
Lawrance Clarke	"	R-Middletown	Othniel Campbell	60+
Thomas Durfee	"		Lot Sherman	16-50 A
Abraham Hicks	"		George Crocker	"
Stephen Safford	"		John Bennet	"
Henry Carter	"		Caleb Cook	"
Humphry Sherman	"		John Jenks	"
Joseph Eley	"		John Stafford	"

1777 MILITARY CENSUS
TIVERTON, RHODE ISLAND

Page 6 (cont)

Noles Negus	16-50 A	
John Coggishall	"	
Wilson Osband	"	
Paul Perry	"	
Gideon Gifford	"	
Elijah Borden	"	
John Perry	"	
Joseph Sowle	"	
Job Durfee	"	
Prince Durfee	"	
Stephen Negus	"	
George Westgate	"	
Joseph Cook Jn^r	"	
David Durfee	"	
Jonathan Coggishall	"	
Wanton Sherman	"	
Peter Thatcher	"	
Robert Springer	"	
Benjamin Springer	"	
Benjamin Howland	"	
William Wilbour	"	R-Newport
Stephen Cook	"	
Isaac Negus	"	
Joseph Hart	"	
James Lowden	"	R-Newport
Pearce Perry	"	
Hercules Gifford	"	

Totals:
39 16-50 A   1 60+

Page 7

Isaac Cook	16-50 A
Philip Cory	"
Philip Manchester	"
Philip Gray	"
Daniel Gray	"
David Gray	"
Thomas Gray	"
Sanford Almy	"
Jeremiah Cook	"
Russel Cook	"
Job Cook	"
William Cook	"
William Willcox	"
Stephen Taber	"
John Davenport	"
Gideon Willcox	50-60 A
Abner Soule	16-50 A

Page 7 (cont)

Nathaniel Briggs	16-50 A
Ephrajm Davenport	16-50 U
Pardon Davenport	16-50 A
Samuel Sanford	"
Thomas Cory	"
Philip Cory ye 2^d	"
Israel Brownell	"
Godfrey Cook	"
Thomas Cook	16-50 U
Nathaniel Cook	"
Redford Dennis	16-50 A
Charles Brownell	16-50 U
William Willcox	16-50 A
Thomas Willcox	"
Joseph Taber	50-60 U
Gideon Taber	16-50 A
Jacob Taber	"
Walter Cook	16-50 U
George Cook	16-50 A
Peleg Cook	"
William Cook	"
Walter Moon	"
Nathaniel Crandell	16-50 U
Jeremiah Manchester	16-50 A
Isaac Sanford	"
Thomas Lawton	"
Samuel Simmons	"
Aaron Tripp	"
Samuel Taber	"

Totals:
38 16-50 A   6 16-50 U
1 50-60 A   1 50-60 U

Page 8

Godfree Manchester	16-50 A	
Thaddeus Manchester	"	
William Gray	"	
Philip Gray	16-50 U	
Peleg Burroughs	"	
William Burroughs	16-50 A	R-Newport
Pardon Gray	16-50 A	
Job Gray	"	
Edward [blank]	"	
Daniel Brown	"	
Abraham Brown	"	
Isaac Brown	"	
Benjamin Brown	"	
John Bennet	"	

1777 MILITARY CENSUS
TIVERTON, RHODE ISLAND

Page 8 (cont)

Thompson Taber	16-50 A	
John Taber	"	
Philip Lake	"	
Joseph Lake	"	
Philip Bennet	"	
Jonathan Lake	16-50 U	
Job Lake	"	
John Willcox	16-50 A	
John Round	"	
Ephrajm Chamberlin	"	
Water Earl	50-60 U	
Joel Lake	"	
David Round	16-50 A	
Obadiah Dennis	"	
Thomas Dennis	"	
Godfree King	"	
Job King	"	
Stephen King	"	
Noak Lake	"	
Joseph Hawksey	"	R-Newport
Jonathan Jeffes	"	R-Newport
John Cook	"	
Job Manchester	"	
Smiton Hart Jn[r]	"	
John Taber [?S[r]]	"	
Jacob Davids	I "	
John Brooks	N 16-50 A	
Primus Stafford	N "	
Sharper Almy	N "	
Forten Gray	N "	
Othniel Campbell	16-50 U	

Totals:
   38 16-50 A   5 16-50 U
   2 50-60 U   1 I   4 N

Page 8 Reverse

Enlisted
Soldiers of the Town of Tiverton

Christopher Manchester Cp[n]
Edward Slocum Leu[t]
Water Taber
Sanford Hart
Thomas Butts
Daniel Cook
Noah Palmer
Isaac Willcox
Ephrajm Willcox
Benjamin Willcox

Page 8 Reverse (cont)

~~Sanford Hart~~
Giles Brownell
Charles Brownell
Benjamin Willcox y[e] 2[d]
Pearce Horswell
Jonathan Devol
Silas Devol
Jeremiah Dencas
Milford Holms
Abner Willcox
Ichabud Simmons
Joshua Cuttawon

Total: 21

Enlisted Soldiers of the Town of Tiverton
James Tompkins
Noel Taber

Page 9

William Cory		
son of Tho[s]	16-50 A	
Lemuel Durfee	"	
Stephen Devol	"	
Joshua Pettey	"	
Phinehas Perry	"	
Joseph Clarke	"	
James Durfee		
son of Benj[n]	"	
Samuel Slocum	"	
Jeremiah Dwelly	"	
Pardon Cook	"	
John Negus	"	
Thomas Fish Jn[r]	"	
Isaac Jennings	"	
Benjamin Cook	"	
Lot Sherman	"	
Rodman Thomas	"	
Samuel Soule	"	
Reuben Sherman	"	
John Tallman	"	R-Portsmouth
Joseph Tallman	"	R-Portsmouth
William Borden	"	R-Portsmouth
Job Cook	"	
John Murfee	"	R-Newport
William Philips	"	R-Newport
Samuel Peckham	"	R-Newport
Benjamin Hambly Jn[r]	"	
William Manchester	"	
Abner Cook	16-50 U	

1777 MILITARY CENSUS
TIVERTON, RHODE ISLAND

Page 9 (cont)

Elijah Cobb	16-50 A
Ebenezer Sherman	60+
David Sherman	16-50 A
Humphry Sherman	"
Richard Dwelly	"
Philip Lamunyon	"
David Stafford	60+
John Stafford	16-50 A
Thomas Estes	[blank]
Robert Estes	16-50 A
Joseph Estes	"
Seth Thomas	"
Samuel Stafford	"

Page 9 (cont)

Isaac Manchester	16-50 U	
Isaac Manchester Jn^r	16-50 A	
Thomas Manchester	"	
Philip Taber	"	
Joseph Crandell	"	R-Newport
Samuel Crandell	60+	R-Newport
Ezekiel Crandell	16-50 A	R-Newport
Elijah Devol	"	
Gilbert Manchester	16-50 U	
Elijah Devol	16-50 A	

Totals:
  44 16-50 A   3 16-50 U   3 60+

Page 9 Reverse

Agreable to the Requirements of the General Assembly I have Endevoured to Collect
the best Information of the male persons according to said requirement and present the same as is before Demonstrated
            p^r Peleg Simmons Jn^r Committeeman

Newport ss) In Tiverton on the 18th of April 1777 Cometh Peleg Simmons Jn^r
            Subscriber hereof and maketh Oath to the truth of ye foregoing

        Before   Walter Cook Justice peace

Separate sheet not numbered:

  Totals:
    292 16-50 A   24 16-50 U   7 50-60 A   14 50-60 U   55 60+   11 Aff

                                                        Total: 403

WARREN, RHODE ISLAND

Page 1

Cromell Child	16-50 A	
John Child	60+	
John Child 3rd	16-50 A	
Joseph Hardin	60+	
Moses Turner	16-50 A	
Benjamin Diman	"	
Revd Charles Thompson	"	
James Bushee	50-60 U	
Wilkins Treby	16-50 A	R-Newport
William Sandford	"	R-Bristol
Isaac Olney	"	R-Providence
Sylvester Child Esqr	"	
James Child 2nd	"	
Caleb Eddy	"	
George Neal Prisoner	"	T-Berwick on Tweed

Page 1 (cont)

Jeremiah Comstock	16-50 A	
Samuel Luther Esqr	"	
Allin Cole	"	
Martin Luther Esqr	50-60 A	
Luther Sallisbury	16-50 A	
Ebenezer Cole Esqr	60+	
Ebenezer Cole Junr	16-50 A	
Benjamin Cole Junr	"	
Joseph Smith	"	
Daniel Richards	"	
Benjamin Weaver	"	T-Freetown
Isaac Gorham	"	
William Lewis	"	
John Eastabrooke	60+	

1777 MILITARY CENSUS
WARREN, RHODE ISLAND

Page 1 (cont)

Edward Eastabrooke	16-50 A	
William Barton Esqr	"	
Amos Haile	"	
Barnard Haile 3rd	"	
Shubeal Burr	"	
Samuel Burr	60+	
Josias Lyndon Esqr	60+	R-Newport
Samuel Wheaton	16-50 A	
Barnard Hill Junr	"	
Norton Thurston	"	R-Newport
Joseph Eddy	"	
Oliver Eddy	"	
William Rude	"	R-Newport
William Rude Junr	"	T-Newport

Totals:
35	16-50 A	1	50-60 A
1	50-60 U	6	60+
3	T	6	R

Page 2

Brought forward:
  35-0-1-1-6-0-0-3-6-0-0

Simeon Togood	16-50 A	
Jeremiah Jolls	"	R-Bristol
Jonathan Pearse	"	R-Newport
Peleg Eastabrooke	"	
Nelson Miller	"	
Thomas Eastabrooke	"	
Nicholas Campbell	"	T-The Island of Malta in the Mideteranian Sea
Hezekiah Child	16-50 A	
Benjamin Child	16-50 U	
Haile Child	16-50 A	
William Child 2nd	"	
Benjamin Cranston	"	
Caleb Thurber	"	
Barnebe Luther	"	
Samuel Hicks	"	
John Thurber	"	
Warren Eastabrooke	"	
Barnard Haile	"	
Samuel Cranston	"	
Nathan Bowen	"	
Amos Bowen	50-60 U	
Charles Collins	16-50 A	

Page 2 (cont)

Thomas Aaronshire	50-60 A	R-Newport
William Hoar Junr	16-50 A	
Benjamin Hoar	"	R-Bristol
William Hoar	60+	R-Bristol
Curtis Cole	16-50 A	
Barnard Sallisbury	50-60 A	R-Bristol
John Child Esqr	16-50 A	
Philip Morse	"	R-Newport
Philip Knight	"	
Caleb Thomas	16-50 U	
Benjamin Eastabrooke	60+	
Daniel Eastabrooke	16-50 A	
Barnard Hill	60+	
Thomas Cole	50-60 A	
James Cole	16-50 A	
John Topham	"	R-Newport

Totals:
64	16-50 A	2	16-50 U
4	50-60 A	2	50-60 U
9	60+	4	T	14 R

Page 3

Brought forward: 64-2-4-2-9-4-14

James Webb	16-50 A	R-Newport
Benjamin Sherburn	"	R-Newport
Samuel Maxwell	60+	
Joseph Belcher Junr	16-50 A	R-Newport
Caleb Carr	"	
Joseph Belcher Esqr	"	R-Newport
William Belcher	"	R-Newport
David Melvil	"	R-Newport
James Belcher	"	R-Newport
Samuel Miller	"	
Thomas Pearse	"	R-Portsmouth
Edward Wing	"	
Martin Eastabrooke	"	
Jonathan Carr	"	
Edward Chase	Cert	
Level Maxwell (Cert)	16-50 A	
William Haile	"	
James Naning	"	R-Bristol
John Haile	"	
Peter Cole	60+	
Caleb Turner	16-50 A	
Seth Snell	"	
Josiah Bowen	"	

1777 MILITARY CENSUS
WARREN, RHODE ISLAND

Page 3 (cont)

John Bowen	16-50 A	
William OBryan	"	
Jesse Baker	"	
Nathan Miller Esqr	"	
Samuel Miller 2nd	"	
Caleb Miller	"	
Peter Turner	"	
James Miller 2nd	"	
William Bedum Prisoner	"	T-Hustwit Yorkshire
Thomas Leman Prisoner	"	T-Ayer Ayershire
Caleb Cranston	"	
Benjamin Cranston Junr	"	
Edward Eddy	"	
William Child	"	
Samuel Fish	"	
James Child	"	
Caleb Child	"	

Carried Forward:

101	16-50 A	2	16-50 U
4	50-60 A	2	50-60 U
11	60+	2	Cert
6	T	23	R

Page 4

Brought forward:
101-2-4-2-11-0-2-6-23

Cromell Child 2nd	16-50 A
John Wilber	"
Jonathan Bowen	"
Jonathan Bowen Junr	"
Stephen Bowen Junr	"
Joseph Ormsbe	"
Thomas Ormsbe	[blank]
William Bliss	16-50 U
James Bliss	16-50 A
Jonathan Bliss	"
Daniel Kelley	"
Joseph Kelley	"
Jeremiah Child	"
Rufus Whitaker	"
William Turner Miller	"
Nathaniel B. Whitting	"
Jacob Saunders	"

Page 4 (cont)

Thomas Stacy	16-50 A	R-Newport
Peter Reynolds	"	
Nathaniel Hill	16-50 U	
John Hardin	16-50 A	
Stephen Bowen	60+	
John OKelley	16-50 A	
Barnard Miller	50-60 A	
Elkenah Cole	16-50 A	
Joshua Whitting	"	
Nathaniel Bowen	60+	
John Bowen	16-50 A	
James Bowen	"	
William Bowen	"	
Joseph McMillion	"	
Paul Chase	Aff	
William Linzey	16-50 A	R-Bristol
Marmaduke Mason	"	
Alexander Mason	"	
Edward Mason	"	
James Mason	"	
Nathan Haile	16-50 U	
Ephraim Pearse	"	
Oliver Sallisbury	60+	
Fredrick Luther	Aff	
John Butterworth	60+	

Carried forward:

131	16-50 A	6	16-50 U	
5	50-60 A	2	50-60 U	
15	60+	2	Aff	
2	Cert	7	T	24 R

Page 5

Brought forward:
131-6-5-2-15-2-2-7-24

James Grave	16-50 A
Ezra Ormsbe	"
John Ormsbe	16-50 U
William Arnold	16-50 A
William Arnold Junr	"
Peleg Arnold	"
Ebenezer Luther	"
Gideon Luther	"
Nehemiah Luther	"
Robert Eastabrooke	60+
Benjamin Eastabrooke 2nd	16-50 A

1777 MILITARY CENSUS
WARREN, RHODE ISLAND

Page 5 (cont)

Job Sallisbury	16-50 A	
Samuel Pearse	"	
Jeremiah Pearse	"	
James Miller	"	
William Luther	"	
Luther Cole	"	
Caleb Sallisbury	"	
Isaiah Cole	16-50 U	
Richard Haile	50-60 A	
Jonathan Haile	16-50 A	
Richard Haile Junr	"	
James Cole	"	
Smith Bowen	"	
Samuel Bowen	60+	
Samuel Bowen Junr	16-50 A	
Sampson Simms	"	
Elisha Phinney	"	
Benjamin Cole Esqr	50-60 A	
Benjamin Smith	60+	R-Bristol
Daniel Lufavour	16-50 A	R-Bristol
Ichabod Cole	"	
Isaac Cole	"	
Thomas Cole 3rd	"	
John Kinnecutt Esqr	60+	
John Kinnecutt Junr	16-50 A	
Edward Kinnecutt	"	
Edward Sheldron	16-50 U	
Shubeal Kinnecutt	16-50 A	
Allin Usher	"	R-Bristol
Jabez Luther	Aff	
Jabez Luther Junr	16-50 A	
Mark D'Wolf	60+	
John D'Wolf	16-50 A	

Carried Forward:

164	16-50 A	9	16-50 U	
7	50-60 A	2	50-60 U	
20	60+	3	Aff	
2	Cert	7	T	27 R

Page 6

Brought forward:
   164-9-7-2-20-3-2-7-27

John Brown	16-50 A	
Edward Cole	"	
Joseph Butterworth	60+	
Benjamin Barton	16-50 A	
Joseph B. Barton	"	
Hezekiah Butterworth	"	
Benjamin Butterworth	60+	
Samuel Hicks	Aff	
Oliver Round	16-50 U	
Richard Barton	16-50 A	
Daniel Cole	"	
Landal Cole	"	
Daniel Cole Junior	"	
Seth Cole	"	
David Barton	"	
Haile Barton	"	
John Sisson	50-60 A	
George Sisson 3rd	16-50 A	
John Sisson Junr	"	
Caleb Sisson	"	
George Sisson	50-60 A	
George Sisson Junior	16-50 A	
Jonathan Sisson	"	
James Sisson	"	
Edward Gardner	"	
John Mason	50-60 A	
William Sallisbury	16-50 A	
Gardner Mason	"	
Samuel Mason	"	
Rufus Chase	"	R-Bristol
Andrue Cole	"	
Edward Cole 2nd	"	

Totals:

189	16-50 A	10	16-50 U	
10	50-60 A	2	50-60 U	
22	60+	4	Aff	
2	Cert	7	T	28 R

State of Rhode Island and Providence Plantations, Warren April 16th 1777.
Whereas the Honorable General Assembly of this State in their Last Session
appointed me a Committee man to Take the number of Male persons in the Town of
Warren from 16 years old and upwards making proper distinction between those
from 16 to 50 able to bear Arms and then from 16 to 50 unable to bear Arms

1777 MILITARY CENSUS
WARREN, RHODE ISLAND

and those from 50 to 60 able to bear arms as well as those from 50 to 60 unable
to bear arms as also from 60 and upwards &c I do Report as follows That there is
in the Town of Warren 189 Male persons from 16 to 50 able to bear Arms and 8
from 16 to 50 unable to bear arms 10 from 50 to 60 able to bear Arms and 2 from
50 to 60 unable to bear Arms. Likewise 22 from 60 and upwards as also 4 who
have taken the affirmation and one who hath a Certificate from the Friends Meeting in which numbers are Included 7 Transient persons and 28 Residents.

p^r William Turner Miller Committee

Bristol Ss Warren April 16th 1777) Then personally appeared the within named
William Turner Miller and made Solemn Oath to the truth of the within List according to the best of his knowledge before me

William Barton Justice of Peace

10 from 16 to 50 unable to bear Arms
2 who have Certificates

WARWICK, RHODE ISLAND

Page 1

Thomas Tibbitts	50-60 A	
John Tibbitts	16-50 A	
Thomas Tibbitts Ju^r	"	
Jonathan Tibbitts		
Thomas Rice Ju^r Esqr	50-60 A	
John Rice	[blank]	
Reuben Rice	N 16-50 A	
Thomas Rice		
son of Randal	16-50 A	
Caleb Potter	"	R-Coventry
James Jerauld	"	
Samuel Gorton	60+	
Jonathan Gorton	16-50 A	
Elisha Wightman	"	
John Wightman	"	
Daniel Wightman	"	
Philip Wightman	"	
John Ladd	50-60 A	
Joseph Ladd	16-50 A	
Philip Arnold	50-60 A	
Andrew Arnold	16-50 A	
Quash Arnold	N 15-60 A	
Wm Burk	16-50 A	
John Hackstone	50-60 A	
Wm Hackstone		
son of John	16-50 A	
Nathaniel Arnold	60+	
Nathaniel Arnold Ju^r	16-50 A	

Page 1 (cont)

Nathan Arnold	16-50 A
Thomas Babcock	"
Benjamin Babcock	"
Asa Wightman	"
Waterman Tibbitts	"
James Greene	
son of W^m	"
James Greene Ju^r	"
Cuff	N

Totals:

25 16-50 A	5 50-60 A		
3 60+	1 R	3 N	

Page 2

Benj^a Hutson (CS)	16-50 A	
Olney Stone (CS)	"	
Timothy Daily	I 16-50 A	
Thomas Price	60+	
Benj^a Fairbanks	16-50 A	
Benj^a Arnold	50-60 U	
Philip Arnold		
son of Benj^a	16-50 A	
Stephen Arnold		
son of Benj^a	16-50 U	
Henry Arnold	16-50 A	
Thos Arnold		
son of Benj^a	"	

1777 MILITARY CENSUS
WARWICK, RHODE ISLAND

Page 2 (cont)

Africa Arnold	N	60+	
Wall Arnold	N	50-60 U	
Cuff Arnold	N	16-50 A	
Benedict Weever		16-50 A	
Stukely Stafford		50-60 U	
Stukely Stafford Ju^r		16-50 A	
Keelor Stafford		60+	
Peter Potter		16-50 A	R-Cranstown
Charles Shearman		"	
James Greene			
Potowomut		60+ Cert	
Jabez Greene		16-50 A Cert	
James Green			
son of James Decea^d		" Cert	
Benj^a Pierce Ju^r		" Cert	
Amos Shearman		"	
Anthony Nichols		" Cert	
Richard Green			
Potowomut		50-60 A	
Stephen Tifferny		16-50 A	
Cato Green	N	16-50 A	
Jack Minthorn	N	"	R-Newport
Cuff Spencer	N	"	
Jacob Greene		16-50 A	
Wm Green son Natha^l		"	

Totals:

23	16-50 A	1	16-50 U
1	50-60 A	3	50-60 U
4	60+	5	Cert
2	R	6	N

Page 3

Joseph Baker	16-50 A Cert
Nathan Howard	"
Robert Edmunds	"
Jonathan Arnold	16-50 U
Caleb Gorton	16-50 A
Edward Gorton	60+
Edward Gorton Ju^r	16-50 A
Thoms Greene	
son of Rich^d	"
Ishmael West	I 16-50 A
Benoni West	I "
Thos Watt	N "
Caleb Watt	I "

Page 3 (cont)

James Watt	I	16-50 A
[torn]iobin Eldridge	N	"
Thomas Stone		50-60 A
Stukely Stone		16-50 A
Josiah Stone		"
Amos Kimbel		"
Pardon Wood		"
George Briggs		"
Stephen Briggs (CS)		"
Giles Briggs		"
Adam Comstock (CS)		"
Samuel Greene		60+
Christopher Greene		16-50 A
Wm Hackstone		60+
Caleb Arnold		50-60 A
Joseph Arnold (CS)		16-50 A
Samuel Arnold (CS)		"
John Walton		"
Samuel Walton		"
Caleb Greene		"

Totals:

26	16-50 A	1	16-50 U		
2	50-60 A	3	60+		
1	Cert	2	I	3	N

Page 4

Thos Remington Ju^r	16-50 A
Job Briggs	60+
Joseph Bennit	16-50 A
John Bennit	60+
Thos Davis	16-50 A
Samuel Davis	"
Moses Budlong	60+
Moses Budlong Ju^r	16-50 A
Samuel Budlong	"
Rhodes Budlong	"
Solomon Howard	60+
Nathan Budlong	16-50 A
John Bennit Ju^r	"
Benja Howard	"
Jonathan Baker	60+
Samuel Davis (CS)	16-50 A
Samuel Littlefield	"
Abraham Colebee	"
Wm Wood Ju^r	"

1777 MILITARY CENSUS
WARWICK, RHODE ISLAND

Page 4 (cont)

Bell Davis	16-50 A	
Aron Davis	60+	
Henry Straight	16-50 U	
Ebenezer Allen	"	R-Portsmouth
Barnet Hill	16-50 A	
Nathaniel Hackstone	"	
Stephen Card	"	
Wm Hackstone son of Nathl	"	
Co^{ll} John Low	"	
Richard Low Prisoner	"	
Chat Low	N 16-50 A	
A John Johnson	60+	
Peleg Johnson (CS)	16-50 A	

Totals:
    23 16-50 A   2 16-50 U
     7 60+   1 R   1 N

Page 5

Israel Tripp	60+	
Samuel Tillinghast	60+	
Daniel Tillinghast (CS)	16-50 A	
Wm Havens	16-50 A	
James Whipple	"	
Edward Coddington	"	R-Newport
Wm Webb	"	
Isaac Briggs	"	
John Joice	"	
Isaac Gammet	16-50 U	
Reding Heys	"	
Ruel Remington	16-50 A	
Job Briggs Ju^r	"	
Joseph Brown	"	
Daniel Colvin	"	R-Coventry
Samuel Gorton, Cooper	"	
Moses Baker	"	
Pardon Baker	"	
Abraham Baker	"	
Nathan Gorton	"	
Joseph Gorton son of Nathan	"	
Wm Gorton	60+	
John Gorton son of W^m	16-50 A	
Benj^a Budlong	"	
James Greene	60+	

Page 5 (cont)

Jeremiah Philips	16-50 A	R-Cranstown
James Greene Ju^r Nesoket	"	
Thos Greene	50-60 A	
John Budlong	16-50 A	
Samuel Bennet	"	
Samuel Bennet Ju^r	"	
Thomas Remington	50-60 U	

Totals:
    24 16-50 A   2 16-50 U
     1 50-60 A   1 50-60 U
     4 60+   3 R

Page 6

Jonthan Allon	50-60 U	R-Portsmouth
Barnet Allen	16-50 A	R-Portsmouth
Beriah Allen	"	R-Portsmouth
Anthony Low	50-60 A	
Anthony Low Ju^r	16-50 A	
Charles Holdon Elder	60+	
Wm Gorton Ju^r	16-50 A	
Wm Gorton the 3^d Prisoner	"	
Oliver Gorton	"	
Edward Gorton the 3^d	"	
Caleb Greene son of Rich^d	"	
Daniel Brayton	"	
John Warner Ju^r	"	
John Wells	60+	
John Green son of Rich^d	16-50 A	
Nathl Mumford	"	R-Newport
Richard Mumford	"	R-Newport
Godfrey Greene	"	
Cato Mumford	N "	R-Newport
Thos Greene Son of Rich^d	16-50 A	
Benj^a Gorton Mariner	"	
Beckus Gorton	N 50-60 U	
Tom Gorton	N 16-50 A	
Randal Holdon	50-60 A	
Anthony Holdon son of Randal	16-50 A	
Randal Holdon Ju^r	"	

1777 MILITARY CENSUS
WARWICK, RHODE ISLAND

Page 6 (cont)

David Arnold	16-50 A	
Nathan Westcot Ju^r	"	
Thomas Westcot	"	
Caleb Westcot	"	
Robert McNear	"	
Thos Wicks	60+	
Saul Wicks	N 50-60 U	

Totals:

25	16-50 A	2	50-60 A
3	50-60 U	3	60+
6	R	4	N

Page 7

Samuel Bennit	16-50 A	R-Cranstown
John Edmunds	"	R-Coventry
Wm Church	"	
Anthony Church	"	
Daniel Snell	"	
Wm Bennet	60+	
Jonathan Bennet	16-50 U	
Benjamin Vaughan	16-50 A	
Wm Spencer	"	
Oliver Baker	"	
Jeremiah Baker	"	
Elisha Baker Ju^r	"	
Job Whipple	"	
Elisha Baker	60+	
James Baker	16-50 A	
George Baker	"	
Moses Burlingame Ju^r	"	
A Benj^a Ellis	60+	
Benj^a Ellis Ju^r	16-50 A	
John Greene		
Son of Rich^d	16-50 U	
Andrew Barton	60+	
Joseph Barton	16-50 A	
Wm Potter	50-60 A	
Olney Potter	16-50 A	
Pardon Potter	"	
Wm Holdon	60+	
Wm Holdon Ju^r	16-50 A	
Charles Holdon Ju^r	"	
Anthony Holdon	"	
John Holdon (CS)	"	
John Holdon Esqr	60+	

Page 7 (cont)

Thos Holdon	16-50 A	
Peter Holdon	N 16-50 A	
Jacob Holdon	N "	

Totals:

25	16-50 A	2	16-50 U
1	50-60 A	6	60+
2	R	2	N

Page 8

Co^l Christopher Greene

Prisoner	16-50 A	
Job Greene son of Chri^o	"	
Jack Roberts	I 16-50 A	
Boston	N 16-50 U	
Caleb Hatheway	16-50 A	
Nathan Hatheway	"	
Thomas Cruff	"	
Isaac Matteson	16-50 U	
John Levalley	50-60 A	
Peleg Levally	16-50 A	
John Levally Ju^r	"	
Peter Levally Ju^r	"	
Peter Levally	"	
Josiah Levally	"	
Wm Levally	"	
Thomas Bartholick	"	
Moses Matteson	"	
Spencer Merril	"	
Joseph Arnold		
Son of Thos	"	
Charels Arnold	"	
Nathaniel Arnold		
Son of Thos	"	
Thos Arnold Son of Thos	"	
Thos Rice Esqr	60+	
Thos Rice the 4^h	16-50 A	
Wm Rice Son of Thos	16-50 U	
Anthony Remington	16-50 A	
Tony Rice	N 60+	
Abraham Chace	50-60 A	
Lory Chace	16-50 A	
Gorge Irish	16-50 A	R-Middle Town
John Weeden	"	R-James Town

1777 MILITARY CENSUS
WARWICK, RHODE ISLAND

Page 8 (cont)

Charles Attwood	16-50 A		
Wm Philips	"		
Thos Biddlecome	"		
Nehemiah Tubbs (CS)	"		

Totals:

28	16-50 A	3	16-50 U
2	50-60 A	2	60+
2	R	2	N	1 I

Page 9

Stephen Arnold 16-50 A
Edward Arnold 16-50 U
Benedict Arnold 16-50 A
Anthony Arnold "
Wm Waterman "
?Tony Waterman N 60+
Cesar Finch I 16-50 A
Israel Arnold 50-60 A
James Arnold
 Son of Elisha 50-60 A
David Arnold 16-50 A
George Arnold (CS) "
Samuel Gorton Doc^o 60+
Benj^a Gorton Ju^r 16-50 A
Slaid Gorton "
Wm Gorton "
Wm Wood the 3^d "
?Benoni Price 50-60 U
Mathew &
 Samuel Price 16-50 A
Joseph Arnold "
[torn] Arnold "
Elijah Johnson Ju^r "
Silvester Wicks "
David Wightman "
Reuben Wightman "
Silas Cook 16-50 U
Paul Greene 16-50 A Cert
John Greene
 Son of John 16-50 A Cert
Timothy Green " Cert
Job Carpenter "
Wilbour Carpenter "
Thos Carpenter "
Gideon Arnold "

Page 9 (cont)

Nathanil Millard 50-60 A
Hezekiah Millard 16-50 A
Spicer Millard "
Wm Wood 60+
Thomas Arnold 16-50 A
Randal Arnold "
Thos Remington 50-60 A
Benj^a Remington 16-50 A
John Remington (CS) "
Malachi Hammet (SM) "
John Arnold "
W^m ?Tibbett "
Samuel Baily " R-Richmond

Totals:
 [torn]

Page 10

Benj^a Nichols 16-50 A
Thom Nichols N 16-50 A
Simon I "
Stukely Barton 16-50 A
Benj^a Barton "
Ebenezer Slocum 50-60 U
Saml Sweet 16-50 A
Abraham Shoemake "
Philip Andrew "
Othniel Gorton 50-60 U
Prince Gorton N 16-50 A
Prosperous Gorton N "
Samuel Gorton
 Son of Doc^r (CS) 16-50 A
George Whitford "
Peleg Saulsbury "
Whitman Sweet 16-50 U
Peter Greene 16-50 A
Ebenezer Green "
Wm Greene Son of Eben^r "
Thos Tifferny "
Giles Peirs " R-East
 Greenwich
Thos Slocum "
Elijah Johnson 50-60 A
Elisha Carpenter 16-50 A
Caleb bently 16-50 U
John Allen 50-60 A

1777 MILITARY CENSUS
WARWICK, RHODE ISLAND

Page 10 (cont)

Jo^s & Charles Allen	16-50 A	
Pardon Allen	"	R-E.Green-wich
Jonathan Greene	"	
George Brightman	16-50 U	
Pierce Spencer	16-50 A	
Francis Matteson	60+	
Wm Matteson	16-50 A	
Jeremiah Baker	"	
Wm Arnold Son Elisha	60+	
Thos Arnold Son of W^m	16-50 A	
Wm Arnold the 3^d	"	
John & Daniel Clapp	"	
Thos Watt Ju^r	"	

Totals:

32	16-50 A	3	16-50 U
2	50-60 A	2	50-60 U
2	60+	2	R
3	N	2	I

Page 11

Dutee Jerauld	50-60 A	
Gorton Jerauld	16-50 A	
Samuel Peirce Ju^r	"	R-Pourts-mouth
Nathan Millard	"	
Nathan Millard Ju^r	"	
James Millard (SM)	"	
John Millard (SM)	"	
Caleb Carr	50-60 U	
Caleb Carr Ju^r	16-50 A	
Wm Talman	"	
David Greene	"	
Ben Lippitt	N "	
Ben Pegg	I 50-60 A	
John Greene Son D	16-50 A	
John Ladd Ju^r	"	
Henry Rice	50-60 U	
Henry Rice Ju^r	16-50 A	
Job Rice	"	
John Rice	"	
Squire Millerd	"	
Samuel Millerd	"	
John Millerd Ju^r	"	
Joseph Briggs	"	

Page 11 (cont)

Noah Doud	16-50 A	
Ezekiel Doud	"	
Job Greene Ju^r	"	R-Coventry
Wm Arnold	60+	
James Talman	50-60 A	
Jonathan Slocum	16-50 A	
Pero Slocum	N 60+	
Benj^a Howland	16-50 A Cert	
Peleg Remmington	50-60 A	
Elisha Remmington	16-50 A	
Abel Bennit	"	
Benedict Remmington (SM)	"	
Stukely Wicks	"	
Benj^a Wever	16-50 U	

Totals:

28	16-50 A	1	16-50 U		
4	50-60 A	2	50-60 U		
2	60+	1	Cert		
2	R	2	N	1	I

Page 12

Joseph Green	N 16-50 A	
Jeremiah Green	N "	
Wm Greene Son of John	16-50 A	
Seth Davis	"	
Wm Batty	50-60 A	
Joseph Batty	16-50 A	
Job Smith	"	
Nathaniel Chatman	"	
Thomas Sweet	50-60 A	
Stephen Sweet	16-50 A	
Ambrous Taylor	"	
Oliver Arnold	"	
Jeremiah Clerk	"	
York Clerk	N 16-50 A	
Cesar Clerk	N "	
Sion Arnold	16-50 A	
David Knap	60+	
Peleg Remmington Son of Danl Prisoner	16-50 A	
Simeon Palmer	60+	
Samuel Potter	50-60 U R-Cranstown	
John Rhodes	16-50 A	

1777 MILITARY CENSUS
WARWICK, RHODE ISLAND

Page 12 (cont)

Wm G. Rhodes	16-50 A	
Simeon Arnold	16-50 U Aff	
Lemuel Arnold	16-50 A	
Christopher Vaughn	"	
Caleb Batty	50-60 A	
Benj^a Batty	"	
Sampson Batty	"	
Newport Batty	N 50-60 A	
Joseph Hicks	60+	
Rufis Barton	60+	
Benj^a Stone	60+	
Joseph Whitney	16-50 A	
James Carder	60+	
James Carder Junr	16-50 A	

Totals:
   24 16-50 A   1 16-50 U
    3 50-60 A   1 50-60 U
    6 60+   1 Aff
    1 R   5 N

Page 13

Silas Casey	16-50 A	
Wanton Casey	"	
Moses Casey	N 16-50 A	
Walter Casey	N "	
John Casey	16-50 A R-to Newport	
	Cert	
Gideon Freeborn	16-50 A	
Daniel Austin	16-50 U R-to Newport	
Peleg Olin	16-50 A	
Dutee Weever	"	
Benj^a Jenkins (CS)	"	
Eliazer Trivett	60+	R-Newport
John Trivett (CS)	16-50 A R-Newport	
Oliver Gardner	"	
John Howland	"	R-James Town
Robin Howland	N "	R-James Town
Dick Howland	N "	R-James Town
John Lilly	16-50 A	
Peleg Eldrid	"	R-James Town
Eldridge Spink (SM)	"	
Wm Conklin	"	T-Old
		Countryman
George Harrison	"	R-Newport
Daniel Remmington	60+	

Page 13 (cont)

Daniel Remmington Ju^r	16-50 U	
Holdon Rhodes	16-50 A	
John Gorton Elder	16-50 U	
John Gorton Ju^r	16-50 A	
Bowen Gorton	"	
Charles Briggs	"	
Aron Wilen (CS)	"	R-Maryland
John Stafford	"	
Nathan Price	60+	
Wm Price	16-50 A	
Randal Price (SM)	"	

Totals:
   27 16-50 A   2 16-50 U
    1 50-60 A   3 60+
    1 Cert   1 T
   10 R   4 N

Page 14

Barner Wicks	N 16-50 A	
Henry Wicks	N "	
Benedict Arnold		
Prisoner	16-50 A	
Joseph Lippitt Esqr	60+	
Thomas Lippitt	16-50 U	
Parris Lippitt	N 50-60 A	
Jube Lippitt	N 16-50 A	
Prisoner		
Benj^a Gorton	16-50 A	
Abraham Anthony	60+ Cert	
David Anthony	16-50 A Cert	
Job Anthony	"	Cert
John Wicks	"	
Moses Lippitt Ju^r	"	
Wm Lippitt	"	
Cuff Lippitt	N 16-50 A	
Jeremiah Westcot	16-50 A R-Cranstown	
John Lippitt	"	
Primus Lippitt	N 50-60 A	
Prince Lippitt	N 16-50 A	
Sili Lippitt	N "	
James Lippitt	N "	
Wm Warner	16-50 A	
Sam. Warner	N 16-50 A	
Stephen Low	60+	
Stephen Low Ju^r	16-50 A	

1777 MILITARY CENSUS
WARWICK, RHODE ISLAND

Page 14 (cont)

Tony	N 16-50 A	
Thomas Stafford	16-50 A	
Fortune Stafford	N 16-50 A	
Jonathan Pierce	50-60 U R-Portsmouth	
John Greene	60+	
Stephen Greene	16-50 A	
James Greene	N 60+	
Moses Lippitt	16-50 U	
Abraham Lippitt	"	
Cesar Lippitt	N 16-50 A	

Totals:

24	16-50 A	3	16-50 U
2	50-60 A	1	50-60 U
5	60+	3	Cert
2	R	14	N

Page 15

George Arnold	16-50 U	
James Arnold Ju^r	50-60 A	
Philip Arnold		
Son of James	16-50 A	
Moses Arnold	"	
Daniel Cory	50-60 A R-North Kingstown	
Benj^a Arnold		
Son of Simeon	16-50 A	
Israel Arnold	"	
Stephen Smith Ju^r	"	
James Aborn	"	
John Aborn	"	
Thos Howard	"	
Samuel Aborn	"	
Lowry Aborn (CS)	"	
Robert Rhodes	"	
Malachi Rhodes	"	
Silvester Rhodes	"	
Stephen Smith	60+	
James Rhodes	60+	
Job Randal	16-50 A	
Thos Remmington		
Son of Peleg	"	
John Randal	"	
Jeremiah Randal	"	
Joseph Randal	"	
Zachariah Rhodes (CS)	"	

Page 15 (cont)

Aborn Thornton (CS)	16-50 A	
Christopher Thornton	"	
Solomon Thornton	"	
James Whitney	"	
John Rice		
Son of Benj^a	"	
Wm Holdridge	"	
John Stone	"	
Olney Stone	"	
James Arnold the 5th	"	
Gilbert Potter	"	
Stephen Greene	"	
Rhodes Greene	"	

Totals:

31	16-50 A	1	16-50 U		
2	50-60 A	2	60+	1	R

Page 16

Benoni Waterman	60+	
Col^l John Waterman	16-50 A	
Benj^a Waterman	"	
John Waterman Ju^r	"	
Cuff Waterman	N 16-50 A	
Prince Waterman	N "	
Ebenezer Matteson	16-50 A R-Portsmouth	
Abraham Lockwood	"	
Nathaniel Cole	"	
John Cole	"	
John Warner Esqr	50-60 A	
Thos Warner	16-50 A	
Joseph Whipple	"	
Adam Lockwood	"	
Benajah Lockwood	"	
Caleb Green		
Son of Jonath^n	"	
Joshua Straight (SM)	"	
Amos Lockwood	"	
John Allen	50-60 A R-Portsmouth	
Durfy Allen	16-50 A R-Portsmouth	
Zebulon Utter	50-60 U	
Josiah Arnold	50-60 A	
Christopher Arnold	16-50 A	
Jesse Arnold	"	
Sampson Spywood	I 16-50 A	
Philip Greene Esqr	60+	

1777 MILITARY CENSUS
WARWICK, RHODE ISLAND

Page 16 (cont)

Wm Greene Esqr	
Son of Philip	16-50 A
Jack Greene	N 16-50 A
Pero Greene	N "
Cesar Greene	N "
Prims Greene	N 60+
Richard Greene	16-50 A
Benjaman E. Greene	"
Lewis S. Greene	"
Aron Saulsbury	16-50 U

Totals:

27	16-50 A	1	16-50 U	
3	50-60 A	1	50-60 U	
3	60+	3	R	
6	N	1	I	

Page 17

Elihu Greene	16-50 A
Christopher Greene	
Son of Nathl	"
Perry Greene	"

Page 17 (cont)

The Sum Total:

444	16-50 A	26	16-50 U	39	50-60 A	16 50-60 U	59 60+ 2 Aff
13	Cert	1	T	41	R	59 N	11 I

Page 17 (cont)

Daniel Sweet	16-50 A
Daniel Sweet Ju^r	16-50 U
Benjamin Pierce	50-60 A
Nathaniel Pierce	16-50 A
Thos Spiner	"
John Spencer	50-60 A
Sweet Briggs	16-50 A
Hugh Essex	50-60 A
John Essex	16-50 A
Corps Essex	"
Daniel Scranton	60+
Wm Corey (SM)	16-50 A
Oliver Corey (SM)	"
William Greene Esqr	"
Cesar	N 50-60 U
Cato	N 16-50 A
Cudjo	N "
Tony	N " R-Newport
Charles Ward	16-50 A R-Westerly

Totals:

16	16-50 A	1	16-50 U
3	50-60 A	1	50-60 U
2	R	4	N

April 17th 1777 These may Certify that James Jereld who was appointed at the Last Sessions of Assembly to Take the Number of all the male Persons of Sixteen years of age and upwards in the Town of Warwick Appeared before me and Solomly Declard that the within List by him Taken is a true and Perfect List to the Best of his Judgment

James Arnold   Assistant

Page 17 reverse

This List Contains the Whole agreeable to the Act of the General Assembly

1777 MILITARY CENSUS
WESTERLY, RHODE ISLAND

Page 1

Joseph Babcock Jr	16-50 A	
Amos Pendleton	"	
Joseph Saunders	50-60 A	
David Taylor	50-60 U	
Humphry Taylor	Aff	
Christopher Babcock	50-60 A	
William Greene	16-50 U	
Joseph Davis	16-50 A	
Elhanah Babcock	"	
Edward Bliven	50-60 A	
Peleg Sisson	"	
Samuel Champlin	"	
John West	"	
Job Bennet	50-60 U	
	N 1	
John Greene	16-50 A	T-Exeter
William Scrivan	50-60 A	
Samuel Tribby	50-60 U	T-Newport
	N 1	
John Lewis	50-60 U	
Joshua Vose Jr	16-50 A	
George Sheffield	50-60 U	
Ethan Clarke	16-50 A	T-Hopkinton
	N 1	
John Tefft	16-50 A	
Nathan Babcock 2d	"	
Nathan Lanpher	50-60 U	
John Latham	50-60 A	
Sumnor Chapman	"	
John Bours	16-50 A	
	N 2	
Joseph Clark Jr	50-60 A	
Ebenezer Brown	"	
Joseph Hall	"	
John Ross	"	
Joseph Lewis	"	
Thomas Sisson	50-60 U	
Isaac Babcock	"	
Oliver Gavit	16-50 U	
James Saunders	50-60 A	
Nathan Barber	16-50 A	

Totals:

11	16-50 A	2	16-50 U		
15	50-60 A	8	50-60 U		
1	Aff	3	T	5	N

Page 2

William Babcock	50-60 A	
Daniel Maxson	16-50 A	
Jeremiah Willcox	50-60 A	T-South Kingston
Robert Burdick	60+	
Jonathan Burdick	60+	
David Burdick	60+	
Nathan Babcock	60+	
Joshua Babcock Esq	60+	
Ichabod Babcock	60+	
Samuel Brand	60+	
Richard Berry	60+	
William Chapman	60+	
Joseph Clarke	60+	
Joseph Crandal	60+	
Joseph Crandal son of Eber	60+	
Joseph Crumb	60+	
Daniel Collins	60+	T-Stonington
William Davis	60+	
William Davis son of Peter	60+	
Peter Davis	60+	
Jonathan Foster	60+	
Ezekiel Gavit	60+	
William Hiscox	60+	
Ephraim Hiscox	60+	
Thomas Hiscox	60+	
Daniel Lanpher	60+	
David Lewis	60+	
John Maxson	60+	
Sanford Noyes	60+	
William Pendleton	60+	
John Peckham	60+	
Isaac Peckham	60+	
Ebenezer Rathbun	60+	
William Ross	60+	
	N 1	

Totals:

1	16-50 A	2	50-60 A		
31	60+	2	T	1	N

Page 3

Seth White	60+	T-State Boston
Christopher Sugar	60+	
Elias Thompson	60+	

1777 MILITARY CENSUS
WESTERLY, RHODE ISLAND

Page 3 (cont)

Joshua Thompson	60+	
	N 2	
Joshua Vose	60+	
	N 1	
Theodaty Vosse	60+	
Elisha Willcox	60+	
Isaiah Willcox	Aff	
Oliver Dodge	Aff	
John Bliven	Aff	
Stephen Willcox	Aff	
David Willcox	Aff	
John Lewis 3[d]	Aff	
James Babcock Carp[n]	Aff	
David Willbur	Aff	
Artillery etc.		
James Babcock Jr	16-50 A	
	N 1	
Peleg Pendleton L	16-50 A	
John Pendleton	"	
Nathan Pendleton	"	
Amos Pendleton Jr.	"	
Andrew Pendleton	"	
Isaac Pendleton	"	
Timothy Beegly	"	T-Newport
James Cheesebrough	"	T-Stonington
Amos Dickins	"	T-New Shoreham
Joseph Burdick	"	T-New Shoreham
Oliver Burdick	"	
Langworthy Lanpher	"	
Nathan Babcock Jr	"	

Militia first Company

Joseph Pendleton Cap[t]	"	
Joshua Pendleton Lieu[t]	"	
Ephraim Pendleton Ens[n]	"	
George Foster	"	

Totals:
    17 16-50 A   7 60+
     8 Aff   5 T   4 N

Page 4

Nathan Crary	16-50 A	T-Stonington
Silas Champlin	"	
Oliver Lewis	"	

Page 4 (cont)

Hezekiah Lewis	16-50 A	
Elias Lewis	"	
Samuel West	"	
Robert Thompson	"	
John Allen	"	
John Willbur	"	
Jeremiah Willbur	"	
Robert Willcox	"	T-South Kingston
Maxson Burdick	"	
Arnold Willcox	"	T-South Kingston
Ezekiel Gavit Jr	"	
Simeon Pendleton	"	
Jabez Cheesebrough	"	
Naham Babcock	"	
Samuel Brown	"	
Simeon Lewis	"	
Enock Crandal	"	
William Sheffield	"	
Samuel Babcock	"	
William Rhodes	"	
Caleb Pendleton	"	
Joseph Willbur	"	
Isaac Thompson	"	
John Thompson	"	
Samuel Brand Jr.	"	
John Burdick Jr	"	
Frederick Chase	"	
Aziel Gean	"	
Hezekiah Willcox Jr	"	
Benjamin Lanpher	"	
Caleb Pendleton Jr	"	

Totals:
    34 16-50 A   3 T

Page 5

Militia

William Lewis	16-50 A	
Walter Brand	"	
Benjamin Pendleton	"	
David Latham	"	
Seth White Jr	"	
James White	"	T-State Boston
Elias Hedges	"	T-Long Island
Noah Bradford	"	T

1777 MILITARY CENSUS
WESTERLY, RHODE ISLAND

Page 5 (cont)

Adam Stales	16-50 A
Samuel Babcock Jr	"
Daniel Willcox	"
Peleg Willcox	"
Philip Driskell Jr	"
William Driskel	"
Thompson Burdick	"
William Babcock Jr	"
Joseph Latham	"
Nathan Barber Jr	"
[blank] Barber	"
Lewis Crandal	"
Arnold Kinyon	"
Jonathan Lanford	"
Samuel Thompson	"
Jonathan Foster Jr	"

The 2^{d} Company Militia

John Gavit Capt	16-50 A
Stephen Saunders Lieut	"
William Bliven Ens^{n}	"
Wm Sweet Peckham	"
Joseph Peckham	"
John Ross Jr	"
James Ross	"
Edward Ross	"
Phineas Crandal	"
Joseph Noyes Jr	"
Sanford Noyes Jr	"

Totals:
   35 16-50 A   3 T

Page 6

Militia

Henry Babcock	16-50 A
Samuel Champlin Jr	"
Aaron Davis	"
Clarke Crandal	"
Joseph Saunders Jr	"
Roger Clarke	"
Joshua Chase	"
Jesse Ross	"
Lebbeus Ross	"
Charles Hall	"
Charles Hall Jr	"
Asa Burdick	16-50 U

Page 6 (cont)

Isaac Hall	16-50 A
Thomas Hall	"
Abel Peckham	"
Bradick Peckham	"
Charles Saunders	"
Cornelius Stetson	"
Augustus Saunders	"
Peleg Saunders Jr	"
Benjamin Hull	"
Thomas Hull	"
Rhodes Hale	"
William Ross Jr	"
Edward Saunders Jr.	"
James Saunders Jr	"
Nathan Greenman	"
Isaac Carr	" T-Newport
Walter White	" T-Hopkinton
John Scriven	"
William Scriven Jr	"
Isaac Peckham Jr	"
Hezekiah Gavit	"
Isaiah Gavit	"
Christopher Crandal	"
Eldridge Crandal	"
John Brand	"
John Prentice Babcock	"
Jeffery G[avit]	16-50 U

Totals:
   37 16-50 A   2 16-50 U   2   T

Page 7
Militia

Henry Champlin	16-50 A
Jude Taylor	"
Gideon Frazier	"
Rowland Champlin	"
Sanford Gavit	"
George Gavit	"
Stephen Gavit Jr	"
Valentine Willcox	"
Ichabod Babcock 3^{d}	"
James Babcock 3^{d}	"
Daniel Babcock	"
Arnold Bliven	"
George Bliven	"
William Davis 3^{d}	"

1777 MILITARY CENSUS
WESTERLY, RHODE ISLAND

Page 7 (cont)

James Davis	16-50 A	
Nicholas Davis	"	
Stephen Rathbun	"	
Paul Rathbun	"	
Jonathan Sisson	"	
Thomas Sisson Jr	"	
John Sisson	"	
George Sisson	"	
Edward Bliven Jr	"	
Ebenezer Rathbun Jr	"	
William Thompson	"	
David Clarke	"	
Samuel Greene	"	
Peleg Ross	"	
Peleg Ross Jr	"	
Nathaniel Lewis	"	T-Charles Town
Henry Crandal	"	
Arnold Crandal	16-50 U	
James Peckham	16-50 A	
Thompson Burdick	"	
Joseph Varin	16-50 U	T-Stonington
Joshua Burdick	"	
James Crandal	16-50 A	
Benjamin Willcox	16-50 U	

Totals:
  34 16-50 A   4 16-50 U   2 T

Page 8
Militia

Isaac Babcock Jr	16-50 A	
Amos Babcock	"	
Jesse Babcock	"	
Hezekiah Hall	"	T-Hopkinton
Elisha Sisson	"	
Peleg Sisson Jr	"	
Daniel Peckham	"	T-Middle Town
William Babcock 3d	"	
Oliver Champlin	"	
Joshua Saunders	"	T-Charles Town
Jonathan Crandal	"	
Joshua Peckham	"	T-Middle Town
Thomas Babcock	"	

Page 8 (cont)

3d Company Militia

George Stillman Capt	16-50 A
Peleg Saunders Lieut	"
Asa Maxson Ensn	"
David Saunders	"
Stephen Lewis	"
Clarke Stillman Jr	"
Joseph Potter	"
Haron Lanpher	"
Arnold Burdick	"
David Hiscox	"
William Clarke	"
Amos Maxson	"
Amos Lanpher	"
George Clarke	"
Thomas Clarke	"
Paul Maxson	"
John Chapman	"
Joseph Davis Jr	"
Joshua Clarke	"
Paul Babcock	"
Timothy Chapman	"
John Cottrel Jr	"
Charles Greene	"
Joshua Saunders	"

Totals:
   37 16-50 A   4 T

Page 9
Militia

Nathan Hiscox	16-50 A
Abram Perkins	"
Simeon Pendleton	"
Elias Cottrel	"
Thomas Brand	"
Thomas Edwards	"
David Lanpher	"
Joseph Crandal 3d	"
James Pendleton Jr	"
Perry Brombly	"
Elijah Berry	"
Samuel Clarke	"
Joseph Stillman Jr	"
Daniel Lanpher 3d	"
Daniel Lanpher Jr	"
Abraham Lanpher	"

1777 MILITARY CENSUS
WESTERLY, RHODE ISLAND

Page 9 (cont)

Silas Baily	16-50 A	
Nathan Clarke	"	
Gideon Pendleton	"	
Stephen Pendleton	"	
Arnold Clarke	"	
Nicholas Clarke	"	
George Potter	"	
Christoʳ Clarke	"	
William Holmes	"	T-Stonington
William Smith	"	
John Stillman Jr	"	
David Corp	"	T-West Greenwich
Nahor Lanpher	"	
Joseph Crumb Jr	"	
David Crumb	"	
Samuel Lanpher	"	
George Stillman Jr	"	
Nathan Lanpher Jr	"	
Elias Crandal	"	
Nathan Stillman	"	
Wait Stillman	"	
Sylvester Crumb	"	
Plumb Chapman	"	

Totals:
    39 16-50 A   2 T

Page 10

Samuel Allen	16-50 A
John Cottrel	50-60 A
Stephen Gavit	50-60 U
Thomas Ross	"
Hezekiah Saunders	16-50 A
Joseph Maxson	"
John Burdick	50-60 A
Philip Driskil	"
William Crumb	50-60 U
Samuel Pendleton	50-60 A
Andrew Champlin	"
Isaac Ross	"
Oliver Babcock	16-50 U
Nathan Bliven	16-50 A
James Brown	50-60 U
[torn ?John] Stillman	"
[torn ?Samuel Bliven]	16-50 A

Page 10 (cont)

Abel Larkin	16-50 A	
Joseph Gavit	Aff	
William Vincent	16-50 A	
Theodaty Hall	50-60 U	
Elisha Clarke	50-60 A	
Thomas Rathbun	"	
Elisha Sanford	"	T-Newport
Ichabod Clarke	"	
George Potter	16-50 A	
Peter States	"	
Joseph Hiscox	50-60 U	
Edward Saunders	"	
Samuel Berry	16-50 A	
Simeon Burdick	50-60 A	
Daniel Clarke	"	
Silas Greenman	"	
David Maxson	"	
Phineas Clarke	16-50 A	
Joshua Crandal	16-50 U	
Hezekiah Willcox	16-50 A	
William Crandal	50-60 A	
Col. Jonᵃ Hedges	"	T-Long Island

Totals:
    12 16-50 A   2 16-50 U
    16 50-60 A   8 50-60 U
     1 Aff   2 T

Page 11

William Chapman Jr	16-50 U
Joseph Stillman	16-50 A
Arnold Lewis	"
Adam Crandal	"
Joshua Hiscox	"
Edward Hiscox	"
George Lanpher	"
Elijah Crandal	"
Benjamin Herrick	"

Totals:
    8 16-50 A   1 16-50 U

1777 MILITARY CENSUS
WESTERLY, RHODE ISLAND

Page 11 (cont)

Totals:
   265 16-50 A   11 16-50 U   33 50-60 A   16 50-60 U   38 60+   10 Aff
    28 T   10 N   346 Westerly Residents

Pursuant to the Act of the General Assembly to me Directed have according to the
best of my Knowledge taken a List of all the Male persons in the Town of Westerly
in the State of Rhode Island Agreeable in my Judgment to the subsequent List with-
out sensible Error is Given under my Hand at Westerly April 16th 1777

                         Joseph Crandal) Commttee Man

To my Time Horse Ride & Expences   )
Four Days Which I Submit to the   ) £9/6
Honorable the General Assembly   ) Jos. Crandal

State of Rhode Island Providence Plantations Kings County Westerly 16th April 1777
The above Subscriber Joseph Crandal Esq. Personally appeared & made Oath that he
had justly & truly made the foregoing Lists According to the best of his Knowledge

                        Before --- Joseph Clarke Justice Peace

WEST GREENWICH, RHODE ISLAND

Page 1

George Matteson	16-50 A	R-?
Gorge Jenkins	"	R-?
Samuel Jordun	"	R-?
George Vaughan	50-60 A	
Job Whitford Ju	16-50 A	R-?
Gardner Briggs	"	R-Rhod Island
Justous Ellas	"	
George Niles	"	
George Vaughan Jur	"	
Gideon Ellis Jur	"	
Henry Hopkins	"	
Henry Sweet	16-50 U	
Abel Casey	16-50 A	
Hezekiah Myus	"	
Henry Olin	50-60 A	
Henry Olin Jur	16-50 A	
Hezekiah Gorton	"	
Henry Tanner	"	
Henry Reynolds Jur	"	
Henry Matteson	"	
Henry Reynolds	50-60 A	
Henry Nichols	16-50 U	
John Albro	16-50 A	

Page 1 (cont)

Jonathan Dean	16-50 A
Thomas Stone	"
Job Strait	"
Joseph James	"
John Matteson	
Son of abr	"
Jishmael Comstock	"
Job Matteson	"
John Niles	60+
Joseph Wood	16-50 A
John Casey	50-60 A
Jeremiah Weight	16-50 A
Job Whitford	16-50 U
Joseph Weaver	16-50 A
Samuel Rathbon	"

Totals:
    29 16-50 A   3 16-50 U
     4 50-60 A   1 60+   5 R

Page 2

John Tillinghast	60+
John Sweet	16-50 A

1777 MILITARY CENSUS
WEST GREENWICH, RHODE ISLAND

Page 2 (cont)

Samuel Philips	60+
Jeremiah Austen	16-50 A
Joseph Nichols	60+
Jonathan Cumstock	Aff
Jonathan Matteson	60+
Jonathan Matteson Jun	16-50 A
John Matteson	60+
Job Matteson Ju^r	16-50 A
John Matteson Ju^r	"
Gideon Weight	"
John Hall	"
James Moon	50-60 A
Joseph Green	"
Josiah Sweet	"
Judadiah Alesworth	16-50 A
Joseph Draper	"
John Briggs	"
John Parker	"
John Weight	"
John Casey Ju^r	"
James Tanner	"
John Strait	60+
Josiah Matteson	50-60 A
John Case Ju^r	16-50 A
John Case	50-60 A
Eleazer Burlinggame	16-50 A
Alexander Stone	"
James Reynolds	60+
Joseph Niles	60+
John Stanton	16-50 A
Josiah Brown	"
Joseph Case	"
Joseph Jefry	"
Joseph Hogekins	"
Job Herrington	"
Job Herrington Ju^r	"
Whitman Herrington	"
Timothy Weaver	"
Benjamin Weaver	"
Caleb Shippey	" R-State of Masachuset Bay
Nathanael Harloo	"

Totals:
29 16-50 A   5 50-60 A
 8 60+   1 Aff   1 R

Page 3

Thomus Colegrove	16-50 A
Jessey Colegrove	"
Job Whitford Jun	"
Sweet Whitford	"
Joseph Niles Jun	"
Samuel Niles Jun	"
Job Spencer	"
Charles hopkins	"
William hopkins Jun	"
Robart Carr	"
Ruben hopkins	"
Eabennezer Thomas	"
parden tillinghast Ju	"
thomus tillinghast Ju	"
John tillinghast Ju	"
William Case	"
Clark Rathboun	"
presarvid hall Jun	"
Gustous? Ellis	"
Jeremiah Ellis	"
Oliver Cottrill	"
William Gardner	"
Samuel Gallup	"
Uriah Stone	"
Uriah Matteson	"
William Baker	"
William Manchester	"
William Nichols	"
William Cumstock	"
William Sweet Ju	"
William hopkins	60+
William Spink	16-50 A
William Matteson	"
William Sweet	60+
William Davis	16-50 A

Totals:
  33 16-50 A   2 60+

Page 4

Stephen Briggs	16-50 A
Samuel Reynolds	"
Simon Gates	"
Samuel Tanner	"
Samuel Niles	50-60 A
Samuel Casey	16-50 A

1777 MILITARY CENSUS
WEST GREENWICH, RHODE ISLAND

Page 4 (cont)

Samuel Hopkins	60+	
Samuel Hopkins Ju	16-50	A
Samuel Spencer	60+	
Samuel Wattson	50-60	A
Sanford Case	"	
Silous Matteson	16-50	A
Samuel Kiney	"	
Thomas Nichols	50-60	A
Thomus hovey	16-50	A
Thomus Gorton	"	
Thomus Reynolds	"	
Timothy Hall	50-60	A
Thomus Straight	60+	
Thomus Weaight	50-60	A
Thomus Tillinghast	16-50	A
Thomus Cook	60+	
Thomus Rogers	50-60	U
Tibbits Hopkins	50-60	A
Thomus Whitford	16-50	A
Matthew Remmonton	"	
Thomus Rathborn	"	
Thomus Matteson	"	
Thomus Willcox	"	
Thomus young	"	
Thomus Joslon	"	

Totals:
19 16-50 A   7 50-60 A
 1 50-60 U   5 60+

Page 5

Nathun Matteson	16-50	A
Nathanal Rathbons	"	
Nathanial Niles	60+	
Nathanial Brown	16-50	A
Nichalis Matteson	50-60	A
[blank] Conglon	16-50	A
Nichols Whitford	"	
Phillip Greene	60+	
presarvied hall	60+	
peter Crandel	16-50	A
purden tillinghast	"	
paskeo Whitford	60+	
phillip Sweet	60+	
pentous? Sweet	16-50	A
peter Lee	60+	

Page 5 (cont)

Paul Kiney	16-50	A
pelek Greene	"	
Richard Esex	"	
Ruffus austen	"	
Robart Godforey	"	
Robert Hall	"	
Robart austen	60+	
Ruffus Ellis	16-50	A
Robart hazard	"	
Randel Spencer	"	
Richard Winsor	"	
Robart Copander	[blank]	
John Cophander	16-50	A
Christpher Cophander	"	
Richard Matteson	"	
David Matteson Ju	"	
Abel Matteson	[blank]	
Ruffus Matteson	16-50	A
Sheffield Corey	"	

Totals:
24 16-50 A   1 50-60 A   7 60+

Page 6

John Brown	16-50	A
John hopkins	60+	
Jonathan Matteson		
sun Jo	16-50	A
Joseph hopkins Ju	"	
Joseph Dolver	16-50	U
Joseph Dolver Ju	16-50	A
Josiah Matteson Ju	"	
John Young	"	
John Kinyon	"	
John Reynolds	50-60	A
Joseph phulps	60+	
John Matteson Sun Jos	16-50	A
Joseph Gardner	"	
Benjamin Gardner	"	
James Matteson	60+	
Jonathan Greene	16-50	A
Jonathan Niles	"	
Job angel	"	
Jousha Carr	"	
John Weathers	"	
Joseph austin	"	

1777 MILITARY CENSUS
WEST GREENWICH, RHODE ISLAND

Page 6 (cont)

James Weaver	16-50 A
John Spink	"
James Convars	"
John Ellis	"
Joseph Reynolds	"
Job Straight	"
Michel Stafford	"
Muylon Kiney	60+
Nichols Johnson	16-50 A
Nichols Brown Jun	"
Nichols Ellis	"
Nichols Myous	"

Totals:
27 16-50 A   1 16-50 U
1 50-60 A   4 60+

Page 7

David Kynyoun	16-50 A
David Lews	"
David Matteson	"
David Hall	"
David Whitford	"
David Culver	"
David aylworth	"
David Hall Jun	"
David Straight	"
David Matteson	
sun Jont.	"
Danial Aurstin	"
David aylworth Jun	"
David Cumstock	"
Epheram Kittel	"
Edmond Kittel	"
William Kettel	"
William Vaghan	"
Clamment Weaver	"
Eseck Carr	"
Ebenezer Matteson	"
Edward Bulloson	"
Edmon Matteson	"
Elisha Case	"
Edward Kittel	"
Elisher Greene	"
Ellis austin	"
Ezekel Matteson	"

Page 7 (cont)

Elisha arnold	16-50 A
Elezer arnold	"
Edward Borse	"
Ebenezer Sweet	16-50 U
	60+
Ebenezer Hopkins	16-50 A
George Whitford	"
George Dyre	"
	50-60 A
Griffen Sweet	[blank]
Giden Ellis	[blank]
Thomas Matteson	
Sunto abraham	16-50 A
Giden Tripp	"
Robart Tripp	"

Totals:
36 16-50 A   1 16-50 U
1 50-60 A   1 60+

Page 8

Abel Greene	16-50 A
	60+
Arter aylworth	60+
amos Raynolds	16-50 A
	60+
Abel Matteson	"
Ams Ellis	[blank]
abel potter	[blank]
Addam Richmond	16-50 A
amos frink	"
amo Hall	"
Abraham Gammet	"
Alexander Hopkins	"
Abel potter Jun	"
Benjamin Greene	[blank]
Benjamin Jenkins	16-50 A
Benjamen tillinghast	50-60 A
Bendiek Covey	16-50 A
Benjamen Tanner	"
Benjamin Spink	"
	60+
Benjamin Johnson	"
Benjamen austen	"
Benjamin young	60+
Benjamin allin	16-50 A

1777 MILITARY CENSUS
WEST GREENWICH, RHODE ISLAND

Page 8 (cont)

Benjamon Weaver	[blank]
Caleb Carr	16-50 A
Caleb Arnold	16-50 U
Caleb Greene	16-50 A
Caleb Reynolds	"
	60+
Charles Carr	[blank]
Christpher Choandel	16-50 A
Caleb Baley	"
	Aff
Joseph Baley	16-50 A
Charles Cumstack	"
	60+
Caleb hall	[blank]
Jacob Lews	[blank]
Danial Lews	16-50 A

Totals:
    24 16-50 A   6 60+[sic]   1 Aff

Page 9

John Ellis	16-50 A R-Ne?
Daniel Ellis	"
Charles Winmore	"
amos Jakways	"
Job Cleveland	"
E-----h Briggs	"
Stephen Lewis	"
William Gials	50-60 A
Silous James	16-50 A
Danial Bates	"
Artur aylworth Jun	"
Judiah aylworth Ju	"
Stephen aylworth	"
Timothy hull Ju	"
abel potter the 3^{d}	"
James potter	"
William potter	"
William Kynnon	"
Solomon Baker	"
William headely	"
Joseph matteson	"
John Draper	"
Garner tanner	"
Joseph Jenny	"

Totals:
    23 16-50 A   1 50-60 A

Page 10

William Gillis	16-50 U	
William Barker	16-50 A	
Weareght Ellis	"	
Simmon Whitford	"	
Ruben Whitford	"	
Leuis Whitford	"	
John Comstock	16-50 U	
Samuel Dyre	"	
Walter Nichols	[blank]	
Benjamin Rows?	16-50 A	
George Tennent	[blank]	R-Newport
Jonathan Whitford	"	R-Newport
Jeremiah Ellis	50-60 U	
Pelick andrew	16-50 A	
William Constabel	"	
Samuel Spencer Jun	"	
Giden Myers	"	
Barney Hirrick	"	
Caleb Gates	"	
Simon Gats	"	
Luke Greene	"	
Pelick andrew	"	
Thomus andrew	"	
Thomus Weaight	"	
John Berrimen?	"	
Iasiah aylworth	"	
Thomus Stafford	"	

Totals:
    21 16-50 A   3 16-50 U   1 50-60 U

[bottom of page 3 has totals:]
265 16-50 A   10 16-50 U   22 50-60 A
  5 50-60 U   25 60+   1 Aff
  2 Cert   3 R   5 N

State of Rhode Island Ss
        West Greenwich April 18th 1777

    Whereas I the Subscriber was by the
Hon'ble Genl Assembly appointed to take
an Account of all the Male Inhabitants
in the Town of West Greenwich from 16
Years & upwards, agreeable thereto, I
have numbered the Male Inhabitants in
s^{d} Town according to the preceeding
Roll, & find that there are 265 Male

West Greenwich

1777 MILITARY CENSUS
WEST GREENWICH, RHODE ISLAND

Persons from Sixteen Years & upwards to fifty Years of Age able to bear Arms, 10 from 16 Years & upwards to 50 Years of Age unable to bear Arms; from 50 to 60 Years of Age Able to bear Arms 22 Male Persons from 50 to 60 Years of Age unable to bear Arms 5 Male Persons; from 60 Years of Age & upwards 25 Persons. Three Residents. One Person that hath taken the Affirmation, Two that hath Certificates; no Transient Persons; 5 Negros, all w.h Submitted by y[r] Honors hble Serv[t]

                                        Samuel Hopkins Juner

Kings County Ss April 18, 1777

          personally Appeard the above Subscriber and Made Oath to The
          truth of the aforewritten list before me.

                              W[m] Greene Just Sup[r] C[t]

          (Concluded)

                    ▰▰▰▰▰▰▰▰▰▰▰▰▰▰▰▰▰▰▰▰▰▰▰▰▰▰▰

Allen, Samuel 67, 128
  Simeon 65
  Stephen 8
  Stephen (Jr.) 8
  Thomas 3
  Timothy 27
  Volentine 83
  William 8, 72
  Wilm (Cpt.) 75
  Zachariah 69
  Zoheth 42
Allin, Benjamin 132
  Christopher 56
  Jonathan 56
  Nathan 58
  Samuel 58
  Thomas 56
  Thomas (Jr.) 56
  William 57
Allon, Jonthan 117
Almy, Gideon 106
  Gidn 106
  Jack 106
  John 106
  Joseph 106
  Sanford 109
  Sharper 110
  William 106
Alsbary, Job 86
Alsworth, Anthony 35
Alvason, David 35
Alverson, Caleb 52
  John 52
  Uriah 96
  William 52
Ambros, Israel 36
Amos, Richard 106
Amsbary, Jeremiah 27
Anderson, Thomas 27
Andres, Zepheniah 72
Andrew, Benja 18
  Charls 17, 18
  Elnathan 16
  Griffin 19
  James 16, 17
  James (Jr.) 87
  Jeremiah 87
  John 16, 88
  Noel 15
  Pelick 133
  Philip 119
  Silvister 18
  Thomus 133
  Thos 18
  William 16
Andrews, --n 3
  Benoni 34
  Edmund 34
  Epheriam (Jr.) 40
  Epherim 40

Andrews (cont.)
  Jams 85
  John 25, 38, 85
  John (Jr.) 39
  Jonathan 34
  Nathan 42
Angel, Abel 85
  Abraham 87
  Benjamin 87
  James 73
  Jerimiah 83
  Job 131
  John 73
  Jos 73
  Joseph 85
  Nathan 68
  Richard 82
  Samuel 68, 87
  Trimmen 73
Angell, Abraham 27
  Abram 93
  Abrum (Jr.) 90
  Andrew 81
  Benjamin 93
  Charles 92
  Daniel 52, 95
  Eber 93
  Elisha 62
  Enock (Cpt.) 63
  Eseck 62
  Ezekiel (Jr.) 93
  Fenner 94
  George 27
  Gideon 92
  Gideon (Jr.) 92
  Hedibiah 64
  Hope 64
  Isaac 63
  James 62, 63
  Jason 64
  Jesse 82
  John 93
  Jonathan 94
  Joshua 95
  Nehemiah 85
  Oliver 63
  Pardon 82
  Prince 52
  Rufus 63
  Solomon 92
  Stephen 91
  Thomas 27
  William 52
Anis, Obedias 63
Anthony, Abraham 121
  David 121
  Edward (Jr.) 105
  Job 121
  John 12
  Joseph 13

Anthony (cont.)
  Ruben 69
  William 108
Antony, David 63
Antram, Dirias 69
  William 52
Apling, Benjn 70
  John 70
  Thomas 70
  William 70
Appleby, James 90
  John 94
  Thomas 91
  Zebedee 94
Armes, John 75
Armstrong, Edward 102
  Elijah 43
  George 102
  Jese 41
  Michael 102
  Oliver 103
  Thomas 103
Arnold, (?) 119
  Aaron 42
  Abram 92
  Africa 116
  Alfred 70
  Amos 27
  Andrew 115
  Anthony 119
  Aza 92
  Benedick 40
  Benedict 119, 121
  Benja 92, 115, 122
  Benja (Jr.) 18
  Caleb 42, 61, 87, 90,
    116, 133
  Caleb (Jr.) 43
  Charels 118
  Christopher 69, 93, 122
  Christopher (Jr.) 69
  Cuff 116
  Daniel 93
  Daniel (Jr.) 92
  David 38, 70, 71, 118,
    119
  David (Jr.) 38
  Edmond 57
  Edmund 90
  Edward 45, 119
  Eleazer 52
  Elezer 132
  Elijah 94
  Elisha 91, 119, 120,
    132
  Enoch 95
  Ezekiel 93
  George 91, 119, 122
  Gideon 15, 119
  Henry 115

137

Baggs (cont.)
John (Jr.) 78
Bagley, Benja 95
Jooeph 63
Samuel 95
William 64
Bailey, Charke 76
John 35
Richard 76
Richard (Jr.) 76
William 35
Baily, Samuel 119
Silas 128
Baker, Abial 95
Abraham 38, 117
Benajah 88
Benjamin 79
Benjamin (Jr.) 76
Daniel 88
Elijah 79
Elisha 118
Elisha (Jr.) 118
George 82, 96, 118
James 100, 118
Jeremiah 118, 120
Jesse 113
John 87
Jonathan 116
Joseph 116
Josiah 79
Moses 117
Oliver 118
Pardon 117
Reuben 22
Seth 91
Seth (Jr.) 94
Solomon 133
Stephen 44
Thomas 25
William 24, 130
Baley, Caleb 133
George 36
Joseph 133
Josph 35
Lemuel 108
Nathaniel 53
Oliver 108
Samuel 18
William 108
Ballard, Andrew 42
Benja 93, 95
Epherim 39
Icabod 39
Jeremiah (III) 39
Jeremiah (Jr.) 39
Luke 39
Ballou, Aaron 95
Abner 27
Absalom 28
Ariel 27

Ballou (cont.)
Asa 28
Benjamin 28, 93
David 27
Edward 27
Elisha 28
Ezekiel 27
James 28
John 90
John (Jr.) 95
Joseph 28
Levi 27
Moses 95
Nathan 27
Noah 27
Noah (Jr.) 27
Reuben (Cpt.) 28
Richd 93
Seth 41
Simeon 92
William 27
Balloue, Stephen 94
Ballow, David 41
Barber, (?) 126
Benjamin 46, 78
Caleb 78, 79
Ezekiel 78
Ezekiel (Jr.) 78
James 99
John 47
Joseph 48
Joshua 76
Moses 98
Nathan 124
Nathan (Jr.) 126
Nicklis 49
Samuel 76
Thomas 46
William 48
Wm 99
Barbour, John 58
William 56
Bardain, Ebenezar 87
Barding, John 83
Bardne, Comfort 69
Barker, Abraham 66
Benja 104
Isaac 66
Peter 106
William 66, 133
Barnard, Jeseniar 91
Barnes, Benja 38
John 91
Joseph 44
Nathan 90
Barney, Israel 22
Barns, --eas 3
Daniel 40, 43
Elisha 84
John 3

Barns (cont.)
Levi 3
Mathew 43
Peleg 3
Samuel 3
Stephen 43
Thomas 43
William 43, 88
Barrow, Solomon 95
Bartan, Seth 72
Wilm 72
Bartholick, Thomas 118
Bartlet, Able 27
Abner 27, 44
Asa 27
Caleb 41
Daniel 27
Eber 27
Elisha 41
Ezra 44
Israel 28
Jacob 27
Jehu 28
Jeremiah 27
Job 28
John 27
Joseph 27
Joseph (Jr.) 27
Rufus 28
Samuel 91
Bartlett, John 8
John (Jr.) 8
Bartley, Isaac 68
Barton, Andrew 118
Benja 119
Benjamin 114
David 114
Haile 114
Joseph 118
Joseph B. 114
Richard 114
Rufis 121
Rufus 24
Stukely 119
William 112, 115
Basett, Joseph (Jr.) 44
Samuel 18
William 44
Basset, Joseph 91
William 48
Bassett, Caleb 8
Joseph 42
William 8
Bastow, Samuel 73
Bates, Asaph 21
Benoni 23
Danial 133
David 61
James 21
John 28

138

140

Budlong (cont.)
  Rhodes 116
  Samuel 19, 116
Buffington, William 4
Buffum, Benja 91
  Benjamin 90
  David 91
  James 91
  Joseph 90
  Joseph (Jr.) 94
  Moses 94
  William 91
Bugbee, Samuel 72
Bul, Samuel 34
Bull, Nathan 105
Bullingame, Benedick 40
  Benedick (Jr.) 39
  Thomas 40
Bullock, Christopher 81
  Ebnezer 80
  Leanox 6
  Leanox (Jr.) 6
  Simeon 6
Bulloson, Edward 132
Bunday, Silas 63
Bundy, Mark 41
Burdick, Able 47
  Adam 48
  Amos 46
  Arnold 127
  Asa 50, 126
  Clarke 98
  David 124
  Dyre 78
  Edmund 78
  Edward 47
  Elijah 49
  Elnathan 48
  Ephraim 8
  Gideon 8
  Hubart 50
  Hubrart 47
  Ichabod 8
  Jesse 47
  John 128
  John (Jr.) 50, 125
  Jonathan 8, 124
  Joseph 47, 125
  Joseph (Jr.) 48
  Joshua 127
  Libeus 47
  Luke 47
  Maxson 125
  Nathan 48
  Nathaniel 8, 47
  Oliver 125
  Parker 48
  Peleg 48
  Pery 47
  Peter 47

Burdick (cont.)
  Robert 48, 124
  Rufus 47
  Samll 8
  Silvester 8
  Simeon 128
  Thompson 126, 127
  Walter 8
  Weight 47
  William 47
  William B. 48
Burdk, Stephen 48
Burgess, Thomas 39
Burgis, James 22
  Jos. (Jr.) 26
  Thomas 63
Burk, James 71, 97
  Jos 70
  Wm 115
Burket, Arther 68
  Thomas 67
Burlingame, Gidn 82
  Moses (Jr.) 118
  Silas 80
Burlinggam, Benja 19
  Daniel 19
  Eseik 19
  Joseph 19
  Stephen 19
  William 20
Burlinggame, Eleazer 130
Burlingham, Abnor 80
  Chandley 35
Burlison, John 16
  John (Jr.) 16
Burllingame, David 38
  Elisha 43
  Ezikiel 44
  Peter 26
Burllinggame, Abraham 87
  Benja 25
  Caleb 25
  Daniel 28
  Elisha 24
  Hopkins 25
  James 25
  Jeremiah 25
  John 28
  John (Jr.) 28
  Jonathan 25
  Joshua 25
  Nathan 25
  Nehemiah 24
  Pardon 25
  Peter 25
  Peter (III) 24
  Philip 25
  Roger 23, 53
  Samuel 25
  Samuel (Jr.) 23, 25

Burllinggame (cont.)
  Stephen 25
Burllingham, Jeremiah 94
Burn, Simon 7
Burns, Robert F. 1
Burr, David 67
  David (Jr.) 67
  James 70
  Joshua 71
  Levi 73
  Samuel 112
  Shubeal 112
Burrel, James 74
Burrell, Ebenezer 73
  Jos 73
  Jos. (Jr.) 73
Burrington, Abraham 107
  Robert 107
Burrlingame, Thomas (Jr.)
    40
Burrough, Daniel 22
  John 65
  Wm 65
Burroughs, Peleg 109
  William 109
Burton, Benjamin 26
  David 24
  George 26
  John 26
  John (Jr.) 24
  Rufus 26
  William 26
Bush, Richard 103
  Richard (Jr.) 103
Bushe, James 4
Bushee, James 111
Bussey, John 38
  William 40
Butler, Benjamin 28
  Samuel 72
  Samuel (Jr.) 72
Butterrix, Edward 27
Butterworth, Benjamin 114
  Hezekiah 114
  John 28, 113
  Joseph 114
  Noah 28
  Noah (Jr.) 28
Button, Daniel 47
  David 49
  Isaiah 47
  John 47
  Joshua 48
  Rufus 49
  Samll 48, 49
  Siras 50
  William 47
Butts, Thomas 110
Buxston, Henry 41
  John 94

Buxton, Aaron 91
  Caleb 90, 91
  James 91
  Samuel 90, 91
Caff, James 12
Cahoon, Benja 18
  Joseph 18
Cain, Thomas 72
Calvin, Morgan 33
Campbell, Joseph 59
  Nicholas 112
  Othniel 108, 110
Canaday, Alexander 81
Caperin, Charles 93
Caperon, Benjamin 35
Capron, Charles 28
  Jonathan 34
  Joseph 28
  Philip 28
  William 69
Captener, Daniel 49
Capwell, James 15
  Jeremiah 15
  Petter 19
  Stephen 15
  Stephen (Jr.) 15
  William 19
Card, Abraham 98
  Aechus 9
  Augustus 9
  Benjamin 77
  Bowen 58
  Edward 23
  Elisha 98
  Henry 105
  James 98
  Job 9, 35, 58, 98
  John 8
  John (Jr.) 9
  Jonathan 9, 58, 105
  Jonathan (Jr.) 58
  Joseph 35
  Joshua 9
  Joshua (Jr.) 9
  Phillip 57
  Samuel 105
  Shadreck 98
  Stephen 59, 117
  Weeden 8
  William 9, 57, 58, 65,
    98
Carder, James 121
  James (Jr.) 121
Carey, John 53
  Thomas 53
Cargill, James 28
Carpendar, John 85
Carpenter, (?) (Col.) 34
  Asa 28
  Benajah 102

Carpenter (cont.)
  Benja 53
  Caleb 103
  Cud 102
  Cyril 85
  Daniel 102
  Daniel (Jr.) 51
  Elisha 22, 119
  Ephraim 102
  Ephram 67
  Ezekiel 28
  Francis 58
  Garsham 65
  Hezechiah 46
  Israel 53
  James 102
  Jemmy 102
  Job 119
  John 65, 74, 94
  Jonathan 23
  Jonathn 98
  Joseph 90, 103
  Jotham 29
  Jotham (Jr.) 29
  Nathaniel 61
  Nicholas 53
  Oliver 29, 56
  Ollever 74
  Silas 22
  Thoms 103
  Thos 119
  Thos. (Jr.) 104
  Timothy 73
  Warterman 73
  Wilbour 119
  William 25, 28
Carpinter, Comfort 86
Carr, (?) (Cpt.) 6
  Benjamin 52
  Caleb 59, 112, 120, 133
  Caleb (Jr.) 120
  Charles 133
  Daniel 51
  Edward 52
  Edward (Jr.) 51
  Eseck 132
  Isaac 33, 51, 126
  James 51
  James (Jr.) 51
  John 51, 59, 61
  Jonathan 112
  Jousha 131
  Nicholas 51
  Peleg 51, 56
  Quam 102
  Robart 130
  Robert 51
  Samuel 52, 61
  Samuel (Jr.) 51
Carter, Henry 108

Carter (cont.)
  John 68
Cartwright, Briant 49
  Briant (Jr.) 49
Carver, Joseph 82
  Oliver 82
  Solmon 88
Cary, Elias 9
  Mihal 4
  Nathaniel 8
Case, Bandon 105
  Elisha 132
  Henry 99
  Iman 97
  Imanl 105
  Immanuel 104
  Inian 15
  John 130
  John (Jr.) 130
  Joseph 56, 130
  Joseph (Jr.) 56
  Peter 104
  Prince 104
  Sanford 131
  William 101, 130
Casey, Abel 129
  Edward 19
  Gedion 37
  Gideon 34
  John 121, 129
  John (Jr.) 130
  Moses 121
  Samuel 130
  Silas 121
  Thomas 36
  Walter 121
  Wanton 121
Cass, Ebenezer 90
Cassell, John 15
Casson, Job 101
Castoff, John 98
Cato, (?) 8, 123
Ceasor, Jeremiah 54
  John 54
  Joseph 54
Cesar, (?) 123
  William 70
Chace, Abraham 118
  Amas 74
  Barnabas 74
  Barnard 93
  Daniel 61
  Isaac 28
  John 75
  Lory 118
  Samuel 65
  Samuel (Jr.) 65
  William 43, 99
  Willm 65
Chadsey, Jabez 61

Chadsey (cont.)
  Jabez (Jr.) 61
  Richard 18
Chaffield, James 56
Chamberlain, Mildred
    Mosher 1
Chamberlin, Ephrajm 110
  Samuel 29
Chambers, James 33
Champlin, Andrew 128
  Asa 9
  Bristol 13
  Chriso 100
  Conga 13
  Cudd 100
  Dick 101
  Elijah 104
  Elijah (Jr.) 104
  Geo. 100
  Hazard 101
  Henry 126
  Jabez 9
  Jack 102
  James 13
  Jeffery 49
  Jeffry 104
  Jesse 9
  John 9
  Jonathan 9
  July 101
  London 13
  Michal 9
  Nathan 47
  Newport 105
  Oliver 127
  Robert 98
  Rowland 126
  Samll 47
  Samuel 124
  Samuel (Jr.) 126
  Sharper 100
  Silas 125
  Stepn 101
  Thomas 7
  Thomas (Jr.) 7
  Thos 101, 102
  William 9, 100
  Wm 99
Chaniel, Benjamin 64
Chapel, Caleb 103
  James 102
  Richard 100
  Scranton 104
  Stephen 98
  Thomas 102
  William 102
Chapman, John 127
  Plumb 128
  Sumnor 124
  Timothy 127

Chapman (cont.)
  William 124
  William (Jr.) 128
Charles, Ephraim 13
Charls, (?) 7
Chase, Abner 106
  Benjamin 106
  Edward 112
  Frederick 125
  John 28
  Joseph 28
  Joseph (Jr.) 28
  Joshua 126
  Paul 113
  Rufus 114
  Stephen 28
Chatman, Nathaniel 120
Cheats, John 13
  Joshua 13
Cheesebrough, Jabez 125
  James 125
Cheseborough, Silvester
    56
Chetson, Abnor 41
Chever, Edward 50
Chickley, Wilm 71
Child, Benjamin 112
  Caleb 113
  Cromell 111
  Cromell (II) 113
  Haile 112
  Hezekiah 112
  James 113
  James (II) 111
  Jeremiah 113
  John 111, 112
  John (III) 111
  Sylvester 111
  William 113
  William (II) 112
Chillson, Joseph 90
  Joseph (Jr.) 93
Chlson, John 63
Choandel, Christpher 133
Christophers, William 5
Church, Anthony 118
  Caleb 49
  Charles 9
  Isaac 9
  Nathaniel 78
  Nathanil 6
  Peter 8
  Samuel 7
  Wm 118
Cillcox, William 103
Clap, Benjn 67
  Isaac 67
Clapp, Daniel 120
  John 120
Clark, Aaron 95

Clark (cont.)
  Abraham 9, 23
  Caleb 9
  Daniel 64
  David 9
  Edward 9
  Eleazar 23
  Elish 9
  Elisha 9
  Ephraim 9
  George 9
  James 9, 81
  Job 9
  John 23
  John Innes 69
  Jonathan 9, 68
  Jonathan (Jr.) 9
  Jos. 73
  Josa 9
  Joseph 9
  Joseph (Jr.) 124
  Joshua 9
  Lemuel 7
  Nathan 9
  Nicholas 74
  Oliver 9
  Rowland 9
  Samuel 65
  Thomas 59
  Walter 22
  William 9
  William (Jr.) 9
Clarke, Aaron 28
  Arnold 76, 128
  Asa 76
  Benja 102
  Christopher 77
  Christor 128
  Cornelius 34
  Daniel 104, 128
  David 127
  Edward 28
  Elias 77
  Elisha 60, 128
  Ethan 124
  George 127
  Gideon 100
  Ichabod 104, 128
  Isaac 77
  Jabez 98
  James 77
  Jemmy 100
  John 28, 77
  Joseph 77, 110, 124,
    129
  Joshua 77, 127
  Josias 102
  Lawrance 108
  Lyman 104
  Moses 76

145

146

Eldred (cont.)
  John (Jr.) 52
  Joseph 60
  Peleg 52
  Samuel 51, 103
  Seth 103
  Thomas 83
  Thos 101
  William 86
Eldrid, Peleg 121
Eldridge, --iobin 116
Elett, Jonathan 94
  Thomas 94
Eley, Joseph 108
Elias, Darling 29
Ellas, Justous 129
Elles, Jonathan 74
Ellet, Robart 74
Ellis, A. Benja 118
  Ams 132
  Benja (Jr.) 118
  Daniel 133
  Giden 132
  Gideon 56
  Gideon (Jr.) 129
  Gustous 130
  Jeremiah 130, 133
  John 132, 133
  Nichols 132
  Ruffus 131
  Weareght 133
Ely, Paul 104
Emerson, William 29
  William (Jr.) 29
Enehes, Ishmal 40
Enos, Jesse 10
  Stephen 10
  William 100
Enoss, Benjamin 78
  John 78
  Joseph 78
Erving, James 101
Esex, Richard 131
Eslick, Isaac 5
Essex, Corps 123
  Hugh 123
  John 123
Esten, Theophilus 84
Esterbroocks, Charles 66
Esterbrooks, Abiel 29
Estes, Elisha 87
  John 29
  John (Jr.) 29
  Joseph 111
  Richard 29
  Richard (Jr.) 29
  Robert 111
  Samuel 29
  Stephen 29
  Thomas 111

Eston, Esek 63
Evens, Daniel 38
  Edward 45
  Richard 38
  Stephen 41, 43
Eyeres, Joseph 10
Fairbank, Jonathan 35
Fairbanks, Benja 115
  William 89
Fairfield, Abraham 39
  Stephen 43
Fales, John 6
  Nathaniel 6
  Nathaniel (Jr.) 6
  Stephen 6
  Thomas 6
  Timothy 6
  William 6
Fanner, Palmer 87
Farnum, Noah 91
Feald, Lemuel 75
Fearweather, George 101
  Saml 101
Fedderman, John F. 25
Feffers, Caleb 30
Feld, Thomas 86
Fen-h, Peter 62
Fenner, Antram 53
  Arnold 53
  Arthar 65
  Arther (Jr.) 65
  Arthur 24, 53
  Daniel 22, 74
  Edward 53
  George 53
  James 21, 53
  Jemes 82
  Jeremiah 19
  Jeremiah (Jr.) 19
  John 42, 53, 77
  John (Jr.) 53
  Joseph 19, 24
  Pardon 53
  Rhodes 53
  Richard 53
  Richard (Jr.) 53
  Samuel 24, 86
  Seth 53
  Stephen 22, 24
  Thomas 84
  William 22
  Wm. 22
  Yankway 40
Field, Abnir 23
  Charles 38
  Daniel 94
  Edward 65, 71
  Isaac 75
  James 22, 23, 71
  James (Jr.) 71

Field (cont.)
  Jeremiah 22
  John 22, 29, 74, 75
  Jos 65
  Joseph (Jr.) 39
  Mical 68
  Nathan 65
  Nehemiah 23
  Solomon 29
  Stephen 53
  Thomas 53, 85
  Thomas (III) 87
  Thos 23
  William 23
  William (Jr.) 23
Files, Peter 67
Filler, Isaac 69
Fillips, Jonathan 67
Finch, Cesar 119
Finney, Jabez 34
  Jeremiah 7
  Josiah 4
  Loring 7
  Thomas 7
Fish, Benjamin 108
  John 108
  Joseph 107
  Moses 89
  Robert 108
  Samuel 113
  Thomas 36, 106
  Thomas (Jr.) 110
  William 108
  Zuriel 108
Fisher, Henry 101
  Jeremiah 29
  Jonathan 29
  Jonathan (Jr.) 29
  Nathan 70
Fisk, Benjamin 23, 86
  Caleb 82
  Daniel 86
  Daniel (Jr.) 86
  Job 86, 89
  Job (Jr.) 81
  John 82, 89
  John (Jr.) 23, 29
  John (Maj.) 29
  Johnston 19
  Joseph 53
  Joseph (III) 53
  Joseph (Jr.) 53
  Nathean 19
  Noah 23
  Oliver 88
  Peleg 80
  Squire (Lt.) 29
  W.m 65
  William 89
Fitton, John 66

Gates, Caleb 133
  Simon 130
Gats, Simon 133
Gavit, Ezekiel 124
  Ezekiel (Jr.) 125
  George 126
  Hezekiah 126
  Isaiah 126
  Jeffery 126
  John (Cpt.) 126
  Joseph 128
  Oliver 124
  Samuel 102
  Sanford 126
  Stephen 128
  Stephen (Jr.) 126
Gean, Eziel 125
George, (?) 7
Gials, William 133
Gibbins, John 62
Gibbs, Abel 21
  Giles 108
  John 74
  Jonathan 108
  Josiah 16
  Josiah (Jr.) (Cpt.) 21
  Samuel 16
  Thos. 18
Gibson, James 16
  James (Jr.) 16
  John 21
Gifford, Annaniah 107
  Elihu 108
  Gideon 109
  Hercules 109
  Richard 106
  William 107
Gillis, William 133
Ginne, Daniel (Jr.) 102
Ginned, Daniel 103
Gladding, Benjm 73
  Daniel 5
  Ebenezer 5
  John 5
  John (Jr.) 5
  Joseph 3, 5
  Joshua 5
  Peter 5
  Solomon 5
  Timothy 74
  William 5
  William (Jr.) 5
Glason, Ezra 99
Glazier, John 34
Glover, (?) 65
  Jonathan 7
Goddard, Nicholas 34
  Towndsend 57
Godforey, Robart 131
Godfrey, Barnett 59

Godfrey (cont.)
  Benja 33
  Caleb 59
  John 71
  Jonathan 62
  Joshua 34
  Samuel 69
Goff, Abner 16
  Caleb 16
  Daniel 16
  Job 15
  Nathan 15
  William 19
Goldthwaite, John 94
Goodfrey, Caleb 71
Goodspeed, Nathan 84
  Stephen 83
Goof, Charles 23
Goold, Benjamin 29
  Jabez 29
  John 29
  John (Jr.) 29
  Nathaniel (Lt.) 29
Gorff, Jacob 94
Gorham, Isaac 111
Gorton, (?) (Dr.) 119
  Beckus 117
  Benja 117, 121
  Benja (Jr.) 119
  Benjamin 26
  Bowen 121
  Caleb 116
  Edward 116
  Edward (III) 117
  Edward (Jr.) 116
  George 19
  Hezekiah 129
  Israel 26
  Israel (Jr.) 26
  John 26, 104, 117, 121
  John (Jr.) 121
  Jonathan 115
  Joseph 117
  Nathan 117
  Oliver 117
  Othniel 119
  Pardon 26
  Peleg 18
  Prince 119
  Prosperous 119
  Samuel 115, 117, 119
  Samuel (Dr.) 119
  Slaid 119
  Thomus 131
  Tom 117
  Wm 117, 119
  Wm (III) 117
  Wm (Jr.) 117
Gould, Adam 103
  Benja 36

Gould (cont.)
  John 103
  Joseph 104
  Nicholas 103
  Thomas 25
Goulding, Joseph 98
Grafton, Jos. 73
  Wilm 73
Granger, John 66
Grant, Abiel 3
  Allen 29
  Benjamin 4
  David 29
  Ebenezer 3
  Gilbert (Lt.) 29
  John 29
  John (Jr.) 29
  Joseph 3, 29
  Joseph (Jr.) 3
  Samuel 29
  Shubal 3
  Thomas 3
Grave, James 113
Graves, Constant 88
Gray, Ammasa 66
  Daniel 109
  David 109
  Forten 110
  Gideon 108
  Job 109
  John 6
  Pardon 109
  Philip 109
  Thomas 6, 109
  Thomas (Jr.) 6
  William 109
Green, Allen 10
  Amos 10
  Amos (Jr.) 10
  Andrew 29
  Benjamin 10
  Benjm 68
  Caleb 69, 122
  Cato 116
  David 10
  Ebenezer 119
  Ebnezer 20
  Edward 10
  James 68, 116
  Jeremiah 120
  John 10, 117
  John Morley 68
  Jonathn 122
  Jos 65
  Joseph 36, 120, 130
  Joshua 10
  Josiah 72
  Nathal 116
  Nathan 68
  Reuben 10

Green (cont.)
 Richard 116
 Richd 117
 Robert 20
 Samuel 10
 Stephen 36
 Thomas 10, 65, 69
 Thomas (Jr.) 10
 Thos. 10
 Timothy 119
 William 10
 Wm 52, 116
Greene, Abel 132
 Abraham 34, 57
 Benja 18, 20, 25, 99
 Benjaman E. 123
 Benjamin 132
 Bowen 20
 Caleb 116, 117, 133
 Cesar 123
 Charles 127
 Charls 18
 Cheafea 20
 Chrio 118
 Christopher 116, 123
 Christopher (Col.) 118
 Coggeshal 105
 D. 120
 David 51, 58, 120
 Ebenezer 16
 Ebenr 119
 Edward 19, 43
 Eliheu 20
 Elihu 123
 Elisha 18, 45
 Elisher 132
 Fons 19
 Gideon 20
 Godfrey 117
 Griffen 34
 Henry 18, 77, 98
 Henry (Jr.) 18
 Increese 20
 Increese (Jr.) 18
 Isaac 16, 18
 Isaac (Jr.) 17
 Jabez 63, 116
 Jack 123
 Jacob 116
 James 16, 18, 115, 116,
  117, 122
 James (Jr.) 115, 117
 Jeremiah 21
 Jesea 19
 Job 19, 118
 Job (Jr.) 120
 Job (Lt.) 21
 John 16, 20, 21, 23,
  56, 118, 119, 120,
  122, 124

Greene (cont.)
 Jonathan 16, 51, 120,
  131
 Joseph 52
 Joseph (Jr.) 51
 Joshua 53, 103
 Judiah 19
 Lawduick 20
 Lewis S. 123
 Luke 133
 Nathan 33
 Nathaneal 16
 Nathean 18, 20
 Nathl 123
 Othanial 16
 Paul 119
 Pero 123
 Perry 123
 Peter 45, 119
 Philip 122, 123
 Phillip 16, 131
 Prims 123
 Rhodes 122
 Richard 118, 123
 Richd 116, 117
 Robert 16
 Samuel 18, 53, 116, 127
 Stephen 16, 19, 122
 Sylvester 33
 Thomas 20
 Thoms 116
 Thos 18, 117
 Timethey 16
 Uzal 18
 Warddel (Jr.) 21
 Warddell 16
 William 16, 19, 123,
  124
 Wm 115, 119, 120, 123,
  134
 Wm. 21, 47
 pelek 131
Greenman, Gideon 103
 James 51
 John 103
 Nathan 126
 Silas 10, 103, 128
Greenold, Jonathan 51
 Robert 51
Griffen, George 10
Griffith, John 78
 Joshua 79
 Phillip 78
Grindman, James 60
 William 56
Grinel, Jonathan 35
Grinlod, William 67
Grinnal, George 10
Grinnel, John 36
 Jonathan 106

Grinnel (cont.)
 Thomas 10
Grinnell, Daniel 108
 Gideon 108
 Nathaniel 108
Grinnold, Stephen 79
 Wisson 65
Guile, John 85
 John (?) 89
 Joseph 83
Gulley, Jona 96
 Stephen 95
 Wm 90
Guy, James 99
Hackker, Joshua 65
Hackstone, Benja 16
 John 115
 Nathaniel 117
 Nathl 117
 Wm 115, 116, 117
Hager, William 22
Haile, Amos 112
 Barnard 112
 Barnard (III) 112
 John 112
 Jonathan 114
 Nathan 113
 Richard 114
 Richard (Jr.) 114
 William 112
Haines, Josiah 22
Hale, Rhodes 126
Hall, Abial 34
 Benoni 60
 Caleb 133
 Charles 126
 Charles (Jr.) 126
 Daniel 60
 David 132
 David (Jr.) 132
 Ebenezar 76
 Elisha 78
 Ephraim 10
 Ephraim (Jr.) 47
 Ezekiel 46
 Gardner 61
 George 10
 Henry 46
 Hezekiah 127
 Isaac 126
 Jacob 49
 Job 78
 John 10, 48, 57, 130
 Jonathan 10
 Jonathan (Jr.) 10
 Joseph 124
 Levi 70
 Nathan 10
 Peter 10
 Robart 33

Hall (cont.)
  Robert 131
  Robt 61
  Rowland 61
  Samuel 103
  Silas 10
  Slocum 57
  Theodaty 10, 128
  Thomas 10, 126
  Timothy 131
  William 57, 60, 61
  William (Jr.) 57
  amo 132
  presarvid (Jr.) 130
  presarvied 131
Ham, John old 74
  Jotham 72
  Levi 72
  Wamoth 72
  Wemath 72
  Wilm 72
Haman, Abraham 63
Hambetton, Francis 43
Hambleton, Joseph 61
Hambly, Benjamin 107
  Benjamin (Jr.) 110
Hamilton, Frederick 33
  William 35
Hamlin, Samuel 72
Hamman, Benjn 66
Hammet, Malachi 119
Hammon, Edward 86
  James 71
  John 80
  Jonathan 66
  Samuel 86
  Stephen 54
  Thomas 80
  Wm (Jr.) 22
Hammond, Amos 83
  Gidean 84
  James 81
  Joseph 59
  Nathaniel 51
  Paine 51
  Thomas 100
  William 59
Hamon, Nathan 62
Handrek, Stephen 92
Handy, Ebenezer 88
  Job 91
Hardin, John 113
  Joseph 111
Harding, Benjamin 7
  Elezer 72
  Richard 3
  Step. 71
  Thomas 72
  Walker 74
  William 3, 6

Harington, Stukely 89
  Thomas 81
Harkness, Adam 90
  Adam (Jr.) 90
  James 91
  Robert 91
Harloo, Nathanael 130
Harres, Stepen 69
  Stephen 88
Harris, Abner 96
  Amaziah 42
  Andrew 23, 53
  Aseal 87
  Benja 53
  Benjamin 63
  C. 56
  Caleb 53
  Charles 88
  Christopher 29, 53
  Christopher (Jr.) 29,
    53
  David 90
  David (Jr.) 92
  Elezer 43
  Eseck 39
  Ezekiel 29
  Gedion 88
  Henry 53
  Isaac 95
  Israel 92
  Jabez 92
  James 22, 95
  Jeremiah 92
  Jesse 95
  John 22, 80
  Jona 92
  Jonathan 42
  Joseph 23, 42, 90
  Josiah 53
  Luke 40
  Nathan 95
  Oliver 29
  Preserved 92
  Richard 92
  Richd (Jr.) 96
  Robert 95
  Stephen 42, 95
  Thomas 54, 83
  Tobe 54
  William 53
Harrison, George 121
  Robert 55
Harry, Chrisr 13
  Daniel 12
  Gideon 13
  Silas 13
Hart, Constant 107
  Eber 107
  Joseph 109
  Nicholas 57, 59

Hart (cont.)
  Nicholas (Jr.) 62
  Peleg 107
  Robart 62
  Sanford 110
  Smiton 106
  Smiton (Jr.) 110
  William 107
Hartshorn, Stephen 67
Harvey, Edward 105
  James 10, 98
  James (Jr.) 10
  John 10
  Joseph 10
  Peter 10
  Uriah 10
  William 10, 45
  William (Jr.) 10
Harzard, Ephraim 57
Haskill, Abner 30
  Amos 30
  Comfort 30
  John 30
  Samuel 30
Haszard, Freborn 59
  Gideon 59
  Jeffry 58
  Jer 61
  Jeremiah 58
  John 59, 61
  Jonathan 60
  Robart 59
  Robert (Jr.) 58
  Robt 58
  Stephen 102
  Thomas 58, 60
  Thos 101, 102
Hatch, Samuel 34
Hathaway, Benjamin 4
Hatheway, Caleb 118
  Nathan 118
Hathuway, Thomas 20
Hathway, Melatiah 30
  Silvanus 30
Havens, Abraham 58
  George 62
  James 59
  John 56
  Robart 57
  Silvester 57
  William 57
  William (Jr.) 59
  Wm 117
Hawkens, Jeremiah 67
  Jos. 75
Hawkings, Joseph 63
Hawkins, Andrew 29
  Benj (Jr.) 39
  Benjn 40
  Charles 91

Hawkins (cont.)
Edward 74
Elijah 44
Elijah (Jr.) 40
Hasakiah 64
John 91, 103
Joseph 43
Mingo 53
Nathaniel 105
Quash 99
Rufus 53
Rufus (Jr.) 53
Thos 103
Uriah 38
Uriah (Jr.) 40
William 44
William (Jr.) 38
Hawksey, Joseph 110
Hayl, Coomer 67
Hazard, Arnold 102
Benja 105
Caleb 98
Caleb (Jr.) 98
Carder 103
Chriso 103
Edward 100
Enoch 99
Geo. Wanton 102
George 92, 102
Godfrey 105
Harry (Jr.) 13
Jack 98, 103
Jacob 103
Jo. 98
Jonathan 10
Jonathan (Jr.) 10
Joseph 98
Mumford 105
Newport 98
Pero 102
Peter 98, 103, 105
Pharash 13
Pharoah 103
Quaco 103
Rich. 105
Robart 131
Robert 10, 97, 105
Robt 97
Samuel 98
Silvester 103
Stepn 98
Thomas 97
Thos 97, 99
Tony 100
Troy 103
Hazzard, Harry 12
Headely, William 133
Healy, Ezra 62
Hearington, James 20
Heath, --anel 3

Heath (cont.)
--g 3
Hedding, James 71
Hedges, Elias 125
Jona (Col.) 128
Heffernan, Elijah 104
Stepn 98
Heley, Recompence 70
Helme, Benedict 103
Gabriel 97
James 97
James (Jr.) 97
Nathl 100
Niles 100
Peleg 62
Powel 97
Prince 97
Rochiel 97
Rowse 60
Rowse J. 97
Samuel 97
William 62
Hennon, John 10
Henry, Benjamin 91
Caleb 22
Pelethiah 99
Robert 24
Samuel 89
Herendeen, Andrew 44
Edmund 95
Elisha 39, 43
Hazakiah 39, 41
Israel 39
John (Jr.) 43
Levi 41
Oliver 42
Othinel 38
Simeon 39, 41
Thomas 39
Thomas (Jr.) 42
William 42
Herin, Matthew 46
William 46
Herindan, Ruphes 81
Herindeen, Josiah 85
Nathl 81
Herindon, Daniel 81
Jencks 86
John (Jr.) 86
Jonathan 81
Josiah (III) 81
Matthew 81
Randol 81
Silas 81
Simeon 86
William 81
Herindoon, John 84
Herndeen, Aaron 94
Abram 95
Ebenezer 90

Herndeen (cont.)
Ezekiel 94
Joseph 90, 94
Preservd 44
Solomon 44
Herndon, Amos 83
Stephen 85
Hernton, Epheram 85
Jonathan 83
Josias 83
Herrick, Benjamin 128
Herring, Newman 79
Herrington, Francis 16
James 21
Job 130
Job (Jr.) 130
Richard 16
Theophalis 21
Whitman 130
William 79
Herris, hanry 80
Hertford, (?) 7
Hews, Jos (Jr.) 67
Spier 4
Heys, Reding 117
Hiams, George 56
Sylvester 56
Hicks, Abraham 108
Elihu 108
John 107
Joseph 107, 121
Samuel 107, 108, 112,
114
Hide, Benjm 73
Higgins, John 5
Higinbotham, Obediah 25
Hill, Asa 47
Barnard 112
Barnard (Jr.) 112
Barnet 117
Benj. 80
Benjamin 89
Caleb 56
Caleb (Jr.) 58
Calob 84
Daniel 102
David 39
Ebenezer 22, 49, 73
Ebenr (Jr.) 22
Henray 87
Henry 102
Israel 43
James 68
John 86
Jonathan 69
Josiah 50
Josiah (Jr.) 49
Nathaniel 113
Nehemiah 87
Roger 30

Hoxsie, Barnabas 77
  Benjamin 10, 77
  Benjamin (Jr.) 10
  Caff 14
  Edward 77
  Elijah 77
  Gideon 10, 77
  Gideon (Jr.) 10
  Jeremiah 77
  Job 77
  John 77
  Joseph 1, 10, 76
  Peleg 10
  Peter 78
  Primas 13
  Samuel 99
  Solomon 78
  Stephen 10, 77
  Thomas 10
  William 77
Hoyl, Jos. 75
  Richard 74
  Wilm 73
Hubbord, Ezra 66
Hudson, John 22
  Stuckely 21
  Thomas 62
Huling, Elexander 60
  Sam 60
Hull, Benjamin 126
  Bristol 98
  Charles 98
  Edward 103
  James 98
  Joseph 97, 104
  London 98
  Peleg 72
  Port 98
  Prince 97
  Silvester 98
  Thomas 126
  Tiddeman 51
  Timothy (Jr.) 133
  Tom 98
  William 98
Humphry, (?) (Jr.) 3
  --h 3
  --y 3
  James 3
  Samuel 3
Hunt, Adam 59
  Benjm 69
  Benoni 62
  Charles 61
  Edward 67
  Ezekiel 59
  George 39
  Jeremiah 59
  John 45
  John (Jr.) 43

Hunt (cont.)
  Joseph 36
  Samuel 59
  Samuel (Jr.) 59
  Seth 42
  Zebedee 22
Hunter, Thomas 25
Hutson, Benja 115
  Daniel 74
  Robart 66
Ichabod, (?) 8
Ide, Joel 70
  John 43
  Joseph 43
Indian, Isaac 92
Ingerham, Jos 65
Ingram, Lawton 70
Ingreham, Jeremiah 7
  Simeon 4
  William 7
Inman, Asa 44
  Elisha 44, 94
  Elisha (Jr.) 43
  Ezikiel 41
  Francis 30
  Isaiah 38
  Israel 44
  Jeremiah 30
  John 41, 64
  John (Jr.) 41
  Joseph 94
  Obadiah 45
  Ozial 45
  Rial 45
  Samuel 40
  Stephen 30
  Stukley 91
Inmand, David 41
Inyan, John 56
Irish, Gorge 118
Irons, James 40
  Jeremiah 45
  Jeremiah (Jr.) 42
  Resolved 41
  Saml (III) 38
  Samuel 45
  Stephen 41
  William 41
Jackson, Daniel 72
  Samuel 69
Jackwise, Saml 102
Jacobs, Isaac 74
  Joseph 69
  Samuel 74
Jakways, amos 133
James, Allen 100
  Benjamin 76
  Edward 76
  Ezekiel 76
  George 76

James (cont.)
  James 76
  James (Jr.) 76
  Jonathan 76
  Jonathan (Jr.) 76
  Joseph 129
  Randal 76
  Robert 76
  Samuel 71
  Silous 133
  Stephen 101
  Thomas 76
  William 76
  Wilm (Jr.) 71
Jaquais, Jona 103
Jaquays, Joseph 103
Jeames, John 72
  Wilm 71
Jeffers, John 56
Jefferson, Benjamin 57
Jeffery, Joe 13
Jeffes, Jonathan 110
Jefry, Joseph 130
Jenck, John 65
  Nathaniel 70
Jenckens, Christopher 61
  Jeremiah F 66
  Jeremiah f. 66
  John 66
Jenckes, Ahab 95
  David 95
  George 93
  Henry 96
  Jacob 95
  Jesse 95
  John 95
  John (Jr.) 90
  Joseph 96
  Joseph (Jr.) 95
  Joshua 93
  Thos 92
Jenckins, John 72
Jencks, Benjamin 62
  Christopher 95
  Daniel 65
  Ealeazer (Cpt.) 62
  Eseck 62
  Jeremiah (Jr.) 67
  Jonathan 70
  Rufas 65
  Samuel 86
Jenkens, Phillip 59
Jenkins, Benja 121
  Benjamin 132
  Gorge 129
  Jonathan 68
Jenks, Amos 30
  Anthony 30
  Benjamin 107
  Daniel 30

158

King (cont.)
Daniel 21
Ebenezer 19
Elisha 87
Esaias 54
George 88
Godfree 110
Henry 15
Isaac 40
Isaiah 54
James 42
Jeremiah 25
Jesea 19
Job 110
John 18, 24
John (Jr.) 25
Jonathan 24
Jonathan (Jr.) 25
Joseph 13
Joshua 82
Josiah 54
Nicholas 54
Olphre 106
Peter 80
Ruben 62
Samuel 86
Stephen 110
Wm Borden 54
Kingsley, Jonathan 57
Judediah 57
Samuel 57
Sawell 57
Sawell (Jr.) 57
Kinnecut, Antone 67, 70
Jos 72
Kinnecutt, Edward 114
John 114
John (Jr.) 114
Shubeal 114
Kinnicutt, Daniel 3
Hezekiah 3
Kinyon, (Enock) 11
(James) 11
(Joseph) 11
(Samuel) 11
Alexander 11
Amos 11
Arnold 126
Benadit 76
Benjamin 48
Caleb 11
Dan 11
Daniel 11
David 77
Elijah 11
Elisha 11
Gardner 79
George 46
James 48
Jarvis 79

Kinyon (cont.)
Jas 11
Jas. 11
John 11, 46, 79, 131
Jonathan 11
Joram 38
Jos. 11
Joseph 17
Joseph (Jr.) 11
Joshua 11
Lodowick 11
Nathan 79
Nathaniel 50
Oliver 77
Peleg 46
Peter 49
Peter (Jr.) 50
Phillip 77
Remington 35
Robert 103
Roger 11
Saml 11
Samll (Jr.) 11
Samuel 76, 103
Solomon 77
Stephen 47
Sylvester 77
Thomas 77, 79
Thomas (Jr.) 79
Thos 77
Thurston 77
Wells 50
William 77
Kirk, William 16
Kittel, Edmond 132
Edward 132
Epheram 132
Kittle, Thomas 21
Knap, David 120
Knight, Andrew 24
Barzilla 23
Benajah 25
Charles 88
David 87, 89
Edward 23
Ezra 19
Henry 23
Israel 89
James 25
Jeremiah 26
Job 23
Jona 25
Jona (Jr.) 25
Jonathan 21, 83, 88
Joseph 25
Nehemiah 1, 26, 27
Philip 25, 112
Reuben 23
Richard 23, 85, 89
Robart 87

Knight (cont.)
Robert 25
Robert (Jr.) 88
Rufus 88
Stephen 23
Thomas 23
William 23
Knigt, Joseph 85
Knoles, Edward 66
John P. 70
Jonathan 70
Knowles, Daniel 11, 49
Daniel (Jr.) 11
Henry 98
James 105
Jeremiah 105
John 78
John (Jr.) 78
Jonathan 78
Joseph 99, 104
Joseph (Jr.) 97
Reynolds 11
Robert 78, 99, 104, 105
Samuel 78
Thomas 11
William 78, 98
Knox, Thomas 16
Kook, Jos 71
Kynnon, William 133
Kynyoun, David 132
Lad, James 17
John 17
John (Jr.) 17
Joy 63
Ladd, John 115
John (Jr.) 120
Joseph 115
William 55
Lake, Giles 108
James 107
Joel 110
Joseph 110
Noak 110
Philip 110
Richard 106
William 6
Lamunyon, Philip 111
Samuel 108
Lanard, Zaphanier 20
Lancksford, Wilm 75
Lane, Ebenezer 49
Lanford, Jonathan 126
Langford, John 34, 36
Langutha, John 108
Langworthy, Amos 50
Benjamin 49
Joseph 48
Samll 48
Lanpher, Abraham 127
Amos 127

Lanpher (cont.)
Benjamin 125
Daniel 124
Daniel (III) 127
Daniel (Jr.) 127
David 127
Ebenezer 47
George 128
Haron 127
Joshua 49
Joshua (Jr.) 50
Langworthy 125
Nahor 128
Nathan 124
Nathan (Jr.) 128
Samuel 128
Lapham, Abner 30
Augustus 92
Jethro 42
John 30
Joseph 30
Saul 30
Solomon 44
Thomas (Jr.) 92
Thos 90
Tom 41
Lar(t?)al, John 66
Larkham, Lot 79
Larkin, Abel 128
Covel 49
Covil 47
David 78
David (Jr.) 78
Edward 78
Elisha 78
Jesse 78
John 49, 78
John (Jr.) 49
Kinyon 11
Moses 11
Nicholas 78
Oliver 78
Samuel 79
Stephen 78
Timothy 49
Larned, Benja 54
Larrance, David 68
John 68
John (Jr.) 66
Jos 66
Thomas 66
Larsher, John 72
Latham, Arther 91
Benoni 54
David 125
John 124
Joseph 91, 126
William 54
Laton, Jeremiah 71
Lawless, William (Lt.) 6

Lawton, Edward 58
John 48
Joseph 50, 61
Joseph (Jr.) 50
Thomas 109
Laylon, Abnor 66
Layton, Robart 73
Lea, William 68
Leach, Stephen 82
Stephen (Jr.) 81
Leazer, Thomas 106
Lech, Oliver 88
Lee, Charles 74
Joseph 30
Levi 30
Peter 11
William 78
peter 131
Lefavour, Daniel 4
Leman, Thomas 113
Lemonere, Solomon 104
Lennard, Gulliver 42
James 45
Robart 66
Leshure, Joseph 43
Lester, Daniel 47, 48
Letson, Ephariam 16
Jeremiah 17
John 16
Micheil 18
Robert 19
Robert (Jr.) 19
William 19
Levalley, John 118
Levally, John (Jr.) 118
Josiah 118
Peleg 118
Peter 118
Peter (Jr.) 118
Wm 118
Levit, Joseph 11
Lewes, Benjaiah 68
Lewis, Amos 49
Arnold 128
Augustus 11
Benjamin 79
Beriah 11
Daniel 46
David 124
Elias 50, 125
Ezekel 84
George 79
Green 49
Hezekiah 125
Israel 77
James 38, 47
Jesse 46
John 13, 78, 124
John (III) 125
Joseph 124

Lewis (cont.)
Mark 50
Maxson 49
Nathaniel 127
Obadiah 45
Oliver 125
Paul 49
Peter 40, 42
Randall 49
Reuben 44
Richard 11, 41
Samll 48
Simeon 125
Stephen 127, 133
Vinten 40
William 111, 125
Lews, Danial 133
David 132
Jacob 133
Leyon, John 16
Lillibridge, Edward 79
Lester 78
Thomas 79
Thomas (Jr.) 79
Lilly, John 121
Lind, William 30
Lindley, Joshua 72
Lindsey, Joseph 7
Samuel 5
William 4
William (Jr.) 4
Lindul, Nathanael 15
Linsey, Thomas 72
Linzey, William 113
Lippet, Loudan 74
Lippit, Moses (Jr.) 121
Lippitt, Abraham 122
Ben 120
Cesar 122
Charles 25
Christopher 25
Cuff 121
James 121
John 121
Joseph 121
Jube 121
Moses 25, 122
Parris 121
Primus 121
Prince 121
Sili 121
Thomas 121
Waterman 25
Wm 121
Liscomb, Samuel 5
Samuel (Jr.) 5
Littlefield, Samuel 116
Lloyd, John 11
Lock, Edward 103
Jona 98

Mitchel, Derius 43
  Elisha 43
  Experience 45
  Ezekiel 45
  Hesediah 38
  James 67
  John 41
  Reuben 45
  Zurial 45
Mitchell, Ephraim 59
  Ephraim (Jr.) 59
  Samuel 61
Moffit, Mierjah 39
Moffitt, William 39
Momford, John 65
Moon, James 130
  Walter 109
Moore, David 76
  David (Jr.) 76
  George 77
  Robert 77
  Silas 76
Moorhead, William 54
Morey, John 59
  Samuel 79
Morgan, Abraham 89
Morres, William 70
Morrey, John 69
Morris, Samuel 24
Morse, Philip 112
Morton, James 90
  Thomas 90
Mory, Antony 71
  Daniel 97
  Joseph 61
  Thomas 88
Mosher, Allen 95
  Gardner 30
  Jonathan 30
  Luthan 30
  Obadiah 108
  Paul 108
Mosier, Eber 78
  Gideon 76
  William 33
Mott, Benja 17
  Stephen 34
  Stephen (Jr.) 34
Mowrey, Augustus 60
  John 57
  Robart 58
  William 60
Mowry, Abel 94
  Abial 93
  Ananias 90
  Ananias (Jr.) 90
  Andrew 44
  Daniel 1, 91
  Daniel (III) 91
  Daniel (IV) 91

Mowry (cont.)
  Daniel (Jr.) 96
  Danl (Jr.) 96
  David 90
  Eleazer 94
  Elisha 90
  Elisha (Jr.) 91
  Esek 93
  Ezekiel 90
  George 91
  Gideon 90
  Hosea 92
  Israel 91
  Job (Jr.) 91
  John 93
  Joseph 91
  Peso 92
  Philip (Jr.) 90
  Stephen 90
  Stephen (Jr.) 90
  Sylvanus 91
  Uriah 90
  Uriah (Jr.) 93
Mumford, Benjamin 3
  Benjamin (Jr.) 3
  Cato 117
  Gardner Wm 99
  Gideon 34
  Jack 102
  Jirrah 79
  John 73
  Nathaniel 102
  Nathl 27, 32, 75, 97,
    117
  Paul 103
  Pawl 3
  Peter 3
  Ray 102
  Richard 117
  Stephen 34
  Wilm 72
Munday, Edward 7
  Jonathan 7
Munro, Archibald 5
  George 5
  Henry 5
  Hezekiah 6
  James 6
  Nathan 6
  Nathan (II) 5
  Nathaniel (II) 5
  Samuel 5
  Simeon 7
  Stephen 7
  William 5, 6
Munrow, Nathean 20
  Samuel 20
Murfee, John 110
Mussy, James 92
Myers, Giden 133

Myls, Timothy 83
Myous, Nichols 132
Myus, Hezekiah 129
Naning, James 112
Nash, John (Jr.) 70
  Jonathan 11
  Nathan 103
Nason, James 62
Nathan, Clarke 28
Neadom, William 50
Neal, George 111
Negus, Benjamin 108
  Isaac 109
  Job 106
  John 107, 110
  Noles 109
  Robert 108
  Stephen 109
  Thomas 107
Newel, Robart 75
Newell, Aaron 30
  Benja 92
  David 30
  Elisha 30
  Jason 30
  Jona 92
Newfield, Elisha 92
  Peleg 92
Newman, Thomas 95
Newport, (?) 7
Ney, Caleb 49
  Caleb (Jr.) 49
  George 78
  Isaac 11
  James 11
  Joshua 49
  Stephen 11
Nichals, Nathean 20
Nicher, Thomas 108
Nicholas, John 25
Nichols, Alexander 33
  Andw 97
  Andw (Jr.) 97
  Anthony 116
  Benja 36, 59, 119
  Caleb 17
  David 17, 77
  George 56
  Henry 129
  Isaac 60
  John 19, 34, 97
  John (Jr.) 21
  Jonathan 17, 36, 56
  Jonathan (III) 17
  Jonathan (Jr.) 17
  Joseph 11, 16, 130
  Richard 17, 35
  Samuel 57
  Samuel (Jr.) 57
  Thom 119

Nichols (cont.)
Thomas 56, 131
Thomas (Jr.) 61
Walter 133
William 130
Nichools, Benjiman 63
Nickols, Daniel 46
Nightingall, Jos 65
Niles, Cesar 102
George 129
Jabez 98
James 12, 13
James (Jr.) 13
Jeremiah 97
John 129
Jonathan 131
Joseph 130
Joseph (Jr.) 130
Mingo 98
Nathanial 131
Philip 97
Pompy 97
Quash 98
Samuel 12, 130
Samuel (Jr.) 13, 130
Silas 98
Simeon 13
Tom 102
Tony 97
Nino, (?) 8
Nocake, Gideon 13
Nooning, James 4
Norrice, John 5
John (Jr.) 5
Northup, Benjamin 59
Daniel 59
David 58, 59
George 61
Gideon 58
Henry 58
Immanuel 60
James 56
John 37, 60
John (Jr.) 60
Joseph 58
Joseph (Jr.) 58
Lebeus 56
Nicholas 58, 59
Rhobt 61
Robart 59
Robt 59
Rowse 59
Samuel 58, 62
Silvester 98
Stephen 59
Stephen (Jr.) 58
Stuckley 59
William 58, 61, 62
Zebulon 56
Nowrey, Robert (Jr.) 61

Noxsie, Amos 13
Noyes, Joseph (Jr.) 126
Sanford 124
Sanford (Jr.) 126
OBryan, William 113
OKelley, John 113
Oakley, William 62
Oatley, Benedict 102
Joseph 102
Samuel 101
Oldfeild, John 35
Oldin, Jonathan 17
Oldridge, John 5
Joseph 5
Olin, Giles 56
Henry 129
Henry (Jr.) 129
John 61
Peleg 121
Olney, Abrham 64
Charles 64
Charles (Jr.) 64
Christopher 72
Cristopher 62
Elisha 93
Emor 54
Epenetus 63
Eseck 62
Ezekiel 54
Ezra 64
George 67
Gidan (Jr.) 63
Gideon 64
Isaac 64, 111
James 92
Jeremiah 67, 93
John 38, 63
Jonathan 72
Jos 67
Joseph 44, 64
Joseph (Cpt.) 1, 63
Nemiah 63
Obediah 92
Peter 67
Richard 69
Samuell (Lt.) 62
Simeon 70
Stephen 40
Thomas (Lt.) 63, 64
Til Merreck 67
Omsbary, Jos 70
Oney, John 13
Orberson, Jacob 66
Ormsbary, Caleb 66
Ormsbe, Ezra 113
John 113
Joseph 113
Thomas 113
Osband, Weaver 106
William 108

Osband (cont.)
Wilson 109
Otter, Zebulon 122
Owen, Daniel 38
John 63
Josiah 64
Solomon 38
Solomon (Jr.) 43
Thomas (Jr.) 43
Thos 44
Oxx, George 5
Samuel 5
Packard, Melser 71
Rodes 70
Samuel 70
Packey, Thomas 13
Packham, James 64
Page, Ambres 68
Benjm 68
Benoni 39
Daniel 41
James 39
Job 68
Joseph (Jr.) 38
Stephen 38
Thomas 67
William 41, 73
William (Jr.) 40
Pain, ?ila 95
Benja 54
Benjamin 90
Benjn 43
David 66
Edward 5
Jehu 63
John 82, 93
Jona 92
Nathan 42
Nathan (Jr.) 39, 44
Obed 92
Royal 5
Square 54
Stephen 5, 45
Thomas 5
William 54
Palman, Jonathan 79
Palmer, Amos 48
Amos (Jr.) 48
Asil 48
Jabis 64
Lawton 49
Nathaniel 49
Noah 110
Simeon 120
Stephen 48
Parce, Daniel 69
Jobe 80
Levy 89
Pardon 19
Petter 86

164

Perry (cont.)
Peter 98
Phinehas 110
Quash 100
Raymond 103
Samuel 11, 98
Simeon 11
Simeon (Jr.) 11
Tom 14, 98
Walter 106
William 98
Peter, Thomas 101
Peters, John 65
Peterson, Ichabod 78
Nathan 100
Petters, Mark 43
Pettes, Benjamen 86
John 74
Pettet, Daniel 75
Pettey, Daniel 106
Isaac 108
Joshua 110
Nathan 106
Pettice, Benjn 82
Pettis, Joseph 47
Stephen 20
William 46
Petty, Joseph 11
Pettys, James 79
Robert 77
Phetteplace, Eseck 41
Ezekiel 41
Job 41
John 42, 43
Jonathan 44
Resolved 42
Samuel 41, 42
Philbrook, Elias 30
Philipes, John 48
Philips, Caleb 26
Elisha 26
Jacob 82
Jeremiah 117
John 108
Michael 30
Samuel 26, 130
William 26, 64, 110
Wm 119
Phillips, Abraham 81
Adam 43
Andrew 44
Bartholomew 76
Caleb 41
Christopher 61
Daniel 90
Danl (Jr.) 95
David 41, 45
Edward 82
Epherim 39
Ezekiel 81

Phillips (cont.)
Gideon 95
Israel 57
James 16, 62, 80
James (Jr.) 16
Jeremiah 45
Jeremiah (Jr.) 45
John 92
Jona 95
Joseph 45
Joshua 42, 93
Levi 63
Luke 42
Nathaniel 88
Peter 60
Reuben 41
Richard 57, 60
Rufus 93
Samuel (Cpt.) 61
Solomon 41
Stephen 95
Thomas 60
William 18, 42
Phillops, David 87
Israel 87
John 83, 86
John (Jr.) 86
Mycal 85
Philmore, Adam 25
Phinney, Elisha 114
Phulps, Joseph 131
Pierce, Benja (Jr.) 116
Benjamin 123
Jonathan 122
Nathaniel 123
Pigsle, Wilcom 41
Pike, Jonathan 64
Peter 64
Pirce, John 46
Pirkens, Elias 80
John 86
Samuel 83
Samuel (Jr.) 80
Pitcher, Andrew 23
George 63
John 23, 63
John (Jr.) 23
Jonathan 22
Jonthan 36
Samuel 64
Pitman, John 103
Joseph 108
Sandres 69
Thomas 75
Pitts, John 68
Natiors 69
Place, Benijar? 85
Daniel 40
Enick 83
Enoc 86

Place (cont.)
Enoch 40
John 40
Joseph 20, 40, 81
Peter 38
Rows 86
Ruphes 81
Samuel 58
Samuel (Jr.) 58
Simeon 40
Stephen 83
Thomas 36, 81
Thos (Jr.) 35
Planting, Obediah 72
Plato, (?) 7
Polock, Henry 42
Wm Willson 97
Pool, John 66
Jos 66
Samuel 66
Pope, John 91
Popple, George 47
John 49
John (Jr.) 50
Theodaty 48
William 48
Porter, Nathan 49
Potter, Abednego 22
Abel 17
Abel (III) 133
Abel (Jr.) 132
Amos 23
Anthony 24
Asa 38
Caleb 25, 49, 115
Cesar 101
Charls 84
Christopher 85, 88
Curnel 89
David 15, 77, 80
Ecd 22
Edward 26
Edward (Jr.) 26
Elisha 17, 79, 88
Ezekiel 15
Ezral 83
Fisher 82
Fons 15
Geo. 104
Georg 74
George 15, 16, 104, 128
Gideon 77
Gilbert 122
Henry 104
Holiman 22
Ichabod 98
Ichabud 18
Ichabus (Jr.) 18
Income 77
James 45, 73, 77, 101,

167

170

171

Smith (cont.)
Israel 42
Jacob 92
James 4, 42, 77, 94
Jehu 75
Jere 92
Jeremiah 44, 58
Jeremiah (Jr.) 58
Jerimiah 64
Jesse 31, 94
Jieal 44
Job 38, 71, 120
John 5, 22, 31, 44, 45,
47, 69, 84, 87, 93,
102
John (III) 95
John (Jr.) 22, 31, 45,
91, 102
Jonathan 31, 42, 90
Jonathan (Jr.) 45
Jones 60
Jos 45
Jos (III) 45
Jos. 74
Joseph 111
Joseph (Jr.) 38
Joshua 74
Josiah 4
Levi 31
Lyonard 41
Martin 43
Nathan 87
Nathanel 3
Nathaniel 5
Nathaniel (II) 5
Neamiah 62
Noah 67
Oliver 95
Peregreen 87
Peter 100
Philip 90
Primas 102
Resolved 94
Resolved (Jr.) 94
Reuben 91
Richard 5, 40, 85, 90
Richard (Jr.) 5
Roysal 47
Rufus 44, 92
Saml 34
Samuel 4, 25, 54, 67,
82, 95
Samuel (Jr.) 84
Simeon 41
Simon 4, 40, 68, 103
Stephen 7, 38, 40, 45,
82, 122
Stephen (Jr.) 122
Thomas 42, 56, 82, 94,
102

Smith (cont.)
Thomas (Jr.) 93
Wait 44
William 39, 51, 71, 128
hope 82
Smitton, Jos 70
Snell, Daniel 118
Seth 112
Snow, Daniel 73
Daniel (Jr.) 73
James 73
James (Jr.) 73
Jos. (Jr.) 73
Samuel 74
Zabadee 88
Sole, David 86
Jonathan 81
Salvenas 86
Solovan, Daniel 71
Solsbory, Archable 75
Somnord, James 70
Sothard, John 72
Wallard 66
Soule, Abner 109
Cornelius 106
Jonathan 106
Samuel 110
William 106
Southwick, George 91
Jonathan 90
Zaceus 91
Sowl, Samuel 34
Sowle, Jacob 108
Job 107
Joseph 109
Spauldin, Aholiab 93
Joseph 90
Nathaniel 93
Spears, Elconey (?) 93
Spencer, A. 36
Benjamin 34, 36
Caleb 36
Charls 18
Christopher 56
Cuff 116
David 19
Domini 106
Griffin 34
Jeremiah 35
Job 130
John 37, 123
Joshua 16
Michal 37
Nicholas 60
Pierce 120
Randel 131
Richard 33
Rufus 36
Samuel 131
Samuel (Jr.) 133

Spencer (cont.)
Silas 35
Stephen 34
T. 36
Thomas 34, 36
Thos 35
Walr 35
Walter 33
William 33, 35, 56
Wilson 35
Wm 118
Spenser, Wilm 73
Spensor, Daniel 68
Spicer, Samuel 88
Spiner, Thos 123
Spink, Benjamin 132
Eldridge 121
Ishmael 56
John 60, 132
Josiah 56
Nicholas 56
Silas 58
William 130
Spolding, Edward 65
Spooner, Benjm 71
George 100
Mason 100
Samuel 73
Wing 33
Sprage, Obidiah 73
Sprague, Abraham 31
Amos 31
Benja 23
Bomer 40
Daniel 54
Daniel (Jr.) 54
David 99
Ebenezer 40, 54
Eleazur 63
Elijah 41, 43
Enoch 91
Gideon 31
Jedediah 38
John 43
Jona (Jr.) 23
Jonas 43
Jonathan 23, 31
Nathaniel 23
Nehemiah 93
Peter 23, 39
Reuben 40
Richd 43
Rowland 34
Rufus 54
Samuel 40
Seth 31
Stephen 23
William 24, 54, 90
Spraugue, Elias 93
Joseph 91

Thomas (cont.)
Seth 111
William 62
Thompson, Abner 93
Charles (Rev.) 111
Ebenezer (Maj.) 65
Elias 124
Isaac 125
John 69, 125
Joshua 125
Peter 39
Robert 125
Samuel 126
William 127
Thoms, George 56
John 56
Thomson, Edward 93
Thomston, Samuel 94
Thorn, William 50
Thornton, Aborn 122
Benj. 38
Christopher 55, 122
Daniel 55, 69
Elihu 54
Elisha 91
Ephraim 55
Esek 55
Jeremh 44
John 54
John (Jr.) 45
Jos 68
Joseph 55
Levi 39
Noah 55
Richard 55, 94
Solomon 55, 122
Solomon (Jr.) 55
Stephen 42, 55
Thrasher, Azariah 88
Threp, Palmer 83
Throop, John 7
William 8
Throp, Amos 69
Thurbar, Stepen 72
Thurber, Amos 31
Barnabas 31
Caleb 112
John 112
Samuel 73
Samuel (Jr.) 73
Thurbor, Edward 71
Edward (Jr.) 73
Martin 73
William 69
Thurill, Charls 8
Thurman, John 25
Thurston, Gardner 49
George 50
George (Jr.) 50
James 31

Thurston (cont.)
John 101
Joseph 50
Norton 112
Thomas 108
William 48
Tibbett, Wm (?) 119
Tibbits, Jonathan 35
Tibbitts, Henry 35
John 115
Jonathan 115
Nathaniel 59
Thomas 115
Thomas (Jr.) 115
Waterman 115
Tiffeny, --eazar 3
Hezekiah 3
Tifferny, Stephen 116
Thos 119
Tiffle, John 90
Petor 90
Rufus 90
Tifft, Daniel 74
David 74
David (Jr.) 74
Tiffte, James 94
Robert 94
Tift, Samuel 87
Tiler, Nicholas 37
Tillinghas, William 69
Willm 69
Tillinghash, Gibbs 65
Tillinghast, Benja 37
Benjamen 132
Benjn. 1
Charles 57
Daniel 65, 117
Daniel (Jr.) 65
Henry 67
John 65, 129
John (Jr.) 130
Jonath 73
Jos 65
Jos. 73
Nicholas 67
Parris 67
Philip 34
Samuel 80, 117
Thomus 131
Thos 35
William 65
parden (Jr.) 130
purden 131
thomus (Jr.) 130
Tillingst, Nicholas P. 36
Tillson, Joseph 31
Tindal, Jonathan 76
Tingley, Ephariam 15
Tinkcom, Hazakiah 44
John 40

Tisdale, Lemuel 100
Togood, Simeon 112
Tompkins, James 110
Samuel 24
Tony, (?) 122, 123
Toohigh, John 13
Topham, John 112
Torrey, John 97
Joseph 97
Oliver 97
Tourje, John 59
Peter 61
Thomas 98
William 98
Tourtelot, Abraham (Jr.) 40
Benjn 38
Tourtelott, William 44
Tower, Benjamin (Cpt.) 31
Enoch (Cpt.) 31
Ichabod 31
John 65
Levi (Cpt.) 31
Townsend, Christopher 25
Track, Daniel 31
Edward 31
Traffarn, --h 3
Trask, Ebenezer 92
Treby, Wilkins 111
Treddles, Charles 13
James 13
Trep, Abial 83
Tribby, Samuel 124
Trip, John 63
Samuel 33
Tripp, --der 3
Aaron 109
Abial 81, 106
Benjamin 16
Edward 55, 63
Giden 132
Israel 117
James 18
John 108
Robart 132
Rufus 106
Seth 55
Trivett, Eliazer 121
John 121
Truman, Thomas 55
Tubbs, Nehemiah 119
Tucker, Bennoi (Jr.) 44
Israel 91
Jabez 12
John 42
Jonathan 44
Joseph 83
Joseph (Jr.) 87
Joshua 12
Moris (?) 93

175

176

Wells (cont.)
  Edward 50
  Elias 48
  Elisha 48
  Elnathan 50
  Henry 50
  James 48, 80
  James (Jr.) 48
  John 60, 80, 117
  Jonathan 50, 55
  Jonathan (Jr.) 50
  Joshua 50
  Joshua (II) 48
  Matthew 48
  Peter 35
  Randall 50
  Roger 48
  Samuel 76
  Shedarak 39
  Thomas 1, 47, 50
  Thomas (II) 50
  Thomas (Jr.) 50
  Thompson 48
  Thos 33
Wels, John 72
Wescot, Caleb 118
  Thomas 118
Wescott, Antony 74
  Ford 68, 71
  Jabesh 68
  John 68
  John (Jr.) 68
  Samuel 71
  Uriah 66
Wescotte, Caleb 100
Wesott, Jabesh (Jr.) 72
West, Aseph 7
  Benjm 74
  Benoni 116
  Charles 81
  Francis 49
  Hix 7
  Ichabod 103
  Ishmael 116
  James 5, 100
  John 7, 81, 104, 124
  Jonathan 49
  Mical 48
  Nathan 104
  Nathaniel 7
  Oliver 6
  Samuel 7, 125
  Thomas 81
  William 7, 85
  William (Jr.) 87, 104
  Wilm 49
Westcot, Arnold 18
  Benja 21
  Benjamin 24
  Daniel 24

Westcot (cont.)
  Ephraim 21
  Ephraim (Jr.) 21
  George 83
  Jacob 24
  Jeremiah 121
  John 88
  Jonathan 24
  Josiah 23
  Josiah (Jr.) 24
  Nathan (Jr.) 118
  Oliver 85
  Peleg 80
  Reuben 24
  Samuel 24
  Silas 21
  Stephen 18
  Stuiley 24
  Stukly 18
  Urian 24
  William 25
  William (Jr.) 25
  Zorobable 26
Westcut, Caleb 80
Westgate, George 109
  John 108
  Silvenius 107
  Stukely 57
Wever, Benja 120
  Daniel 18
  Elijah 20
  George 18
  John 20, 49
  John (Jr.) 49
  Jonathan 18
  Lankfard 19
  Lodwick 49
  Nathean 18
  Robert 20
  Thomas 39
Whaley, Jeremiah 60
  Job 16
  John 61, 99
  Joseph 16
  Samuel 16, 99
  Samuel (Jr.) 99
  Thomas 57, 99
  Thos 16
  Thos (Jr.) 16
Whealock, Daniel 45
Wheat, William 66
Wheaton, Samuel 112
  Wilm 72
Wheeler, Bennett 68
  Henry 81
Whelan, Hezekiah 88
Whelar, Silas 71
Wheler, Henry 40
  James 88
Whetan, James 72

Wheton, Benjm 70
  Decon 70
  Ephram 70
  James 70
  Nathaniel 71
  Seth 71
  William 70
Whightman, George 56
  George (III) 58
  Holmes 56
  John 59
  Oliver 57
  Paul 59
  Volintine 57
  Volintine (Jr.) 59
Whippe, Saml 96
  William 67
Whipple, Amos (Cpt.) 32
  Andre 64
  Asa 31
  Azariah 67
  Benadick 85
  Benejah 40
  Benja 95
  Benjamin 32, 63
  Benjman (Jr.) 64
  Calvin 31
  Christopher 31
  Comfort 32
  Cristphor 63
  Daniel 31, 45, 64
  Daniel (Jr.) 32, 39
  David 31
  Eleazer 32
  Eleazer (Jr.) 32
  Elezer 63
  Elijah 42
  Enock 45
  Ephraim 32
  Ephram 64
  Eseck 40
  Ethan 62
  Ezekiel 62
  Ibrook 32
  Ibrook (Jr.) 32
  Israel 31
  Israel (Jr.) 31
  Jabesh 70
  James 117
  Jeremiah 31, 32
  Jeremiah (Jr.) 31
  Jesse 62
  Job 32, 118
  Joel 32
  John 31, 45, 62, 96
  John (Jr.) 31
  Jonathan 38, 64
  Jos. 92
  Joseph 31, 64, 122
  Joseph (Jr.) 63

Whipple (cont.)
  Moses 31
  Nathan 39
  Peck 31
  Pete 31
  Preserved 32
  Samuel 31
  Simon 31, 93
  Simon (Jr.) 32
  Stephen 32, 38, 92
  Thomas 64
  Willm 65
  Wm 96
Whitaker, Rufus 113
  William 32
  Zachariah 55
Whitan, Samuel 88
White, Asa 45
  Borok 94
  Christopher 50
  David 88
  Ebenezer 74
  Edward 68
  James 125
  John 72
  Noah 42
  Oliver 50
  Oliver (II) 50
  Oliver (Jr.) 50
  Samuel 92
  Seth 124
  Seth (Jr.) 125
  Walter 126
  William 5, 50, 64
Whitehorn, Georg 67
  James 99
  Richard 73
  Samuel 101
Whiteman, John 95
  Stephen 94
Whitfard, Nicholas 20
Whitford, Benjamin 61
  Christopher 81
  David 132
  George 119, 132
  Job 129
  Job (Jr.) 129, 130
  Jonathan 133
  Leuis 133
  Nichols 131
  Robart 35
  Ruben 133
  Simmon 133
  Stutely 81
  Sweet 130
  Thomas 61
  Thomus 131
  paskeo 131
Whitman, Benjaman 89
  Benjamin 83, 84

Whitman (cont.)
  Fedrick 58
  Jacob 66
  James 57
  James (Jr.) 36
  Jeremiah 18
  Michal 37
  Noah 38
  Olney 17
  Robert (Jr.) 84
  Squair 41
  Stephen 82
Whitnee, Joshua 95
Whitney, James 122
  Joseph 121
Whiton, Comford 73
Whittemore, Jos 72
Whitterur, (?) 74
Whitting, Joshua 113
  Nathaniel B. 113
  Stephen 7
Wiate, Yelverton 18
Wickham, Mark 100
  Samuel 100
Wicks, Barner 121
  Henry 121
  John 121
  Saul 118
  Silvester 119
  Stukely 120
  Thos 118
Wight, Aaron 89
  Benjn 80
  Eleazar 88
  John 85
  John (Jr.) 88
  Joseph 89
  Peter 89
  Samuel 89
  William 25
Wightman, Asa 115
  Daniel 115
  David 119
  Elisha 115
  James 35
  John 35, 115
  Philip 115
  Reuben 119
Wilbar, Joshua 67
Wilber, Clerk 50
  Gideon 46, 50
  Job 82
  John 113
  Peter 47
  Thomas 46
Wilbore, Benjamin 77
  John 77
  Peter 78
Wilbour, Abnar 85
  Danl 96

Wilbour (cont.)
  George 82
  Jesse 12
  John 85
  Joseph 55, 85
  Knight 85
  Olaver 85
  Samuel 85
  Simeon 87
  Thomas 87
  William 95, 109
Wilbur, Jonathan 17
Wilcocks, Jire 42
Wilcox, Smitten 34
Wilen, Aron 121
Wiley, John 74
  John (Jr.) 74
  Robart 74
  Samuel 74
Wilkerson, Benjamin 87
Wilkinson, Abad 90
  Benjamin (Lt.) 32
  Daniel 32
  Daniel (Jr.) 32
  David 91
  Israel 90
  Israel (Jr.) 91
  Jepthtah 32
  Jeremiah 32
  Jeremiah (Jr.) 32
  Joab 32
  John 32, 92
  John (Jr.) 93
  Jos. 93
  Joseph 87
  Nedabiah (Lt.) 32
  Ozial 92
  Phillip 57
  Robert 91
  Simeon 93
  Simon 32
  Stephen 32
  William 32, 45
Wilkison, Samll 46
Willbur, David 125
  Jeremiah 125
  John 125
  Joseph 125
Willcox, Abner 110
  Arnold 125
  Benjamin 110, 127
  Benjamin (II) 110
  Daniel 31, 104, 126
  David 78, 105, 125
  Edward 12, 76, 104
  Edward (Jr.) 12
  Elisha 125
  Ephrajm 110
  Gideon 109
  Hezekiah 128